The Talking Machine

Frontispiece 1
Courtesy of Allen Koenigsberg.

THE TALKING MACHINE
AN ILLUSTRATED COMPENDIUM
1877-1929

with photographs by the authors

Timothy C. Fabrizio &
George F. Paul

Schiffer Publishing Ltd

77 Lower Valley Road, Atglen, PA 19310

This book is respectfully dedicated to Claire Heffernan Fabrizio, Barbara Ann Paul, Jessica and Timothy Paul, and to Raymond R. Wile, pre-eminent archivist and exemplar to all those who would write of the history of recorded sound.

"THE TALKING MACHINE"

It is even more entertaining, however, when it PLAYS the music by the Great Bands. It is "too funny" when it SINGS the late popular songs, which it does so accurately that the voice of the performer may be distinguished. It also WHISTLES with the most artistic skill. It LAUGHS in the most mirth-provoking manner, and CRIES as if its heart would break. It also PRAYS with the greatest solemnity, and QUOTES SCRIPTURE by the chapter. It CROWS as definitely as any rooster, and BARKS and SNORES as natural as life. So human is it in all its ways, you get to wondering if it EATS.

From an 1897 brochure of the Talking Machine Company,
Rochester, New York

Library of Congress Cataloging-in-Publication Data

Fabrizio, Timothy C.
    The talking machine: an illustrated compendium.
1877-1929/Timothy C. Fabrizio & George F. Paul: with
photographs by the authors.
      p. cm.
    Includes bibliographical references and index.
    ISBN 0-7643-0241-8
    1. Phonograph--History. 2. Phonograph--Collectors and
collecting. I. Paul, George F. II. title.
TS2301.P3F3 1997
    621.389'33'075--dc21   97-364
                           CIP

Published by Schiffer Publishing, Ltd.
77 Lower Valley Road
Atglen, PA 19310
Phone: (610) 593-1777
Fax: (610) 593-2002
E-mail: Schifferbk@aol.com

Please write for a free catalog.
This book may be purchased from the publisher.
Please include $2.95 for shipping.
Try your bookstore first.

End papers.
Courtesy of George F. Paul.

Book design by "Sue"

Printed in China.

We are interested in hearing from authors
with book ideas on related subjects.

CONTENTS

ACKNOWLEDGMENTS

The authors would like to offer their gratitude to all who have helped and supported them in this project. Most importantly, we thank the collectors who opened their hearts and homes to us so that we could provide the reader with the vast scope of machines illustrated here: Robert Adams, Julien Anton, Terry Baer, Lou Caruso, Aaron and Thea Cramer, Peter Dilg and the Baldwin Antique Center, Howard Hazelcorn, Charles Hummel, Jim Kellish, William Kocher, Allen Koenigsberg, Dan and Sandy Krygier, Robert and Marilyn Laboda, Rob Lomas, Alan Mueller, Steve and Ellie Saccente, Sam Sheena, Norm and Janyne Smith, Dr. Jay Tartell and David Werchen. We would also like to take the opportunity to acknowledge individuals who have been important in our development as collectors and researchers: the glorious Jean-Paul, Sylvie and all the little Agnards, the fabulous Doug Anderson, Ernie Bayly, Lynn Bilton, Martin Bryan, the venerable James Card, Doug Defeis, Domenic DiBernardo, the late Felix C. Fabrizio, the late Milford Fargo, Mike Field, Will Frye, Bert Gowans, Tim Gracyk, the late Jim Hadfield, the unforgettable Mark Kaplan, Bill Klinger, Philippe LeRay, Bruce and Charlotte Mager, the late Walter Malone, Charles and Mary McCarn, Ted McCorkle, Artie Miller, Walt Myers, Kurt Nauck, John, Joan and Steve Paul, Richard and Jill Pope, Billy Rau, the late Leon Rothermich, the inscrutable Yves Rouchaleau, Sam Saccente, Steve Smolian, Madame Marie-Claude Stéger, Dave White and, of course, Ray Wile. And special thanks to Sue Chichester and Ginnie Hartson for their computer expertise at critical moments. To these and many others who have enriched our lives we say, "Thank you." We would also like to draw to your attention the Bibliography, which catalogues the writings of dedicated enthusiasts and scholars, many of whose works have enhanced our own libraries. These authors should be applauded for the insights they have contributed to the history of recorded sound. Lastly, we express our gratitude to our editor, Dawn Stoltzfus, and to Douglas Congdon-Martin, who came looking for Tim one October day and thereby began a most pleasant association.

INTRODUCTION

The talking machine has only recently begun to achieve credibility in the field of antiques. As many instruments approach the end of their first century, they are passing from "old record players" to well-appreciated amalgams of rich wood, bright metal, and fascinating archaic technology. Too long have they been the poor relation of music boxes, which attained a high-minded cachet decades ago and prices which reflected the upscale image of cultured clockwork music. The redoubtable (and often raucous) talking machine, perhaps because it was always a purveyor of pop, barking out Jolson more often than Caruso, languished in a netherworld of discarded fashion. Of the museums displaying them over the past half century, too many spent too little time accurately describing or equipping them. They were simply not as important, in a curatorial sense, as more ancient pieces, but they are getting there. To some they have already arrived, and demand to be given their due.

Although today it is difficult to envision the talking machine's novelty, we are charmed by its ingenuity and antiquity. Listen carefully: beyond the colorful horns, spinning gears and shining cabinets are the voices and artistry of a vanished society. Reflected in those recordings are the humor, bigotry, love, intolerance, loyalty, yearning and hopes of our past. To see and hear the talking machine is to discover in a new context the people we were—and the people we have become. The talking machine is a time capsule, and the discovery of one, along with a box of records, will allow you to make a wonderful journey to the time of Melba, Billy Murray, Theodore Roosevelt, Caruso, Casals, Ada Jones and hundreds of others. All are awaiting you through the "machine that talks."

The purpose of this book is to present a truly accurate history of the acoustic talking machine, with properly labelled illustrations of correctly fitted-out instruments. Yet, beyond this lofty-sounding aspiration, we wish to show the splash and color of these marvels of a former age. If your heart has not already been won by the plucky talking machine, we hope to warm it with these pages.

Timothy C. Fabrizio
George F. Paul

CHAPTER ONE:

THE BEGINNINGS OF THE TALKING MACHINE, 1877 TO 1893

THINKERS & INVENTORS

Thomas A. Edison was quoted as saying that the Phonograph was the only thing he ever invented that worked the first time. Notwithstanding any degree of truth or myth contained in this statement, it suggests that the creation of a machine that talked was a simple, decisive act: a burst of genius. Indeed, the story has elements of such a master-stroke, but happenstance has robbed Edison of his autonomy. Slightly before Edison achieved his first successful results in sound reproduction, a Frenchman, Charles Cros, described in detail how similar results could be produced. Though Cros never demonstrated his theory, and it is unlikely that Edison knew of it, credit must go to Cros for anticipating, though barely, what Edison was to accomplish. That, however, is the extent of what Monsieur Cros did. His luster is tarnished by his failure to act concretely.

The year was 1877. During the summer Edison was experimenting with a mechanism to repeat and relay telegraph messages. At the same time, he was working on telephone apparati at the behest of the Western Union Company, which wished to develop a system not dependent on the patents of Alexander Graham Bell. Sound and its properties were very much on Mr. Edison's mind, and one account has him pricking up his ears to the humming of the telegraph repeater as it relayed a message alternately described as having been indented on a paper tape or incised into a wax disc. To him the purring of the machine sounded like indistinct speech. This put him in mind to adapt the process to receive and store sounds. Another story has him pricking his finger on a wire attached to the diaphragm of a telephone receiver as his voice caused strong vibrations. In this version, he instantly thinks how this cutting or indenting action can be employed to capture sound vibrations

on a medium. In either event, he was ready to put into practice the basic idea Monsieur Cros had suggested in his sealed paper, accepted by the Academy of Sciences in Paris on April 30 of that same year.

Charles Cros (1842-1888) himself was an interesting character: a poet, visionary, and inventor, of course. What he proposed was really an improvement of the Phonautograph of Leon Scott de Martinville. This device, developed in 1857, visually described sound waves on a carbon-coated drum which rotated and tracked laterally under a bristle connected to a diaphragm. When sound was concentrated on the diaphragm, the contour of the vibrations was traced on the moving drum. Cros suggested using a photo-engraving method to permanently save the undulations traced on the Phonautograph cylinder, which thereafter could be used to recreate the same sounds by vibrating a diaphragm in a reversal of the "recording" process. He called the proposed device a Paleophone, or "voice of the ancients." Although Edison was not to pursue the engraving process for storing sound, as Emile Berliner would later do, that summer he was thinking along the same lines as Cros without being aware of it. However, by the time Cros' secret paper was published in the periodical "La Semaine du Clergé" (October 10, 1877) and finally read before the Academy which had held it unopened for seven months (December 3, 1877), Edison had nearly completed a working device he named the Phonograph, or "sound writer."

Beginning on July 18, 1877, Edison began to evolve the concept of a talking machine in his laboratory at Menlo Park, New Jersey. By August 17 the device had been developed to the point where its use as a telephone repeater, to relay messages between stations, was considered. On September 7, a statement with accompanying sketches was prepared to announce the invention of the newly dubbed Phonograph, but was not released as improvements continued. In the November 17 issue of *Scientific American*, an article appeared including a letter attributed to Edward H. Johnson, an associate of Edison, which described and roughly illustrated the Phonograph, though primarily in terms of a telephone repeater indenting a "record" of waxed paper tape. Newspapers picked up and trumpeted the revelations, a dangerous situation for Edison, whose work was far from complete and not yet protected by patent.

Into November the experiments continued on the evolving Phonograph which, by the end of that month, had taken on the form in which it was to be introduced to the public: the so-called "Tinfoil Phonograph". According to the diary of Edison's associate Charles Batchelor, he and John Kruesi finished the Phonograph on December 6, 1877. Whether the first words Edison spoke into it were the familiar lines of "Mary Had A Little Lamb," as has been widely recounted, can never be verified, and is just as likely a charming myth. However, it did produce results with enough volume to be recognized.

The Tinfoil Phonograph was demonstrated at the offices of *Scientific American*, which printed an article with illustration in the December 22 issue. It is important to note that whereas Edison had most certainly experimented with incised wax recording, the final medium he chose was indented tinfoil, stretched over the surface of a drum or mandrel into which a spiral groove was cut to allow the foil to indent. He admitted that this was done to get the Phonograph out in a hurry, for exhibition purposes, as the public was clamoring for information. In the near future, the Volta Laboratory Associates were to show the effectiveness of incised wax recording, though it would require years to perfect and the contributions of many hands, not the least of which would be Edison's.

Having received a very unsophisticated patent for the Phonograph in the U.S. (February 19, 1878), Edison applied for a much more detailed and extensive British patent which he received on October 22, 1878 (No. 1644). He had filed a caveat, or preliminary specification, in the U.S. for a patent of equally broad scope, but this was later denied. A complicated set of circumstances probably involving an oversight in timing by Edison had bereft him of potent ammunition for his future battles in American courts. Yet, for the time being the initial U.S. patent was sufficient to encourage willing investors.

In April, 1878, the Edison Speaking Phonograph Company was formed by a group of businessmen from the telephone trade, including Gardiner Greene Hubbard as president. Hubbard was a leading promoter of Alexander Graham Bell's telephone as well as the

inventor's father-in-law, which was to have implications later on. The machines, usually sold for $95.50, were within the reach of only the wealthy. Many would be purchased for scientific study; others were bought for exhibition. The failure of the Phonograph in its nascent form was that no valuable application could be found for it. Therefore, the fortunes of the Speaking Phonograph Company flagged rapidly as the Tinfoil Phonograph, only suitable for novelty purposes, was abandoned by Edison whose attention turned elsewhere. This void invited the necessary improvements to an invention with boundless promise to be made by others. The most notable problem to be solved was a way to create a permanent record, since indented sheets of tinfoil proved impossible to replay once removed from the mandrel. Ironically, it was the French who initiated the next development.

1-1

Thomas A. Edison at about the time he invented the Phonograph. *Courtesy of the Aaron and Thea Cramer Collection.*

1-2
An 1878 Bergmann and Company Tinfoil Phonograph used for exhibition purposes. *Courtesy of the Charles Hummel Collections.*

1-3
A Brehmer Brothers Tinfoil Phonograph of the 1878-1879 period. *Courtesy of the Charles Hummel Collections.*

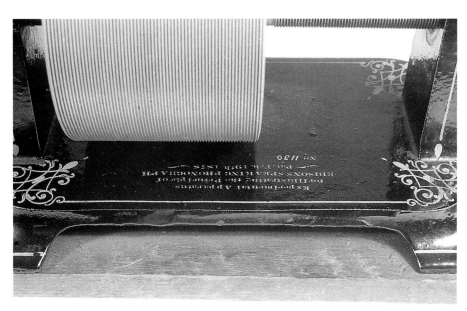

1-4
The bedplate of a Parlor Tinfoil Phonograph showing its attribution to the Edison Speaking Phonograph Company. *Courtesy of the Charles Hummel Collections.*

11

1-5
A French-made Hardy Tinfoil Phonograph with mandrel of extremely narrow dimension. *Courtesy of Allen Koenigsberg.*

1-6
The Hardy Tinfoil Phonograph in its original carrying case, with original tinfoil in upper right-hand compartment. *Courtesy of Allen Koenigsberg.*

1-7
An original wooden holder with its tinfoil still intact. *Courtesy of the Charles Hummel Collections.*

1-8
Another exhibition
Tinfoil Phonograph with
elegant decoration.
*Courtesy of the Charles
Hummel Collections.*

1-9
An American Tinfoil
Phonograph typical of
those made by local
precision instrument
manufacturers.
*Courtesy of Charles
Hummel Collections.*

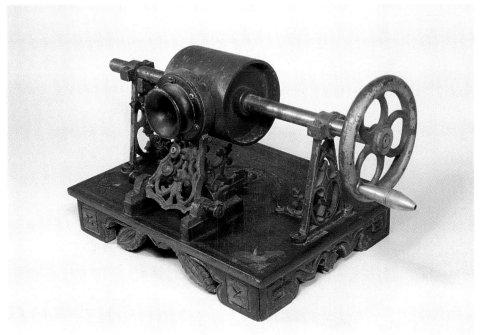

1-10
An exquisite example of a "craftsman"
Tinfoil Phonograph, possibly by Alex
Poole of Newark, New Jersey. *Courtesy of
Allen Koenigsberg.*

1-11
A stylish European Tinfoil Phonograph by C. Lorentz circa 1880. *Courtesy of Julien Anton Collection.*

1-12
A Tinfoil Phonograph made by the D & H Precision Tool Company of Newark, New Jersey. *Courtesy of the Howard Hazelcorn Collection.*

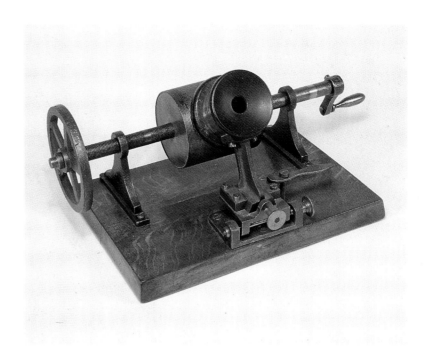

1-13
A rather dainty European Tinfoil
Phonograph with a mandrel
diameter of only 2 13/16". *Courtesy
of the Howard Hazelcorn Collection.*

1-14
A talking machine built circa 1879 by Frank Lambert. The machine's base is 6" by 11" milled steel. The length of
the shaft and winding wheel is 15". The 2 5/8" engraved lead cylinder contains the world's oldest playable
recording (as of this writing), containing the words: "One o'clock, Two o'clock, Three o'clock…" through
"Twelve o'clock," except "Ten o'clock," which is inexplicably omitted. The development of an engraved vertical
recording in 1879 is surprising, and had its existence been widely known during the 1880s and 1890s, talking
machine history would certainly have been altered. *Courtesy of the Aaron and Thea Cramer Collection.*

THE STORY OF THE GRAPHOPHONE & THE NORTH AMERICAN PHONOGRAPH COMPANY

In 1880, Alexander Graham Bell received an honor known as the Volta Prize from the French government. He took the money he received and set about to create an environment wherein he could work on the problems of reproducing sound. This subject had no doubt been on his mind at a time when Gardiner Greene Hubbard must have discussed the unfulfilled potential of Edison's Phonograph. Bell established the Volta Laboratory in Washington, D.C., and enlisted the assistance of a modelmaker who had worked with him before, Charles Sumner Tainter. He also brought in his cousin, Chichester Bell, an expert in physics. Together, they investigated every angle of the subject. They tried transmitting sound by light rays, magnetic recording, and reproduction by compressed air and jets of water. However, the greatest success would be achieved when they began to experiment with the use of wax as a medium for storing sound vibrations.

Because Hubbard's company controlled the Phonograph patent, any work done under his aegis could be protected. He gave the Volta associates a Tinfoil machine manufactured by Brehmer Brothers with which to experiment. By filling the existing spiral groove in the mandrel with wax, Bell and his team developed a method of incising by the action of a cutting stylus, thereby creating a more or less permanent record that could be replayed at will.

The prodigious work of the Volta Lab yielded a variety of patents, the most effective of which was to be No. 341,214, granted May 4, 1886, for recording and reproducing sound. Initially, the Volta experimenters did not foresee what powerful weapons their patents would become. They could never have envisioned the "talking machine wars" of fifteen years later. In fact, they attempted to share their work with Edison, approaching the Speaking Phonograph Company in 1885 about obtaining a license to make improved Phonographs. When Edison balked, they formed the Volta Graphophone Company on January 6, 1886, to be based in Washington, D.C. This firm would function as the patent holder and sometime research lab of the Graphophone interest, the name of the device suggesting they had turned Edison's Phonograph on its head to get it to work better. Yet, the Graphophone had changed considerably since its earliest incarnation as a modified Tinfoil Phonograph. Though it still gave inconsistent results, it had been improved by the use of interchangeable, gravity-pressure floating heads for recording and reproducing a removable cylindrical record: a cardboard tube 1 5/16" wide by 6" long, coated with ozocerite wax.

A manufacturing and distributing arm was needed, and, on May 13, 1887, the American Graphophone Company was organized, which had as its principal backers and general agents men like James O. Clephane, Andrew Divine, and John H. White who were Supreme Court or Congressional reporters. They saw the potential of the device for aiding transcription, though they would fail utterly to appreciate the value of pre-recorded music.

Thomas Edison, meanwhile, turned his attention to what was going on in the realm of sound reproduction. He vigorously objected to the Graphophone interest, claiming that he had anticipated the developments. Unfortunately, his American patent was not broad enough to include the areas covered by the Volta work. Fearing the loss of control over his invention, Edison began working on it with Ezra T. Gilliland, and an Edison Phonograph Company was formed to hold any new patents, though in direct violation of the Speaking Phonograph contract of 1878.

It was now that a man entered the scene who had made his fortune as the part-owner of a glassworks near Pittsburgh, Pennsylvania, and who was seeking to invest his money. Jesse H. Lippincott already had been a member of a failed syndicate formed to negotiate a sales contract with American Graphophone, and by early 1888 was familiar with the terms which that company demanded. It was immediately a point of discussion that the Graphophone interest be combined with the Edison Phonograph Company, which had yet to produce a marketable version of the redesigned machine on which Edison and Gilliland were working.

On March 29, 1888, a contract between Lippincott and American Graphophone was approved, with a very optimistic fifteen-year duration. Lippincott at once negotiated with Edison to obtain the rights to handle his Phonograph. In June of 1888, the so-called "Improved Phonograph" was introduced, featuring an electric motor drive and incised wax cylinder, though solid wax. Before any of the "Improved Phonographs" could be sold, Edison was added to the Graphophone contract. Had an agreement between the Phonograph and Graphophone factions not been reached, through the intercession of Jesse Lippincott, Volta would have sued Edison for his unlicensed appropriation of the incised wax record.

Edison's secondary status was not reflected in the new firm's title, the "North American Phonograph Company," nor was the inventor's lesser role suggested by the decision to market the Graphophone as the "Phonograph-Graphophone". It should be remembered, however, that the Phonograph already had public recogni-

1-15
An Edison Talking Doll, 1890, with
original costume and mechanism
detached. *Courtesy of Allen Koenigsberg.*

tion, albeit of theoretical rather than practical achievement. So, the Phonograph became, despite appearances,
a licensed Graphophone, with a clause which required a
royalty to be paid to American Graphophone on each
Edison machine delivered to Lippincott.

Soon enough, it became clear that neither machine
was terribly reliable. Yet the Graphophone, with its
thinly-coated cardboard single-use cylinder of narrow
diameter and its treadle power, was no match for the
electric motor Phonograph, employing a reusable, wider-
diameter solid wax record. The territorial or "local" companies which had been organized around the country
under the umbrella of North American to lease both
types of machine to the ultimate users were experiencing public rejection of the Graphophone. For even the
simplest office dictation the Graphophone proved un-
workable. Musical applications, although they were tried,
were out of the question. Customers, who could lease
either type of machine for $40.00 a year, were request-
ing Phonographs in replacement of Graphophones. Yet,
Jesse Lippincott was required by contract to purchase
5000 of the unpopular machines per year (at $48.76,
exclusive of treadle stands).

Only one local company seems to have had an even
success with placing the Graphophone: the Columbia
Phonograph Company, which held the Washington, D.C.,
Maryland, and Delaware territory. Even it soon found
that the most profitable aspect of the business was in
selling pre-recorded cylinders in the Edison solid wax
format (actually metallic soap resembling wax). Edward
D. Easton, president of Columbia, unlike the other
former government and law stenographers in the talking machine business, understood the entertainment
potential of records. It was propitious that the well-respected United States Marine Band was available to him,
and he jealously guarded his relationship with it. According to a contemporary Columbia account, the Band
was returning to the recording studio several times a
week in order to maintain the inventory of cylinders.
When Edison agents invaded to record the Band, Easton
sued. A cash cow sometimes bringing in orders for 1000
records a day (at about $1.00 each) was worth protect-
ing.

Mr. Easton became a member of the Board of Direc-
tors of American Graphophone, and embarked upon a
trip around the country to interview the branches of

North American. The unanimous cry was for the Phonograph and Graphophone to be combined, by which a single, superior machine might be obtained. However, it was already too late. Lippincott was in trouble. He could not hold up under his commitment to accept Graphophones which nobody wanted.

As of July 1, 1890, the Graphophone factory in Bridgeport, Connecticut, all but shut down, remaining open only to supply parts and make repairs. Company minutes relate that early in 1891 James G. Payne, president of American Graphophone, travelled to Jesse Lippincott's office in New York City to speak with him about the status of the contract. He was informed that Lippincott was in Boston seeking medical treatment. The only man in America authorized to be the primary handler of both types of talking machine was losing his health. On May 2, 1891, the ailing financier was forced to assign his estate for the benefit of his creditors.

Though North American sputtered on during the next three years to eventual receivership, the Graphophone Company had sold its last machine to the firm designated its sole licensee. North American would continue only as an outlet for Edison Phonographs, which were workable despite their flaws.

Edward Easton, who went on to become the president of American Graphophone, would report that the American Graphophone Company "from January 1891 until May 1, 1893…endeavored to establish a business selling Graphophones in competition with the Phonographs of the North American Phonograph Company. During this period…the total receipts from agents and the public for machines and supplies amounted to about $2500." He would note that expenses outstripped income by a rate of 30 to 1.

The few remaining employees of American Graphophone were not supported by the elemental relationship with Easton's Columbia, which was thriving in the record business. The skeleton crew at the Graphophone Company pieced together an improved model using the tops of the old treadle-powered machines combined with little 2.5 volt motors. Detachable mandrels were made of aluminum, brass, and even felt-covered wood so that Edison-style records could be used. The feed screws were changed from the Graphophone's 160 threads-per-inch to Edison's 100 tpi, allowing the machines to play and record in the Edison system. Cut adrift, they worked up any combination of materials to effect a sale. During the following years, Edison would, as the Graphophone interest had most feared, begin an attempt to recover the rights to his favorite invention from the slowly deflating North American Phonograph Company.

1-16

A prototype Graphophone from the former archives of Columbia. This illustrates the design which was subsequently manufactured by Western Electric Company as the Type "A" treadle Graphophone with certain modifications. (Only 300 Type "A"s were built.) *Courtesy of the Charles Hummel Collections.*

1-17
A selection of the earliest talking machine cylinders. (Left to right): 1886-1893 Bell-Tainter ozocerite-coated over paper core; 1889-1890 Edison cylinder with string-core (an attempt to reduce breakage) with a contemporary unmarked container behind; a typical Edison cylinder of the North American period with shallow "channel" on the flat rim (which was intended to hold a ring-shaped paper label); 1892-1893 Columbia cylinder with paper label adjacent to playing grooves; a square box containing a North American Edison cylinder; unusual 1895 Columbia record developed by John C. English, which imitated the "channel-rim" of the Edison cylinder. *Courtesy of George F. Paul.*

1-18
A Type "B" treadle Graphophone as manufactured from May 1889 to September 1889. *Courtesy of Sam Sheena.*

1-19
The Type "B" pulley plate. *Courtesy of Sam Sheena.*

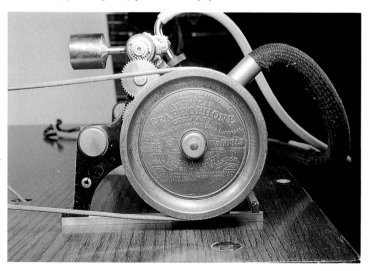

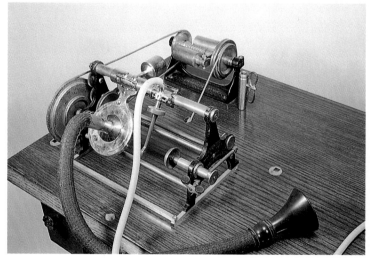

1-20
Close-up of the Type "B" playing mechanism. The recorder is in place, and the long beak-like reproducer is to the right. *Courtesy of Sam Sheena.*

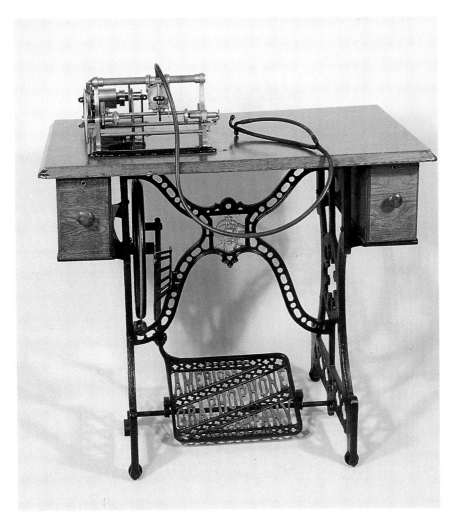

1-21
A Type "C" treadle Graphophone introduced in December 1889 and manufactured until July 1, 1890. *Courtesy of the Howard Hazelcorn Collection.*

1-22
The pulley plate of the Type "C" treadle Graphophone. *Courtesy of the Howard Hazelcorn Collection.*

1-23
The Type "C" treadle Graphophone with recorder in place on an ozocerite-coated cylinder. The reproducer is mounted on the same trunnion and is cocked back out of position. *Courtesy of the Howard Hazelcorn Collection.*

1-24
An Edison "Improved" Phonograph of 1888 showing the "spectacle device" which allowed rapid interchange of recorder and reproducer. *Courtesy of the Howard Hazelcorn Collection.*

1-25
A close-up of the "spectacle device" which was discontinued in November of 1889 and replaced with the Edison "Standard Speaker". *Courtesy of the Howard Hazelcorn Collection.*

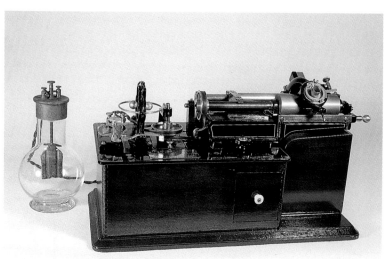

1-26
A North American Phonograph Company era Class "M" Edison electric Phonograph with the "Standard Speaker" and battery cell. *Courtesy of George F. Paul.*

1-27
From the former Columbia archives, a Type "C" treadle Graphophone top with electric motor and repeating mechanism, possibly for coin-slot use. It would have been a design similar to this which Charles Sumner Tainter used in his unsuccessful Columbian Exposition coin-operated Graphophones of 1893. Note the transitional reproducer which retains the narrow shank of the earlier design, but now incorporates a wider area for the diaphragm. *Courtesy of the Howard Hazelcorn Collection.*

1-28
An 1893 Type "E" Graphophone consisting of a Type "C" treadle upper works with a 2 1/2 volt electric motor in a drop-front cabinet. Serial No. 10,431. *Courtesy of the Aaron and Thea Cramer Collection.*

1-29
Close-up of the Type "E" Graphophone showing the narrow diameter nozzle for the transitional reproducer, and a tray to catch record shavings. *Courtesy of the Aaron and Thea Cramer Collection.*

23

THE EARLY TALKING MACHINE IN COMMERCE

Edison's experience with the Phonograph had been disappointing. It would be years before he would find his footing in a business his genius had initiated. Witness the episode of the "Edison Talking Doll", which turned out badly not the least because of Edison's own bad faith.

William W. Jacques and Lowell C. Biggs had founded the Edison Phonograph Toy Manufacturing Company in 1887, whereby Edison would allow his name to be used in connection with a doll mechanism of Jacques' design. This was at a time when various metal foils were thought suitable for reproducing. In 1888, Edison's assistant Charles Batchelor also engaged in talking doll experiments during the development of the "Improved Phonograph". However, neither Jacques' nor Batchelor's mechanism would prevail. Edison stepped in and took over the Doll Company, demoting Jacques.

Edison promoted his own doll motor (patent No. 423,039, March 11, 1890) which, not surprisingly, used an incised solid wax cylinder: the very first entertainment record in the Edison format. Some Edison dolls, with metal bodies, wooden limbs, and Simon and Halbig bisque heads, were finally assembled and put on sale in early 1890. The basic price was $10.00. Most of them came back as defective, since the hand-cranked mechanism and fragile wax cylinder proved unreliable. These problems stalled production and the slighted Jacques left the company, after which nothing would occur. The remaining dolls were stripped of their phonographs and sold off. The "Edison Talking Doll" holds the distinction of being the first "improved" Phonograph to be sold, not leased.

The market for entertainment cylinders, which had proved so successful for Edward Easton's Columbia, was by no means limited to home recitals. Itinerant exhibitors displayed the improved electric Phonographs at fairs and other events, charging customers a nickel apiece to get hooked up to a set of multiple ear-tubes. Though this activity began in a small way, the potential for quick cash was great. As early as November 23, 1889, inventor and businessman Louis Glass had rigged an Edison Phonograph with a repeating mechanism and four selectively controlled sets of listening-tubes (patent No. 428,750, May 27, 1890). Installed at the Palais Royal Saloon in San Francisco, the machine did good business and some fifteen were fitted out.

About the same time, Albert Keller, an associate of the Gilliland family, was developing the coin-op movement for which he would receive a patent in 1894 (No. 518,190). Attached to Edison Class "M" Phonographs and housed in imposing if featureless cabinets, the Keller coin-ops were distributed among some of the local branches of the North American Company in 1890.

George Tewksbury, who would later write a handbook about the Edison Phonograph, adapted some of them with his coin-op device (patent No. 523,556, July 24, 1894). Working as an officer of the local phonograph company in the Kansas territory, he claimed to have operated his machine as early as 1890, though they were actually put on sale a few years later by the United States Phonograph Company of Newark, New Jersey.

Charles Sumner Tainter, who had collapsed from overwork in 1890 and resigned his position as head of the Graphophone factory in Bridgeport, Connecticut, began developing a coin mechanism for Graphophones. He perfected an antecedent of the design which would serve nickel-in-the-slot Graphophones for the next ten years (patent No. 506,348, October 10, 1893). The major problem was the record. Tainter naturally employed the ozocerite-coated cylinder he had helped to develop. It would have been anathema for him to adapt to Edison records, as Easton had done with impunity. Tainter had been galled by the term "Phonograph-Graphophone" which the American Graphophone management had found expedient. He stuck by his own cylinder, and exhibited his coin-op at the 1893 Columbian Exposition in Chicago. Fred Gaisberg, who was working for the Graphophone faction at this time, asserted that the machine could not hold up to rough public use. No doubt poor reproduction from the ozocerite-coated cylinders was also a problem.

Phonograph arcades, with rows of nickel-operated Edison machines for which the records were frequently changed, blossomed in big cities. The Ohio Phonograph Company opened one in Cleveland on September 15, 1890, and in Cincinnati in early November. All this activity increased the need for musical cylinders, especially since they wore out quickly in coin machines. Though all of the local North American franchisees maintained a list of pre-recorded cylinders, Columbia was, by its own loudly trumpeted opinion, the leading supplier. It certainly did the most to market beyond the boundaries of its territory, and the power of this advertising would establish a formidable name for the company.

1-30
An early Edison Class "M" used by an exhibitor, with its eye-catching sign and special wooden base. *Courtesy of the Charles Hummel Collections.*

1-32
An 1891 lithograph entitled "Hear The Music" showing a little girl enjoying a Keller-vintage coin-slot Phonograph.

1-31
A Keller-designed coin-slot Phonograph of 1890. The plunger on the right controls the operation with a single action. *Courtesy of the Charles Hummel Collections.*

1-33
An Edison Class "M" upper mechanism oddly converted by Kumberg in 1893 to allow for motorless operation. *Courtesy of the Julien Anton Collection.*

1-34
A fancy Victorian cabinet in the Eastlake style sold by
the North American Phonograph Company for housing
an Edison Class "M". *Courtesy of the Charles Hummel
Collections.*

1-35
The cabinet, referred to in the catalogue as a "Drop
Cabinet", is shown open to reveal the Edison Phono-
graph raised by a counterweight system. *Courtesy of the
Charles Hummel Collections.*

1-36
An Edison Class "M" Phonograph mounted in
a special table bearing the initials of the
North American Phonograph Company.
Courtesy of the Charles Hummel Collections.

1-37
The "Commercial" Phonograph sold by the Edison-Bell Company in
Britain in 1893. It was this style machine which was first pictured by artist
Francis Barraud in his famous "His Master's Voice" painting. *Courtesy of Sam
Sheena.*

EMILE BERLINER
& THE GRAMOPHONE

While all this was going on, another inventor, Emile Berliner, a German who had immigrated to the United States in 1870, would also find that involvement with the telephone would lead him into the field of recorded sound. In 1878, Berliner sold an improved telephone transmitter to the Bell Company, using the money to finance his own experiments with sound.

In 1887, he took a glass disc coated with a mixture of lamp-black and linseed oil, and traced a spiral on it from a stylus connected to a vibrating diaphragm. A photo-engraving process, such as Cros had predicted, was used to etch a copy of the transparent track of the stylus into a metal plate, making a permanent disc record which could be replayed. For this technique to work, it was necessary for the stylus to vibrate laterally, or side-to-side, displaying the vibrations on the sides of the spiral track. The Phonograph and Graphophone, on the other hand, used an up-and-down or vertical movement when incising the soft wax of the cylinder records they used. The basic difference between these two recording systems would define the camps which were to arise within the talking machine industry.

In 1888, Berliner improved his process by use of a zinc disc thinly coated with beeswax into which the recorded spiral could be cut. The wax was kept moist with alcohol to prevent build-up on the cutting needle. The resulting "master" was etched with acid to produce a permanent groove where the wax had been removed, exposing the metal beneath. Cleaned of the remaining wax, this record could now be played. And in fact some directly-created zinc discs were actually sold when Berliner's machine was later marketed. In practice, the zinc "master" was electroplated with a metal skin of sufficient thickness and strength so that when the two were separated, a "negative" was created from which a large number of identical copies of the zinc recording could be stamped out of a pliable material like hard rubber or celluloid.

Berliner demonstrated his Gramophone, or "writer of sound," before the Franklin Institute in Philadelphia, Pennsylvania, on May 16, 1888. After solving the problem of creating a stamper from the original etched zinc

1-39
A Kämmer and Reinhardt toy Gramophone circa 1891 with paper maché horn and sphere for attaching listening tubes. *Courtesy of the Howard Hazelcorn Collection.*

1-38
An illustration of Scott's Phonautograph (1857) from the published text of the paper on the Gramophone Emile Berliner read before the Franklin Institute on May 16, 1888. Berliner drew inspiration from the Phonautograph, as Charles Cros had done in 1877 when he predicted replayable recording.

disc, the inventor was ready to offer something which would prove a significant advantage over the cylinder record system: the ability to economically and easily turn out multiple copies of any performance. In the field of entertainment records, the Phonograph and Graphophone would be mired in cumbersome technology for the next decade, forced to increase the actual number of machines recording the artist or to use time-consuming dubbing or pantographic copying methods. Despite the advantage of simple record duplication, it was years before Mr. Berliner managed to put his Gramophone on the American market in significant numbers.

1-41
Many 5" Berliner discs carried a paper label pasted to their reverse sides containing the words to the selection. *Courtesy of George F. Paul.*

1-40
On the left, a directly-recorded acid-etched zinc 5" Berliner disc. Although some of these were sold (with ink-stamped title information, as in this example), the primary purpose of the zinc disc was to provide a "master" from which multiple copies of the same performance could be created. The "master" was given a thick electroplated skin of metal which, when separated and processed, became the stamper from which celluloid or hard rubber Berliner discs were pressed. On the right, a 5" stamped celluloid Berliner disc of "The Lord's Prayer." *Courtesy of George F. Paul.*

Berliner travelled to Germany in 1889, where he sold his idea to the toy-making firm of Kämmer and Reinhardt (of Waltershausen, Thuringia). Thus, the Gramophone was first manufactured as a hand-driven toy, with discs of approximately 5" in diameter, pressed from vulcanized rubber or celluloid. These little "plates", as they were called, recorded on one side with the words pasted to the reverse, played at 90 or more revolutions per minute. A steel pin or needle clamped to a reproducing head or "soundbox" released the vibrations through a small horn. In later models, ear-tubes would be used to concentrate the sound, as they did with cylinder talking machines. Even after the introduction of motors to drive the Gramophone some years later, Berliner and his successors continued to produce hand-driven models, though the results could be only described as uneven.

The toy Gramophones remained on sale for several years, from 1890 to 1893 or 1894. They sold well in the British Isles, and many discs were recorded in English. Berliner, having tested the device before the public as a novelty, was anxious to bring a mature Gramophone to an adult market. Ironically, Berliner's patents would prove more valuable to others than to the inventor himself. As the toy business faded, he set up shop in a city already integral to the talking machine business: Washington, D.C.

1-42
An 1893 Type "U" Graphophone factory-equipped with a 2 1/2 volt electric motor. Interestingly, this machine retains the original treadle-type160 threads-per-inch feedscrew. It was intended to play the 6" Type "E" cylinders. These used a narrow "Bell-Tainter" paper core thickly-coated with wax to bring them up to the diameter of an Edison cylinder (2 1/4"). The 6" Type "E" cylinders allowed a lengthened Edison format to be used on the Graphophone without the necessity of a mandrel. Upper works were from a Bell-Tainter Type "C" treadle machine. Serial No. 10772. *Courtesy of George F. Paul.*

1-43
A Type "C" Graphophone with factory-equipped electric motor. The upper works were recycled from a treadle Graphophone (also designated Type "C"). The machine was converted to the Edison 100 threads-per-inch feedscrew and employed a removable Edison-type mandrel. The "A-frames" have been "jeweled" by a machinist, in a manner which will be seen in future Graphophones (such as the "AA"). It is not known why this decoration was added, but it was done purposely to distinguish the appearance. Serial No. 10783.

CHAPTER 2:

THE TALKING MACHINE COMES OF AGE, 1894-1898

The application of the talking machine as a business appliance had met thus far with abject failure. Jesse Lippincott's vision of Phonographs and Phonograph-Graphophones being as commonly used as typewriters was unfulfilled. The prospects of the North American Phonograph Company and the talking machines it was now selling seemed gloomy indeed. Yet, these early talking machines were to be newly appreciated as a result of societal changes brought about by the same industrial revolution which gave them birth.

In cities and towns across America, the workday was beginning to shrink. Automation and power machinery had boosted productivity, reduced necessary working hours and given many wage-earners something that they never had before: leisure time. Recreation, still considered by some to be almost sinful, was gradually becoming accepted. Buggy rides, picnics, bicycling, roller skating, ball games, and band concerts were becoming a part of middle-class American life. People were hungry for entertainment, but most had never even seen a talking machine. As early as 1889, travellers found talking machines modified for coin-operation in railroad stations, ferryboats, hotels, and saloons. The income from these machines surpassed expectations, and by 1891 the conversion of the Edison Class "M" Phonograph to coin-operation had spawned several small companies. The making of entertainment cylinders likewise had become something of a cottage industry, although North American and its local companies supplied entertainment cylinders in substantial numbers. These coin-operated talking machines and the sale of cylinders for them kept some of North American's local companies afloat during this period.

2-1
A custom-made carrying case used by a Phonograph exhibitor to service his coin-slot machines, and a contemporary poster announcing a travelling Graphophone show. *Courtesy of Allen Koenigsberg.*

In addition to coin-operated musical entertainment, talking machine exhibitors were occasionally seen. Unlike the "Tinfoil" exhibitors of fifteen years earlier, this new breed of exhibitor was made up of independent operators who had purchased their talking machines and hoped to recoup their substantial investment and turn a profit through the sale of tickets for demonstrations.

2-2
A talking machine exhibitor plys his trade on the porch of a downtown establishment. *Courtesy of George F. Paul.*

One of these early exhibitors was a Frenchman named Charles Pathé. Impressed by the sight of an Edison Class "M" Phonograph taking in centimes at a brisk rate, Pathé bought one for himself and gave his first exhibition at a fair just outside of Paris in September 1894. Others at the fair were surprised at Pathé's earnings that day, and offered to buy the Edison. Pathé realized that his long-term interests were best served by selling talking machines rather than exhibiting them, so he began buying them wholesale and supplying the French trade. Later, brother Emile Pathé joined Charles to form the company eventually known as Pathé Frères. Thus began several years of importing American machines, and eventually the manufacture of their own models.

Most talking machine exhibitors of the mid-nineties were not so prescient. The surviving handbills and exhibition posters of the period attribute the coming attractions to a variety of "Professors," "Doctors," or simply "Misters," whose names are no longer remembered. The repertoire of these exhibitors differed in several respects from the earlier "Tinfoil" demonstrations. The cylinders were pre-recorded for the most part, and carried from town to town in cases. The improved fidelity of the wax cylinders allowed a much wider variety of recorded entertainment: brass bands, vocal selections with piano accompaniment, artistic whistling, banjo records, cornet solos, xylophone selections, humorous monologues, quartettes, recitations, trombone solos, and popular songs.

Although the acoustic capacity of the wax cylinders was a vast improvement over the tinfoil recordings, the artistic improvement was minimal. The American public of 1894 was generally no more musically literate than in 1878. With very few exceptions, recordings from the nineties consisted of band selections such as "Marching Through Georgia," "The Washington Post March," and "The Star Spangled Banner," sentimental songs such as "My Old Kentucky Home," "Anchored," and "Oh Promise Me," and vocal/instrumental solos such as "La Paloma," "Welcome Pretty Primrose," "Listen To the Mockingbird" and "Loin Du Bal."

The cylinder records themselves were available in relatively limited numbers. There was no means of mass-producing cylinder records. The performer sang or played into a group of recording horns, each connected to a talking machine with a recording device in place. The louder the instrument(s), the more recording machines could be used simultaneously. In this manner, a given number of recordings were made for each performance. If each performance or "round" yielded eight copies, and the company had orders for two hundred copies, the performer was obliged to repeat the selection twenty-five times. Popular titles sold by the hundreds. Pantographs, or cylinder copying machines were used for duplication of cylinders, but their results were variable. Many small cylinder record firms advertised their records as "Each One An Original" or "We Sell No Copies." The truth of these various advertising claims was the subject of lively debate throughout the nineties.

2-3
A cylinder copying machine or "pantograph". Such machines were used by large manufacturers to create enough copies of popular selections to fill demand. Unscrupulous entrepreneurs often used pantographs to duplicate professional recordings, thus avoiding overhead costs. Pantographs were routinely confiscated when found engaged in illegal duplication, but the period was rife with such activity. This example is composed of a modified Edison Class "M" upper works mounted to a "Spring Motor" mechanism. *Courtesy of the Charles Hummel Collections.*

-1894-

The dawning of 1894 found the talking machine business virtually moribund. The North American Phonograph Company was selling, through its local companies, an occasional Edison Class "M" Phonograph from its inventory, but at $150.00 per machine, business was not brisk. The American Graphophone Company was doing an infinitesimally small business in recycling Graphophones made from old Bell-Tainter Type "C" treadle-driven mechanisms. These were modified to play Edison-type cylinders, placed in small wooden cabinets and driven by electric motors. Neither the Edison Phonograph Works nor the American Graphophone Company had manufactured new talking machines for the American market since 1890. Emile Berliner puttered in his laboratory, making a few hand-cranked Gramophones, experimental electric motor Gramophones and 7" celluloid discs while desperately casting about for investors. It was not an environment conducive to investment. Yet, during 1894 changes occurred which would steer the talking machine on a course toward eventual success.

These events were brought about primarily through the activities of the Columbia Phonograph Company of Washington, D.C., and the American Graphophone Company of Bridgeport, Connecticut. For its part, the American Graphophone Company had hired a brilliant Californian, Thomas Hood MacDonald, as general manager of its struggling factory. The early months of 1894 saw MacDonald developing what would become the first practical spring motor for a talking machine. This resulted in the Type "F", or "Spring-Motor Graphophone", introduced in August 1894 for $110.00. The MacDonald motor used a single wide spring and rather robust brass gears. The playing mechanism of the Type "F" Graphophone was a recycled Bell-Tainter Type "C" playing mechanism with a 100 threads-per-inch feedscrew. A removable mandrel was supplied for Edison-type entertainment cylinders. Additionally, a 6" long Type "E" cylinder was offered which used the old Bell-Tainter type paper core, but with a thick, shavable wax surface of standard Edison diameter. These were intended for use as dictation cylinders. It was realized that the continued use of surplus Bell-Tainter mechanisms could only be temporary. Accordingly, MacDonald designed the first full-sized talking machine built solely to entertain: the "Baby Grand" Graphophone. This machine used the same Macdonald motor as the Type "F", but with a smaller cabinet and a newly-simplified playing mechanism which allowed a lower retail price of $75.00. This was, however, a time when an average American salary was $12.00 per week.

In France, Henri Lioret had become interested in talking machines while engaged as a clockmaker in Paris. Avoiding the pitfalls of wax cylinders, Lioret developed a celluloid cylinder along with a lilliputian mechanism to play it. He filed for an American patent on December 20, 1893. It was granted ten months later, and Lioret applied himself to constructing the small machines and cylinders for installation in the talking dolls of the Jumeau firm. The Bébé Jumeau dolls sold well for 38 francs. The talking mechanism was available separately as "Le Merveilleux" for 20 francs. During the nineties, Lioret developed two larger models ("No. 2" and "No. 3") which played celluloid cylinders of longer duration at greater volume. His products were well-made, and evocative of Lioret's clockmaking heritage. These machines were manufactured for approximately eight years. Like others to follow, Lioret was overtaken by larger competition. The dainty "Le Merveilleux" retains the distinction of being the first European-made talking machine to play removable cylinders, and the very first anywhere to use celluloid.

2-4

A French Bébé Jumeau doll with Lioret cylinder mechanism, circa 1895. *Courtesy of Sam Sheena.*

The Columbia Phonograph Company in Washington, D.C., had aspirations beyond being a sales agent for the struggling North American Phonograph Company. On May 1, 1893, Columbia assumed the management of the American Graphophone Company. Columbia's president, Edward Easton, was now in firm control of both companies. Under Easton's direction, Columbia had developed a lucrative trade in wax cylinders, especially those of the United States Marine Band. The alliance of these two companies would open the door to an undreamed-of range of talking machine products, but such potential was only a part of the plan. The Graphophone forces were preparing litigation designed to drive Edison from the field.

In a suit begun in 1893 (the Volta Graphophone Company and the American Graphophone Company vs. the Columbia Phonograph Company), Columbia was actually in league with Volta (a patent-holding company) and American Graphophone. At stake was the legality of the Edison Phonograph due to its use of devices which infringed two key Bell-Tainter patents. Attorneys for the financially-strapped North American Phonograph Company reluctantly defended Columbia, their erstwhile agent-turned-traitor, throughout 1894. Meanwhile, Easton quietly began proceedings under his contract with North American whereby he would legally assume control of Edison Phonograph patents. Edison became aware of this activity and, as principle creditor of the penniless North American Phonograph Company, threw it into bankruptcy on August 21, 1894. Thus ended the unhappy paper alliance of the Edison and Graphophone forces, and thus began several years of virtual anarchy in the talking machine business.

North American's large record-making plant at 120 East 14th St., New York City, was sold on September 5, 1894, to the firm of Walcutt and Miller, which manufactured cylinders for the next fifteen months. Many smaller concerns recorded cylinders and sometimes manufactured their own cylinder blanks. One of the most active of these was the Chicago Talking Machine Company, which was managed by a young man named Leon F. Douglass. At about the time of the Type "F" Graphophone's debut, the Chicago Talking Machine Company began marketing spring motors designed by Edward H. Amet. These motors were mounted in wooden cabinets with a flip-down front door. The owner of an Edison Class "M" Phonograph could remove its playing mechanism and mount it above the Amet motor in minutes. Other short-lived attempts were made to market practical talking machine spring motors. Some of these, such as the "Amet", were well-made and reasonably efficient, but all suffered from high manufacturing costs and limited distribution. The MacDonald motor, in addition to powering the Type "F" and "Baby Grand" Graphophones, was available separately in a cabinet similar to the "Amet", to retro-fit an Edison Phonograph mechanism.

2-6
A very early (circa 1894) single-spring Amet motor powering a Type "U" Graphophone upper works. This machine was sold by the Chicago Talking Machine Company with which Edward H. Amet was associated. *Courtesy of the Howard Hazelcorn Collection.*

2-5
An 1894-1895 Walcutt, Miller & Company cylinder record box.

The Columbia/Graphophone forces took quick advantage of Edison's loss of his North American sales outlet by releasing circulars warning purchasers against using the Edison products:

AMERICAN GRAPHOPHONE COMPANY
Principal Office 919 Penna. Ave.
WASHINGTON, D.C., Oct. 31, 1894

Notice is hereby given that ALL who USE, BUY or SELL the so-called EDISON PHONOGRAPH are INFRINGING the PATENTS of the AMERICAN GRAPHOPHONE COMPANY, and are subject to PROSECUTION in the courts.

The "Improved Phonograph" was originally manufactured under patents of the American Graphophone Co., and put upon the market by Jesse H. Lippincott, to whom authority was specially granted by the American Graphophone Co. After the failure of Mr. Lippincott, the North American Phonograph Co. assumed to carry on the sale of phonographs without license and without payment of royalties; in consequence of which the American Graphophone Co. entered suit against the North American Phonograph Co. This suit was being vigorously pressed up to the time of the bankruptcy of the North American Phonograph Co., which has recently taken place.

The American Graphophone Co. preferred to settle first with the larger infringers, but their disappearance renders this course impossible. It has therefore been determined to give notice to all who use or deal in the phonograph that they must immediately cease so doing or answer to this Company in damages.

Proceedings have already been instituted against the United States Phonograph Co. of Newark, N.J., the New England Phonograph Co., the Ohio Phonograph Co., and the Kansas Phonograph Co.; also against Geo. E. Tewksbury and A.P. Martin of Boston, Mass., James L. Andem of Cincinnati, Ohio, Thomas R. Lombard and E.S. Gresser of Chicago, Ill., and other suits will follow as rapidly as the circumstances permit.

Yours truly,
AMERICAN GRAPHOPHONE COMPANY.
By. E.D. Easton
Vice-Prest. and General Manager

The defendants named in the above circular were among the best-known dealers, distributors, and exporters of talking machines in the country. Anyone in the trade would certainly have been impressed by such a battery of lawsuits. Taken in the context of Edison's apparent lack of viable products, the effect must have been startling.

34

As these combatants formed battle lines, the trade took little notice of a small Gramophone retail store in Baltimore which opened in the Fall of 1894. In order to attract investors, Emile Berliner had judged that his crude hand-cranked Gramophone with its primitive 7" celluloid disc records must prove itself in the marketplace. It was a small, inauspicious beginning for Berliner, but the repercussions would eventually dwarf the giants doing battle all around him.

2-7
A hand-driven Berliner Gramophone originally sold for $15.00. This reasonably-priced machine inaugurated Berliner's activities in the United States. *Courtesy of the Howard Hazelcorn Collection.*

-1895-

An advertisement appeared on February 15, 1895, announcing that John R. Hardin, the appointed Receiver of the now-insolvent North American Phonograph Company would accept bids until March 15 on:

A large stock of miscellaneous phonograph and graphophone machines, tables, cabinets, parts and appliances including obsolete and available material, inventoried by the North American Phonograph Company in the year eighteen hundred and ninety-four at upwards of Forty Thousand Dollars ($40,000).

Shortly thereafter, the Chicago Talking Machine Company circulated an old "North American Price List of Parts for Class 'M' Phonograph" dated April 1, 1894, overstamped with the announcement, "We have purchased the stock of Machines and Supplies of the North American Phonograph Co., and will sell them at 25 per cent discount from this list. We have 8000 good New Jersey, New England, and North American records which we will sell at 75 cents each."

This stock, as noted in the Hardin advertisement of February 15, included obsolete Graphophones. These were the unleasable/unsalable Bell-Tainter Type "C" treadle models which North American had been forced by its contract to purchase. The Chicago Talking Machine Company promptly converted the Bell-Tainter mechanisms to play 100 threads-per-inch Edison-type cylinders on removable mandrels. It sold these Graphophone (and also Phonograph) mechanisms as complete machines by mounting them above Amet spring motors.

Meanwhile, Emile Berliner had received some very good news on February 19, 1895. His patent for the "Gramophone" (No. 534,543) had been granted after a delay of nearly three years. Claim Five of this patent would become the cornerstone of an empire: "The method of reproducing sounds from a record...which consists in vibrating a stylus and propelling the same along the record by...the said record..."

The records pressed by Berliner in 1895 were 7" in diameter and made of hard rubber, since celluloid had been found unable to withstand repeated playings beneath the steel needle, heavy soundbox and horn. Hard rubber had its own disadvantages, including craters in the surface and a short stamper life due to the sulphur content of the rubber. It was now that the speed of the turntable would be set "around" 80 rpm, eventually standardizing at the famous 78 rpm which would serve lateral cut discs for six decades. At first, however, there could be significant variations in speed from record to record. The accuracy of any disc was of little importance, since the only machine offered by Berliner at this time was the hand-propelled model. Although hardly more than a toy, it was the machine on which Emile Berliner pinned his hopes of attracting investors.

Meanwhile, the litigation instituted by the American Graphophone Company against Edison continued. Despite the crack legal staff of Pollok and Mauro, setbacks for American Graphophone sometimes occurred, as described in this broadside of April, 1895:

EDISON PHONOGRAPHS

WHAT THEY SAID
Some time ago the manufacturers of an unsuccessful talking machine took the following extraordinary means of advertising their business among those not familiar with the facts:

"Notice is hereby given that ALL who USE, BUY, or SELL the socalled EDISON PHONOGRAPH are INFRINGING the PATENTS of the AMERICAN GRAPHOPHONE COMPANY, and are subject to PROSECUTION in the courts. Proceedings have already been instituted against the United States Phonograph Co., of Newark, N.J., etc., etc., and other suits will follow as rapidly as the circumstances permit."

This attempt was simply an advertising scheme to traffic in the great name and reputation of Mr. Edison. The fact that Mr. Edison is the inventor of the Phonograph is too well known to be seriously disputed. No one requires to be told that any owner of an EDISON PHONOGRAPH is at liberty to use his instrument as he pleases, and to buy his records whenever he chooses.

WHAT THEY GOT
(In the United States Circuit Court, District of New Jersey, before Judge Green, after full hearing of the case, American Graphophone Co. vs. United States Phonograph Co., et al. Decision on March 26th, 1895.)
"The motion for Preliminary injunction is denied.
Edw. T. Green, J."
"Certified, March 26th, 1895."
Comment would be a waste of time.

THE UNITED STATES PHONOGRAPH CO.
8791 Orange St. Newark, N.J., U.S.A.

Due to his entanglement with North American and his ill-fated ore-mining projects, Edison was unable or unwilling to participate in the development of spring motors for talking machines throughout 1895. Built to capitalize on the many extant Edison Phonograph mechanisms mounted on heavy, battery-driven Class "M" motors were: the redesigned and more-elaborate Amet spring motor, the "Peerless", the Broich, the Greenhill, the Pierce, the Glass, the MacDonald and finally, the Capps... but no *Edison* spring motor!

The Capps motor was a powerful three-spring model known in the retail trade as the "Triton" motor. Frank Capps, of the U.S. Phonograph Company of Newark, New Jersey, filed his patent on December 20, 1895. The Capps motor was sold for $40.00 in a single- drawer cabinet designed, like the others, to accommodate an Edison Phonograph mechanism.

Emile Berliner, after several failed attempts, managed to assemble a small syndicate to back his crude Gramophone. On October 8, 1895, the Berliner Gramophone Company was incorporated with only $25,000 of paid capital. This firm would control manufacturing and sale of Gramophones and records while paying royalties to Berliner's patent-holding organization, the United States Gramophone Company.

The Graphophone/Columbia alliance had also been strengthening its corporate and financial base. This was succinctly described in a later Annual Report of the American Graphophone Company:

In 1895 we entered upon a new era. In that year there was a practical consolidation of the American Graphophone Company and the Columbia Phonograph Company, by the acquirement of the capital stock of the latter. From this point full advantage could be and was taken of the ability and organization of the Columbia Company, for the distribution of our product.

This step was soon followed by the acquirement of the Columbia Phonograph Company, General, then operating a profitable and attractive exhibit at Atlantic City, and under whose charter provisions we obtained a still wider scope. The American Graphophone Company then assumed the position of a manufacturing company only, with the two Columbia Companies as the distributors of its product.

Perhaps the most significant accomplishment of the Columbia/Graphophone forces during 1895 was the introduction in September of the Type "N" Graphophone. It used the same MacDonald motor found in the earlier Type "F" ($110.00), the shaver-equipped Type "K" ($120.00), and the "Baby Grand" ($75.00). For only $40.00, The Type "N" combined for the first time the features of a fixed mandrel, parallel feedscrew and an upright lever-operated carriage. It was the Type "N" which first brought the talking machine and pre-recorded entertainment within reach of the middle class. Approximately 6000 Type "N" Graphophones were built, and they marked the practical beginning of the home entertainment industry.

2-8
The first affordably-priced Graphophone of the new pattern which would finally bring Columbia success: the Type "N" ("Bijou") introduced in 1895 at $40.00. *Courtesy of George F. Paul.*

The forces which had collaborated in this achievement were marketing their products as Columbia Graphophones and Columbia records. From this point onward, we will refer to these consolidated interests in the same manner: simply as "Columbia".

-1896-

Edison had been without a sales organization for sixteen months while coping with litigation leveled at him by the local territorial companies of North American. Some of these suits (with the legal backing of Columbia) would not be settled for a dozen years. Meanwhile, Columbia was developing an affordable product line, strengthening its patents and assailing the validity of Edison's patents in the courts.

In January 1896, Edison established the National Phonograph Company to be the exclusive sales agent for Edison Phonographs in North America. Unfortunately, the only machine Edison had to offer was virtually the same electric-powered (Class "M" or Class "E") Phonograph that had been offered by North American since 1888. Edison's export agent, the United States Phonograph Company of Newark, New Jersey, was manufacturing the Capps-designed "Triton" spring motor. By March 1, an arrangement was made whereby these motors were supplied by the U.S. Phonograph Company to be sold beneath the Edison Phonograph mechanism as the Edison "Spring-Motor" Phonograph. The price, in contrast to the $40.00 Type "N" Graphophone, was $100.00. This clearly was not a machine for the masses. So, in the Spring of 1896, the $40.00 Edison "Home"

2-9
In 1895, the United States Phonograph Company offered a $40.00 triple-spring motor designed by Frank Capps, which would finally be appropriated by Edison in his first spring-driven Phonograph. This machine, known as the Edison "Spring Motor" Phonograph, sold for $100.00 which included a recycled Class "M" upper works. *Courtesy of William Kocher Collection.*

Phonograph was introduced. Alas, its motor (manufactured in Connecticut) was insufficient both in power and speed regulation. Throughout 1896, Edison would sell no spring motors of his own manufacture; only the Phonograph mechanisms mounted above them.

The three-spring Capps Motor used in the Edison "Spring-Motor" Phonograph inspired further competition from Chicago. Attorney Richard N. Dyer later recalled:

> "At or about the time of the grant of the (Capps) patent, the United States Phonograph Company brought to my attention a flagrant infringement upon the Capps patent in a spring motor known as the 'Chicago motor', and placed upon the market by the Chicago Talking Machine Company, of Chicago, Illinois. I was instructed to commence suit against said Company as early as possible."

The three-spring "Chicago Motor" did have a remarkable similarity to the Capps motor, with one notable difference: the "Chicago Motor" was made of aluminum. The first version used a conventional governor and was, like the Amet motor, mounted beneath old Bell-Tainter Type "C" Graphophone or Edison Phonograph mechanisms. The Chicago Talking Machine Company undoubtedly retained plenty of these Bell-Tainter and Edison parts from its 1895 purchase of the North American Phonograph Company inventory. In a wooden cabinet, a "Chicago Motor" and an Edison upper mechanism sold for $100.00 complete. As a result of litigation, slightly later examples of the "Chicago Motor" used a governor of unusual design in an attempt to circumvent the Capps patent. This little-known competitor of Edison's "Spring-Motor" Phonograph made barely a ripple in talking machine history. The designer of the motor remains unknown.

Meanwhile, the Columbia interest had not been idle. Its product line included the old Bell-Tainter-topped Type "K" (or "Standard" Graphophone) offered in both electric and spring-driven models, the Type "N" which had created such a sensation at $40.00 and, in time for the 1896 Christmas trade, the Type "A" which sold for an astoundingly low $25.00. This new model used a cast iron top mechanism rather than the former nickeled brass, and a smaller spring motor. A spring-driven, coin-operated version of the Type "N" was offered for $50.00: the industry's first spring-powered coin machine.

More importantly, Columbia had pursued litigation which, while not driving Edison from the field as it hoped, would ultimately shape the talking machine business for years to come. The catalyst of the Graphophone's legal maneuvers was Edward H. Amet, the designer of "Amet" spring motors for the Chicago Talking Machine Company. Amet had developed and was selling a talking machine which he first called the

"Metaphone" (thus transposing his own name), retitling it within a month or so the "Echophone". The American Graphophone Company brought suit against Amet for using a gravity-weighted or "floating" reproducer and engraved or incised cylinders: both vital elements of Bell-Tainter patents. Amet added a coil spring to the "Echophone's" unusual glass tone-arm in an attempt to escape the Graphophone legal battery, but the case looked grim against him. Edison's attorneys were enlisted late in the proceedings, since an adverse decision against Amet would leave Edison open to the same charge. The Edison forces pointed out that thus far the case had been tried only on affidavits, adding: "This method of making up a record is not only unusual, but can never produce satisfactory results." Additionally, it was revealed that certain parties of the Chicago Talking Machine Company had interests tied to the American Graphophone Company: "We have not at hand proof of collusive action, but it certainly looks suspicious and as if even though no collusion existed at the inception of the suit, the relations of the two parties in interest prevented a complete trial."

Despite the best efforts of the Edison legal staff, the Graphophone forces won a perpetual injunction against Amet. With both sides in formidable legal positions, the only sensible course was a cross-licensing agreement. On December 7, 1896, Edison licensed Columbia to use the tapered mandrel, jewel stylus and Edison-style solid wax cylinder. Edison was now licensed to use a gravity-weighted, "floating" stylus and engraved (as opposed to embossed) recordings. To be sure, it was an uneasy truce, but it allowed the cylinder talking machine to further develop in the marketplace rather than the courtroom.

In Washington, D.C., the Berliner Gramophone Company waited optimistically for business to pick up, even though it had only its crude, hand-driven Gramophone to offer at $15.00. At this point, an astute advertising man, Frank Seaman, was engaged to market the Gramophone, and he established the New York Gramophone Company in February 1896. A better promoter for the Gramophone than Frank Seaman would be difficult to imagine. A close personal friend of Kodak founder George Eastman, Seaman was familiar with the mass-marketing of cameras and film. He immediately placed large, tinted advertisements extolling the virtues of the Berliner Gramophone. Rather than the line cut illustrations used by the talking machine competition, Seaman incorporated half-tone photographs of real people enjoying the charms of the disc record. Edison and Columbia would not yield to such innovative marketing for several years. In hindsight, Frank Seaman can be accurately viewed as the father of talking machine advertising as an art.

2-10
The "Metaphone", a pun on inventor Edward Amet's name, was introduced as the the first low-priced talking machine ($5.00) in November 1895. It would soon be re-named the "Echophone". The wooden mandrel with its reduced center area was an attempt to avoid prosecution under Edison's tapered-mandrel patent. The coil spring beneath the glass tube is missing from this example. *Courtesy of the Howard Hazelcorn Collection.*

2-11
The actual "Echophone" used in the 1896 litigation with Columbia, and marked "EX...1" (Exhibit 1). Amet lost the suit and Columbia took possession of his remaining stock of machines. *Courtesy of the Howard Hazelcorn Collection.*

38

By this time it was clear that, like the Edison Phonograph and the Graphophone before it, the Gramophone needed a spring motor to make it a commercial success. There can be little doubt that Frank Seaman encouraged the Berliner management to pursue such a course. A Berliner accompanist and "talent scout," Fred Gaisberg, investigated an advertisement in the Philadelphia *Public Ledger* in which a spring motor suitable for a sewing machine was offered. The motor was designed and built by a Henry Whittaker, but was too cumbersome for use with the Gramophone. Whittaker called on Belford G. Royal, the foreman of a Camden, New Jersey, machine shop operated by Eldridge R. Johnson. Johnson's shop modified the Whittaker motor, but the Berliner management was not impressed with its performance. This was the end of Whittaker's involvement, but Johnson had become infected with "Gramophonitis". He obtained a Gramophone and began experimenting with spring motors. He later recalled: "The little instrument was badly designed. It sounded much like a partially-educated parrot with a sore throat and a cold in the head, but the little wheezy instrument caught my attention and held it fast and hard. I became interested in it as I had never been interested before in anything. It was exactly what I was looking for."

Adapting a spring motor to a Gramophone entailed problems not encountered in cylinder machines. The weight of the soundbox and horn were substantial, and this drag gradually decreased as the steel needle worked its way from the disc's perimeter toward the center. Johnson approached Levi H. Montross of Camden, New Jersey, for assistance. Montross designed a lever-wound motor, Johnson added a crude governor and on August 10, 1896, was awarded a contract from Berliner for two hundred motors. This first spring-driven Gramophone was encased in a round metal cabinet mounted on a baseboard similar to the hand-wound model. It was offered for $25.00 by Seaman's new National Gramophone Company, which he had established on October 19, 1896.

It seems incredible that the management of the Berliner Gramophone Company could have been unaware of the importance of the new spring motor. Yet, a recording released at this time by the Company as a self-advertisement is fixated on the unsuccessful attempts made during 1894-95 to develop local recording studios whereby purchasers could conveniently make

disc records. Additionally, the record proudly crows that the Gramophone is a reliable machine, since "I haven't even a gear." To Frank Seaman, who was promoting the spring-driven Gramophone as "The Newest and the Best," this anachronism must have been annoying:

No. 637(W) "On The Gramophone" by George Graham. Recorded December 2, 1896:

"I am known far and wide as the 'Berliner Gramophone',
and as a talking machine, I am standing quite alone.
I talk all kinds of talk, about both the old and new,
and whatever you talk into me I can talk back to you.
To be sure, I'm something wonderful, if you will only reflect,
that I can talk every language and in fact every dialect.
Though I've been on the market only a very short time,
the people are finding out that I am right in line.
You can put me in your parlor or your nursery and behold;
I will furnish new amusement for both the young and old.
My records are indestructible; you will find them never wrong;
and they produce properly music, speech and song.
Girls, if your fellow proposes, make him do it through me,
and then you have got him sure and he never can get free;
Because if he should shake you, and off with another (skirt?),
you have the evidence against him in a Breach of Promise suit.
And if the Gramophone before the court is heard,
he surely can't get out of it and go back on his word.
And as for correspondence, why surely there's nothing better,
for into the Gramophone you can talk a letter;
And although your beloved ones you cannot really see,
they can hear your own beloved voice and recognize you through me.
I never get out of order; I haven't even a gear,
and yet I reproduce a voice remarkably loud and clear.
This is an age of invention, yet I am a great surprise;
I can please both old and young; the foolish and the wise.
If you would always be happy and never feel alone,
Why, fifteen dollars will buy you a first-class Gramophone!"

Despite improvements in the shellac-based Berliner discs now being supplied by the Duranoid Company of Newark, New Jersey, these flat little records would probably have elicited a chuckle from the managers of Columbia or the National Phonograph Company. Yet, the end of 1896 found Emile Berliner's Gramophone poised to become a serious competitor of the cylinder format which had been dominant thus far.

-1897-

Effective January 1, 1897, the headquarters of the Columbia Phonograph Company was moved from Washington, D.C., to New York City. The Company had outgrown the venue of the old Volta Laboratory, had put a $25.00 talking machine on the market (the Type "A" Graphophone), achieved a secure patent footing in the courts and was now ready for global marketing from its glamorous new offices in the financial center of the world.

2-12

THE CHICAGO TALKING MACHINE CO.,

Columbia purchased the Chicago Talking Machine Company on August 1, 1897. This pioneer talking machine agency, it will be remembered, had been involved in selling Amet spring motors as well as the mysterious three-spring, aluminum "Chicago Motor" which had run afoul of the triple-spring Capps motor of the U.S. Phonograph Company. In an interesting turnabout, Columbia introduced its first three-spring motor one month after buying the Chicago Talking Machine Company. Although Columbia's new motor was built of more prosaic steel and brass, the similarity to the old "Chicago Motor" was unmistakable.

This new motor was mounted beneath a newly-designed cast upper works using a 6" mandrel and push-button mandrel disengagement, much like the Bell-Tainter upper works which preceded it. The entire mechanism was installed in a plain, oak cabinet and marketed for $50.00 as the Type "C" or "Commercial" Graphophone. Columbia had exhausted the supply of old Bell-Tainter Type "C" upper works used in the Type "K" ("Standard" Graphophone), the last of the "old style" machines in the catalogue. The new Type "C" utilized some of the same features found on the old Bell-Tainter Type "C" mechanisms, but in a more efficient and economical form. An electric-motor version was also available. The paper-core Type "E" cylinder was discontinued. 6" solid wax cylinders of the Edison type were now offered, intended for business correspondence. Pre-recorded 6" brown wax cylinders of this period were not offered in the U.S.A., although they were apparently sold in France.

40

The Columbia forces had recognized by this time that the greater potential profit lay in the sales of records, not talking machines. The more talking machines in the hands of the public, regardless of profit, the greater the number of records that could be sold. With Amet's earlier "Echophone" subdued, Columbia began designing a cheaper machine of its own. In September 1897, the Type "B" Graphophone was introduced. Often called the "Eagle" because of the prominent eagle on the ten dollar gold piece which could be used to purchase it, the Type "B" would be a best-seller for Columbia for six years.

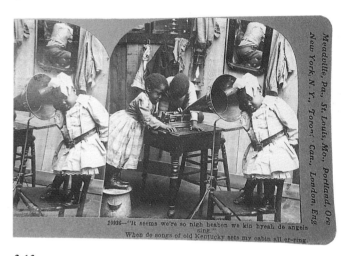

2-13

A contemporary stereo-view depicting children enthralled by an "Eagle" Graphophone to which a large horn of 1890s design has been attached. *Courtesy of Norm and Janyne Smith.*

Business for Edison's National Phonograph Company had been laggard. Sales of Edison "Spring-Motor" and "Home" Phonographs had amounted to only 774 units between March 1, 1896, and February 28, 1897. In January/February of 1897, Edison began fitting an improved spring motor of his own design to the Edison "Home" Phonograph. In the Fall of that year, Edison absorbed the U.S. Phonograph Company, and the manufacture of both types of spring motors used by Edison was finally under his control. During this time, the cylinder talking machine business was dominated by Columbia, with the Edison organization taking a distant second place.

In 1897, another version of the lever-wound spring motor Berliner Gramophone was offered. Rather than a round metal enclosure mounted on a flat baseboard, the motor was housed in a wooden cabinet with attached support arm for the horn/soundbox/traveling arm assembly. Eldridge Johnson and Alfred Clark had developed a closed-face soundbox which made its debut on this machine. On August 19, 1897, Johnson applied for a patent (No. 601,198) on an improved motor and brake for the Gramophone. These features were used in the machine marketed as the Berliner "Improved Gramophone", which sold for $25.00. The "Improved Gramophone" single-handedly enabled the disc record to become a serious competitor of the cylinder. This model would later become part of the world's most famous and best-loved trademark.

2-14
In mid-1897, the spring-driven Gramophone was modified by machinist Eldridge Johnson, employing a new motor and brake. It was this machine, marketed as the "Improved Gramophone" and still selling for $25.00, which would finally gain for Berliner a significant share of the talking machine market.

In mid-1897, a director of Seaman's National Gramophone Company, William Barry Owen, secured the patent rights to the Gramophone in Europe. He promptly sailed for London, and began to cast about for investors, much as Berliner had done earlier in the U.S. For almost a year, Owen entertained potential backers in his stylish rooms at the Hotel Cecil without attracting any British capital.

Back in the U.S., former Berliner employee Joseph W. Jones applied for a patent on a new style of gramophone, one which used a mechanical feed. Such a machine could circumvent Berliner's 1895 patent (No. 534,543) which controlled a mechanism whose soundbox was propelled solely by the record grooves. In addition, Jones began experiments with recordings made in wax. This was an area protected by the Bell-Tainter patents (No. 341,214 & No. 341,288) controlled by Columbia. Jones was clearly a potential threat to both companies.

In November of 1897, young Jones signed a formal agreement with a New York investor, Albert T.

Armstrong. Jones agreed to license his mechanical-feed gramophone to Armstrong (as Berliner had to Seaman) and to supply serviceable disc records as described in his two patent applications: for recording in wax and pantograph copying of disc records. Armed with this contract, Armstrong found partners in the persons of C.G. Conn of Elkhart, Indiana, (a prominent maker of musical instruments) and Emory Foster of Washington, D.C. Conn contributed his design of a dual-horn or "double-bell" soundbox assembly. Jones would furnish the basic machines and Conn would supply the two-horn assembly. As plans for manufacturing slowly took shape, it was decided that the machine would be called the "Wonder".

Despite the immediate success of the "Improved Gramophone", all was not well in the Berliner camp. Frank Seaman had become dissatisfied with the Berliner Company due to its disinclination to lower the price of the "Improved Gramophone". Berliner charged Seaman cost plus a 40% profit. Apparently Seaman had no quarrel with Berliner's profit, but believed that the supplier, Eldridge Johnson, was charging an excessive price for his product. Seaman asked Berliner on several occasions to convince Johnson to cut his price. In line with Seaman's suspicions, several officers of the Berliner Company were financing Johnson. The Company president, Thomas Parvin, owned a share in the Johnson patents. Clearly, if Seaman were to have a less-expensive machine to market, it would not be the "Improved Gramophone".

Taking advantage of Section Eight of his contract with Berliner (which allowed Seaman to provide machines of comparable quality for 5% less than those supplied by Berliner/Johnson), Seaman arranged for production of a different model Berliner Gramophone with Levi Montross, the inventor of the lever-wound spring motor used earlier by Berliner. In the Fall of 1897, the "Montross" Berliner Gramophones were introduced. Although similar in appearance to the "Improved Gramophone", the "Montross" did not have an exposed spring-barrel, and used a horizontal crank which did not revolve as it played. The turntable was covered with a violet material, and the black horn had red stripes rather than gold ones.

The manufacture of "Montross" Berliners was the only instance in which a supplier other than Eldridge Johnson was used. Some 2000 of these machines were built, after which the Berliner/Johnson interests refused to honor Seaman's legal right to arrange outside manufacture. Despite Seaman's repeated protests regarding price and quality of goods, the Berliner Company remained unmoved. In addition, the Berliner Gramophone Company requested Seaman to provide regular financial statements on his National Gramophone Company. Seaman refused. Berliner responded on October 1, 1897, by ceasing to recognize National Gramophone as its sales agency. Frank Seaman's original contract with the Berliner Company had been a personal one and would be observed as such, so far as Berliner was concerned.

During this period, Seaman arranged for sample 7" record pressings by the George Burt Company of Milburn, New Jersey, a manufacturer of billiard balls and poker chips. These pressings were less costly, and of higher quality than the Duranoid pressings Berliner was using. Nevertheless, the Berliner Gramophone Company was again adamant: no change in suppliers of records would be considered. Frank Seaman and his business manager Orville LaDow were losing patience.

2-15
An unusual handbill announcing a Gramophone exhibition. *Courtesy of George F. Paul.*

-1898-

The cylinder and disc talking machine businesses were doing very well financially. The cost of talking machines was no longer a barrier to ownership. Records were selling by the thousands, the public was clamoring for new songs and recorded novelties and all three major companies rushed to deliver. The Spanish-American War generated topical records such as "Under The Double Eagle March," "The Battle Of Santiago," and "Troops Disembarking For Manila." The latter two were examples of "Descriptive Specialties" featuring bugle calls, friendly banter among the soldiers, songs, farewells, and of course the booming of naval guns in battle. These records functioned as newsreels would for a later generation. As America became a world power, nationalist pride poured from the horns of talking machines.

Throughout the Spring of 1898, J.W. Jones, Albert Armstrong, C.G. Conn, and Emory Foster struggled to bring their plans for the "Wonder" to fruition. Jones' patent on a mechanical-feed gramophone (No. 604,829) was granted on May 31, 1898. The next day, C.G. Conn applied for a patent on his two-horned soundbox assembly and a different mechanical feed. The four partners incorporated their business as the Standard Talking Machine Company.

Manufacturing difficulties soon arose. Jones could not supply satisfactory machines or records in sufficient numbers or quality. Consequently, Armstrong found himself selling goods at a discount as "seconds" or "imperfects". In June 1898, the Berliner Company brought suit against the "Wonder" partners for patent infringement, Jones' application for recordings in wax was rejected for the second time and Armstrong et al disbanded the Standard Talking Machine Company. Armstrong later estimated that not more than fifty sample machines were distributed. The "Wonder", hardly sprouted, was swept into oblivion by the winds of litigation.

At the same time (February 1898), Frank Seaman incorporated the Universal Talking Machine Company, with Orville LaDow as President. This company was involved in the conversion of Berliner Gramophones into coin-operated instruments. As well, it shipped Berliner Gramophones marked "Zonophone" to Belgium, which was not subject to patent protection. This was only a temporary operation. Seaman and LaDow must have foreseen eventual secession from Berliner. Accordingly, while the Berliner Company was filing suit against the Standard Talking Machine's "Wonder", the Universal Talking Machine Company hired the patentee of a music box spring motor, Louis Valiquet, to design a new gramophone. Universal also acquired the services of John C. English, a chemist with considerable recording and record-making experience, despite the fact that Frank Seaman's contract with Berliner specifically forbade disc record production.

Meanwhile, in London, William Barry Owen's efforts to attract British investors for the Gramophone had finally borne fruit. Through the interest and influence of E. Trevor Williams, a small group of investors had been formed. In May, 1898, the Gramophone Company was established with rights to market the Gramophone throughout Europe. Offices and a recording studio were set up in the basement of 31 Maiden Lane. Owen was named managing director, while Emile Berliner's brother, Joseph, was sent to Hannover, Germany, to establish a pressing plant. Emile Berliner's veteran "talent scout," Fred Gaisberg, arrived to supervise recording. Machines were shipped from Camden, New Jersey, to London, where they were assembled under the direction of Eldridge Johnson's faithful employee and friend, Belford G. Royal. It was a new company composed of veterans, and was destined to be successful from the very beginning.

Armstrong and Jones needed patent protection if they were to resume their manufacturing activities. Columbia had not been blind to the fact that Gramophone machine and record sales throughout 1898 had skyrocketed. The foremost manufacturer of cylinder talking machines and records was looking for a way to break into the disc market. During September or October of 1898, an arrangement was made between Armstrong, Jones, and the American Graphophone Company whereby the latter would manufacture disc machines and pay a royalty under the Jones machine patent. Jones would again attempt to supply records, this time under the protection of the Graphophone recording patents, while awaiting favorable action on his wax disc recording patent application.

At the same time, on October 22, 1898, Columbia's legal counsel Philip Mauro filed suit against the Berliner Gramophone Company and Frank Seaman's National Gramophone Company alleging infringement of Bell-Tainter Patent No. 341,214 which claimed a loosely mounted reproducer guided by the record groove. The Berliner Gramophone Company, buoyed by the success of the "Improved Gramophone", continued to ignore Frank Seaman's complaints, and prepared to defend itself in court.

The cylinder talking machine market had continued to expand during 1898. In March, Edison introduced the "Standard" for $20.00, which was to become the backbone of the Edison line. The "Home" had been reduced to $30.00 as of August 1897, and the "Spring-Motor" was reduced to $75.00 in late 1898. With a choice of three spring-driven Phonographs finally in place, Edison's sales during 1898 showed healthy growth.

2-16
The Edison "Standard" Phonograph of 1898 sold for $20.00. This was the first Edison Phonograph to use a top works cast in one piece and a parallel arrangement of feed-screw and mainshaft. *Courtesy of George F. Paul.*

2-17
By the end of 1897, the Edison "Home" Phonograph, with its charming decal, had achieved the mechanical design which would endure with little modification throughout its production life. *Courtesy of George F. Paul.*

43

Columbia introduced two extremely popular cylinder machines during 1898. The Type "Q" was a simple one-spring model which sold for as little as $5.00. The Type "AT" was a two-spring refinement of the earlier Type "A" with a more elaborate cabinet. The price remained $25.00.

2-18
The Type "Q" was introduced as the "Five-Dollar Graphophone" in 1898. The cased form shown here sold for $7.50. *Courtesy of Norm and Janyne Smith.*

In December 1898, a Graphophone unlike any other was introduced. It played cylinders of standard 4" length, but of 5" diameter, resulting in a higher surface speed beneath the stylus. Columbia reasoned that such a format would allow the recorded vibrations to be more widely spaced, resulting in less blast and louder reproduction, especially with band numbers. The concept was not new to the recording business, but had been used only in the duplicating of cylinders up to this time. Putting such large cylinders into the hands of the public had not been done before. The "Graphophone Grand" (Type "GG") for $300.00, and the Columbia "Grand" Records at $5.00 each would allow the well-heeled to sample this "Greatest Achievement Of The Talking Machine Art." The 5" cylinder would ultimately accentuate the advantages of the disc in comparison to the cylinder and help bring about the decline of this pioneering format.

Nevertheless, the cylinder record was in the midst of its glory days. Companies such as Hawthorne and Sheble of Philadelphia were marketing a variety of aftermarket items for cylinder talking machines including horns of various styles and sizes, record carrying cases, ear tubes, horn supports, cabinets for machines and/or record storage, repair parts and often a line of cylinder records as well. Other companies offered unique merchandise such as the Polyphone: an attachment for Phonograph or Graphophone which used two reproducers and horns in tandem in order to impart "the sweetness of many echoes instantly combined." The talking machine had begun to show promise to investors.

2-19
A Hawthorne & Sheble "Nonpareil" cabinet, encasing an Edison Spring Motor Phonograph. *Courtesy of George F. Paul.*

One particular afficianado and entrepreneur of this period deserves more than a footnote. He was Gianni Bettini, an Italian who came to America in pursuit of love. He had met young Daisy Abbott at a social function in Paris, followed her back to New York, married her and settled into the life of a wealthy young expatriate. He was a devoted opera-goer, and was fascinated by the possibility of capturing and recreating the legendary voices of his time. The Edison Class "M" Phonograph he acquired did not, he felt, do justice to the art. Bettini devised an apparatus on which he received three U.S. patents and which he called the "Micro-Phonograph". This apparatus consisted of a reproducer with a relatively large mica or aluminum diaphragm (differing from the glass diaphragms then in use). The stylus was attached by a "spider" fixed to the diaphragm at a number of points. The reproducer was assembled in a carriage arm designed to be substituted for that of a Phonograph or held by the trunnion of a Graphophone.

By using the Bettini "Micro-Attachment" the customer would "...obtain perfect reproductions from [the] talking machine." Bettini sold these attachments in America during the late nineties. Of special interest were the cylinder records he offered. Like all Bettini's products, they were expensive: $2.00 to $6.00 apiece at a time when Edison and Columbia offered theirs for fifty cents. The difference lay in the artists. Bettini's performers included luminaries from the Metropolitan Opera as well as European vocal celebrities who toured through New York City. These cylinders were duplicated to order as befit the wealthy patrons of "High-Grade Records, High-Class Music, and only by Leading Performers and World Famed Artists."

Bettini's merchandise sold on a very small scale and, except for his efforts at sophisticated technology, his activities would be of little note if not for his recordings. Some of these contain voices captured in their prime, or artists who recorded only for Bettini. Just after the turn-of-the-century, he moved back to Europe to exploit his products there. However romantic Bettini's legacy, the talking machine industry moved on without him.

The seeds of the talking machine's future had been sown for the previous five years. The major players of the business had taken the field and executed their opening maneuvers. The talking machine was no longer an expensive novelty exhibited in the village square. Thousands of instruments were entertaining families in their own homes. Great potential, though not yet manifest, was envisioned by the captains of industry. The talking machine had come of age.

2-21
A specially-modified Edison Class "M" for exhibition use discovered in Kearny, New Jersey. *Courtesy of the Howard Hazelcorn Collection.*

2-20
An early Edison Class "M" of the North American period later fitted with a "Bettini Micro-Attachment". *Courtesy of Sam Sheena.*

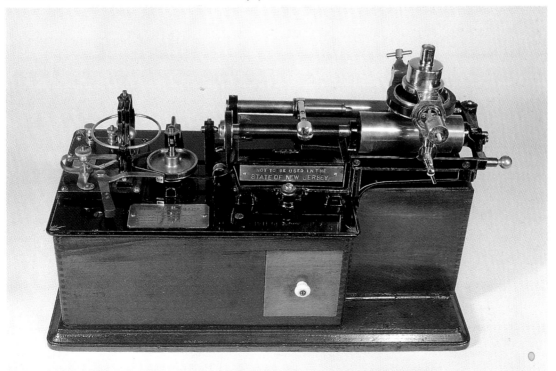

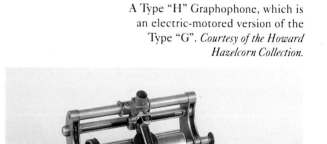

2-23
A Type "H" Graphophone, which is an electric-motored version of the Type "G". *Courtesy of the Howard Hazelcorn Collection.*

2-22
A Type "G" ("Baby Grand"), 1894-1895. This was the first Graphophone constructed without recycled treadle machine parts. *Courtesy of the Charles Hummel Collections.*

2-24
A Type "I" Graphophone using a 110 volt motor. The upper works is recycled from a Type "C" treadle Graphophone. *Courtesy of Sam Sheena.*

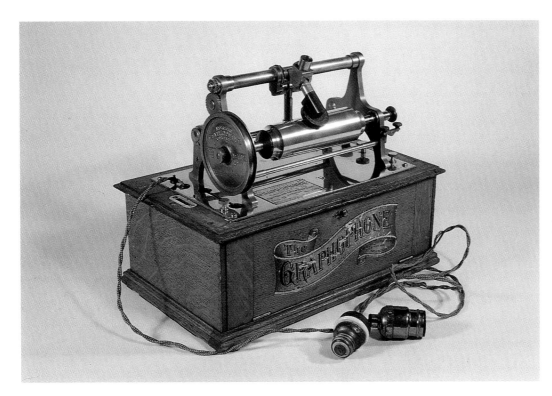

2-25
A Type "U" Graphophone of 1895 with a 110 volt electric motor. *Courtesy of the Charles Hummel Collections.*

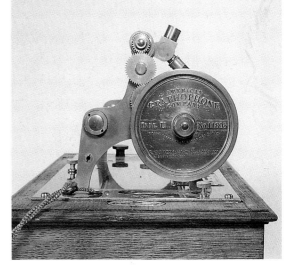

2-26
Close-up of the Type "U" pulley plate. Note that the "North American Phonograph Company", Charles Sumner Tainter's and Jesse Lippincott's names have been effaced. *Courtesy of the Charles Hummel Collections.*

2-27
An 1895 Type "K" with electric motor. Notice that the lower center rod has been raised and a shaver added. *Courtesy of Sam Sheena.*

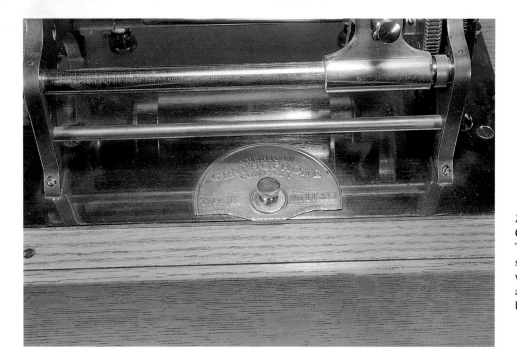

2-28
On spring-motored versions of the Type "K", the upper pulley was smaller, and the large pulley plates were nailed inside the lids or fastened, as in this example, to the rear of the bedplate. *Courtesy of Sam Sheena.*

2-29
A very early example of the McDonald-motored Type "K", in which the motor is made of steel rather than brass. *Courtesy of the Charles Hummel Collections.*

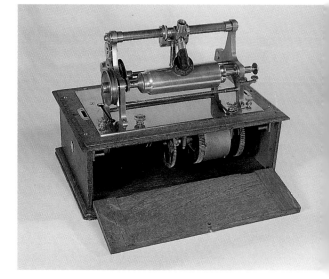

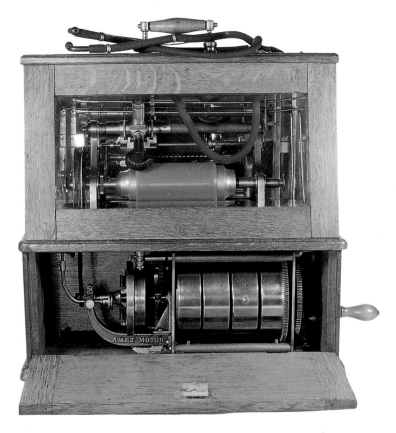

2-30
A coin-slot Type "S" Graphophone powered by a four-spring Amet motor. This machine sold for $100.00 in 1895. *Courtesy of the Howard Hazelcorn Collection.*

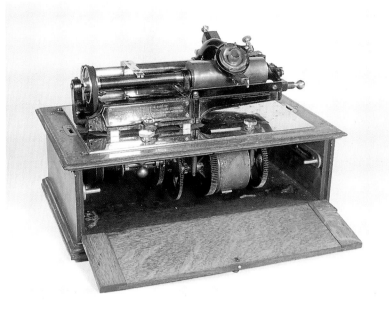

2-31
An Edison Class "M" modified with a McDonald motor in a drop-front cabinet usually associated with Graphophones. *Courtesy of the Charles Hummel Collections.*

2-32
A Class "M" modified in 1895 with an Amet motor using the early-style governor. Notice "AMET MOTOR THE CHICAGO TALKING MACH CO" cast into governor support arm. *Courtesy of the Charles Hummel Collections.*

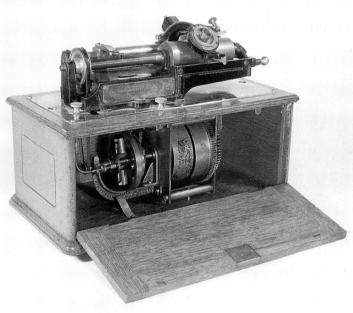

2-33
As Amet continued production through 1895, cabinets became more ornate. *Courtesy of Sam Sheena.*

2-34
The motor of the previous machine showing a transitional governor. *Courtesy of Sam Sheena.*

2-35
The final step of Amet motor evolution. Note that the 3-ball governor is now entirely conventional. *Courtesy of Sam Sheena.*

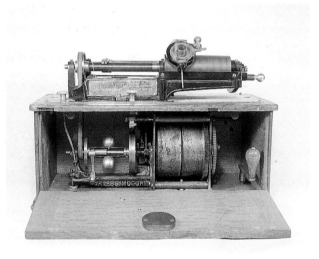

2-36
An Edison Class "M" powered by an Amet-built "Peerless Motor" with a two-ball governor. *Courtesy of the Howard Hazelcorn Collection.*

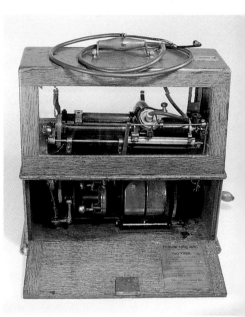

2-37
An Edison Class "M" converted in 1895 to coin-slot operation by the Western Phonograph Company of Chicago. The motor is an Amet. *Courtesy of the Charles Hummel Collections.*

2-38
A close-up reveals details of the Amet motor with the transitional governor and the Western Phonograph Company label. *Courtesy of the Charles Hummel Collections.*

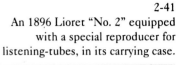

2-41
2-41
An 1896 Lioret "No. 2" equipped
with a special reproducer for
listening-tubes, in its carrying case.

2-39
An 1895 Type "S" coin-slot
Graphophone still using the
old treadle machine upper
works powered by an electric
motor. This cabinet design
would serve Columbia coin-
ops well into the next
century. *Courtesy of Sam
Sheena.*

2-40
An Edison Class "M" Phonograph with an interesting repeating attach-
ment sold by the United States Phonograph Company of Newark, New
Jersey. This style repeater was originally used in the "Kansas" coin-slot
mechanism patented by George Tewkesbury. *Courtesy of the Charles
Hummel Collections.*

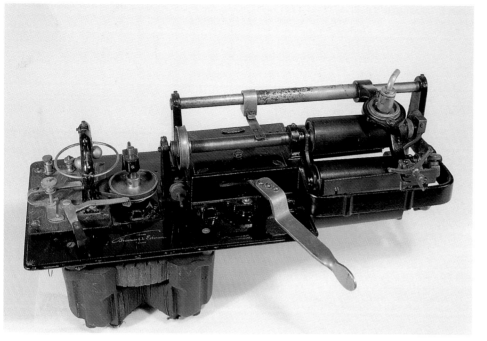

2-43
The 1896 "Chicago Ediphone" of which virtually nothing is known. The Amet motor is the later type with a 3-ball conventional governor. Amet was embroiled in legal trouble during 1896, and the "Chicago Ediphone" could not have long survived. No connection should be made between this early machine and the later Edison machine of the same name. *Courtesy of Allen Koenigsberg.*

2-42
The "Multiplex" attachment offered briefly in 1896. A five-cylinder carousel allowed different selections to be played in succession. *Courtesy of the Charles Hummel Collections.*

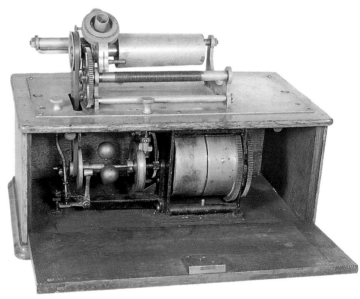

2-44
The re-named "Echophone" used a motor and winding key arrangement different from the "Metaphone". The transmission of sound ("molecular vibration" in Amet's words) was through the hollow glass tube to a resonating chamber composed of wood and rubber. A horn or listening-tubes could be attached. *Courtesy of George F. Paul.*

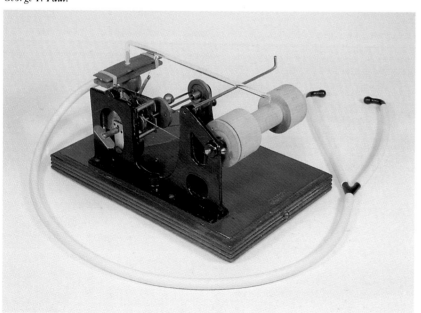

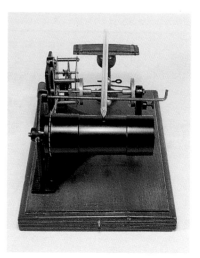

2-45
The final version of the "Echophone" used a mandrel made of gutta-percha. *Courtesy of the Howard Hazelcorn Collection.*

2-46
An 1897 advertisement offering Echophones with subscriptions to Demorest's magazine. *Courtesy of George F. Paul.*

2-49
The Type "A" ("Columbia") of 1896 used a simplified motor and cast-iron upper works to lower the price of a Graphophone to $25.00. *Courtesy of George F. Paul.*

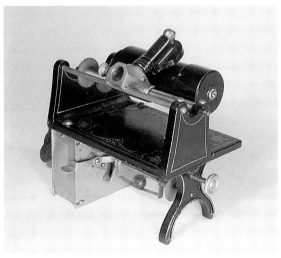

2-47
A "Colibri" of 1897. This unusual machine of French manufacture suggests elements of both Amet's "Echophone" (black recessed mandrel) and the early Graphophone (gutta percha reproducer). The reproducer carriage and half-nut are a single casting which lifts off to be reset at the beginning of the record.

2-48
The unorthodox marking of this machine suggests that it was part of Amet's inventory remaindered by Columbia to a variety of outlets. The emphasis was on quick sales rather than appropriate use of Edison's name!

2-50
The industry's first spring-driven coin-slot talking machine: the 1896 coin-operated Type "N" which sold for $50.00. *Courtesy of George F. Paul.*

53

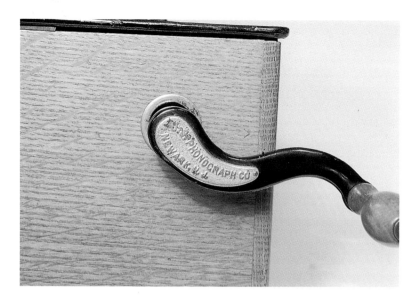

2-51
The crank of this very early "Spring-Motor" identifies the United States Phonograph Company. *Courtesy of the William Kocher Collection.*

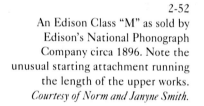

2-52
An Edison Class "M" as sold by Edison's National Phonograph Company circa 1896. Note the unusual starting attachment running the length of the upper works. *Courtesy of Norm and Janyne Smith.*

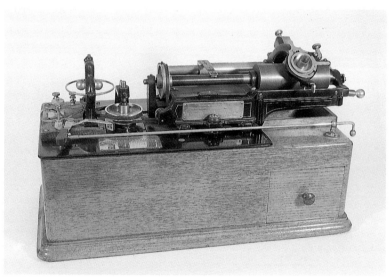

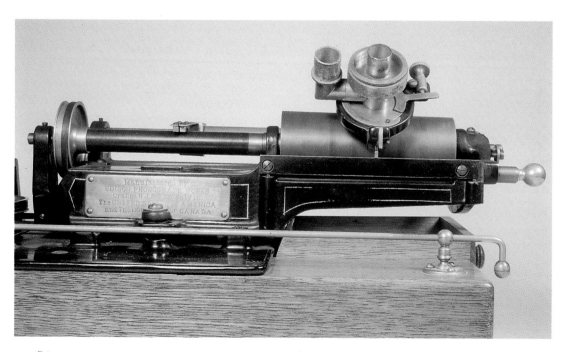

2-53
The seldom-seen Edison "New Duplex Speaker" of 1896 sold for $9.00 and was an attempt to better amplify and distribute the sound. It required the use of two suspended horns. *Courtesy of Norm and Janyne Smith.*

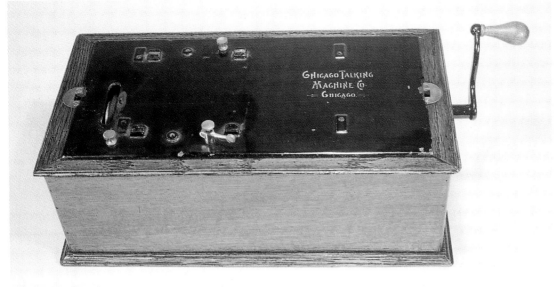

2-54
The Chicago Talking Machine
Company offered this cabinet
and motor (inspired by the
triple-spring motor used by
Edison) to adapt electric
Phonographs and
Graphophones. The motor was
made primarily of aluminum, an
innovative material at the time.
The bedplate is drilled to
accept either Graphophone or
Phonograph upper works.
Courtesy of George F. Paul.

2-55
The "Chicago Motor" was briefly
offered for $40.00. The motor frame,
all gears and main spring barrel were
made of aluminum. *Courtesy of George
F. Paul.*

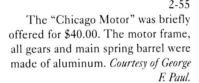

2-56
The "Chicago Motor" coupled
with an Edison Phonograph,
offered complete by the Chicago
Talking Machine Company for
$100.00. *Courtesy of George F.
Paul.*

2-57
The "Chicago Motor" coupled with a
recycled Bell-Tainter upper works.
Courtesy of Sam Sheena.

2-59
A close-up of Edison "Home" Phonograph No.
394 shows the upper casting with open frame
beneath the feedscrew. Cast "fingers" to the
right of the nickeled patent plate hold the lift-
lever in the resting position. Both of these
features were soon abandoned. *Courtesy of the
William Kocher Collection.*

2-58
A very early Edison "Home" Phonograph (No. 394). The "Home" had
been introduced in April of 1896 at
$40.00. *Courtesy of the William Kocher
Collection.*

2-61
A December 1896 advertisement introducing the new lever-wound spring motor Berliner Gramophone. *Courtesy of George F. Paul.*

2-62
The first Berliner with a spring motor, housed in a round metal enclosure, was offered in December 1896, for $25.00. The mainspring was wound by lever action. Levi Montross designed the mechanism with the help of Eldridge Johnson. *Courtesy of Norm and Janyne Smith.*

2-60
The Columbia Type "AE", introduced in 1897 for $40.00, was driven by the same type of 2 1/2 volt electric motor used by the Graphophone Company since 1893. *Courtesy of Sam Sheena.*

2-63
This electric coin-slot Type "N" Graphophone in "large cabinet" sold for $100.00 in 1896-1897. *Courtesy of Sam Sheena.*

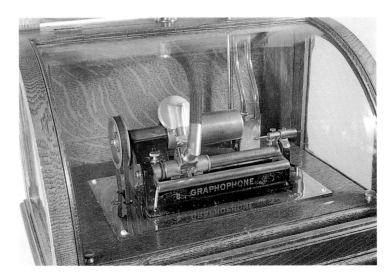

2-64
In 1897, the Type "ASL" coin-slot Graphophone was offered, incorporating the mechanism of the newer Type "A". This example is electrically operated. *Courtesy of Sam Sheena.*

2-65
In early 1897, the lever-wind Berliner mechanism was housed in a square oak cabinet and provided with the new Clark-Johnson soundbox. The price remained $25.00. *Courtesy of Robert Adams.*

2-66
A French "Vichy" automaton of 1896 using a Lioret "Le Merveilleux" cylinder mechanism to imitate the sound of the trumpet. *Courtesy of Sam Sheena.*

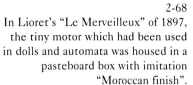

2-68
In Lioret's "Le Merveilleux" of 1897, the tiny motor which had been used in dolls and automata was housed in a pasteboard box with imitation "Moroccan finish".

2-67
The "United States Talking Machine", was made briefly in 1897 and sold for $3.00. Berliner disc records were played by a steel needle vibrating a wooden arm to which eartubes were attached. The turntable was rotated by hand. *Courtesy of Sam Sheena.*

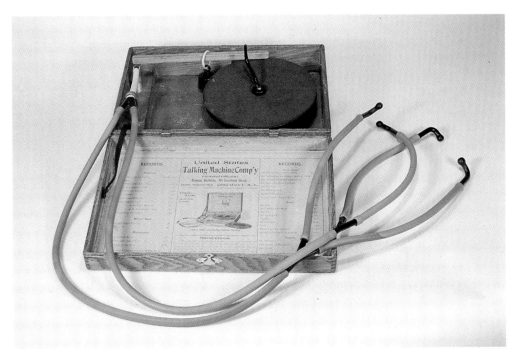

2-69
The Type "AN" Graphophone of 1897 coupled the motor of the Type "N" with the upper works of the Type "A", and sold for $40.00. This combined the powerful McDonald motor with the cheaper-to-produce Type "A" upper works, converting existing stocks of motors into cash.

2-70
The Type "C" Graphophone was introduced in 1897 for $50.00. It was called the "Universal" because it was meant for entertainment as well as business. In the latter capacity, it replaced the Type "C" Bell-Tainter works used in previous business Graphophones. The rocker switch on the right which disengages the pulley during dictation was one of the features continued in the new design. *Courtesy of the William Kocher Collection.*

2-71
Inside the front door of the Type "C" Graphophone was a set of directions. Note the triple-spring motor. It will reappear with minor changes in a number of later models. *Courtesy of the William Kocher Collection.*

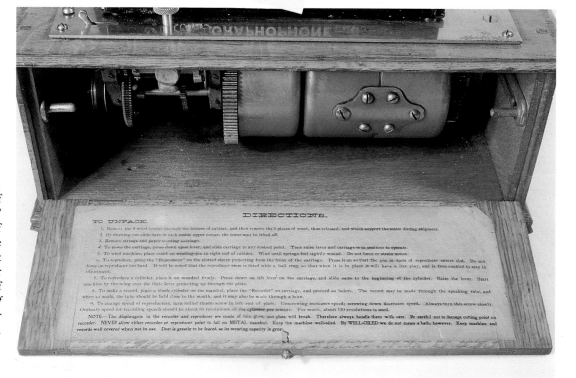

2-72
The "Thornward" is a seldom-seen hybrid Graphophone composed of a Type "N" upper works and a Type "A" motor, offered by Montgomery-Ward of Chicago in 1897. The benefits of this coupling were more apparent for Columbia than for the customer. Type "N" upper works remaining in stock were thereby eliminated. "Thornward" derives from the name of the mail-order company and the family which owned it: Thorn.

2-73
The Type "B" ("Eagle") Graphophone of 1897 was one of Thomas McDonald's finest achievements. A winning combination of simplicity and reliability, it would be copied repeatedly for the next ten years by firms the world over. It sold for $10.00 uncased and for $12.00 in an oak "hand cabinet". It was sold with a 10" black conical horn, but could be equipped, as shown, with horns of larger dimension. *Courtesy of Norm and Janyne Smith.*

2-74
This purpose-built cabinet was used by an exhibitor to allow multiple auditions of a record. The customer paid his nickel, put on a set of listening tubes, and the exhibitor commenced the performance. *Courtesy of George F. Paul.*

2-75
The interior view shows a Type "A"
Graphophone to which the listening-
tubes are connected. *Courtesy of
George F. Paul.*

2-76
An 1898 flyer from the Peter
Bacigalupi agency in San Francisco.

2-77
This Type "AN" Graphophone was
equipped with a medium-sized horn
in the flared-bell style typical of the
mid-1890s. The diagonal horn
support rolls along the front of the
bedplate on a small wheel. *Courtesy of
the Howard Hazelcorn Collection.*

2-78
In his efforts to offer a lower-priced spring-driven Gramophone, Frank Seaman engaged Levi H. Montross to produce an alternative to Johnson's "Improved Gramophone". The motor of the "Montross" machine was wound with a horizontal crank, unlike the Johnson model. The correct horn had a red stripe to match the color of the turntable felt. *Courtesy of Dr. Jay Tartell.*

2-79
The horn support of the "Montross" machine was simplified to a bent rod. As a result of a suit by Johnson in May 1898, each unsold "Montross" machine received a plate numbering it consecutively. This may been seen immediately above the horn support receptacle. 2000 were built; this example is No. 1617. *Courtesy of Dr. Jay Tartell.*

2-80
A.T. Armstrong's "Double-Bell Wonder" of 1898 was offered for $18.00, proving that a lower-priced alternative to the "Improved Gramophone" was possible. J.W. Jones had patented a mechanical-feed device for these machines, but none have been discovered. The brass plug on the top of the cabinet indicates the intended location of the device. *Courtesy of the Howard Hazelcorn Collection.*

PLAYS, SINGS, TALKS, LIKE A THING OF LIFE.

The Wonder Double=Bell Talking Machine.

Two distinct, nickel-plated brass bells, like a band instrument—instead of a tin horn—producing the sweetest, clearest tone and double the volume of sound of others. **The Wonder Talking Machine is not a Toy.** Is simple, compact, dust-proof, durable. Mechanically perfect. Volume enough to fill the largest auditorium, yet can be adapted to any parlor. Indestructible records, made by a new process. A whole entertainment in itself.

Price, $18. Best, yet costs least.

Money returned if not satisfactory. Invented and manufactured by **C. G. CONN**, maker of the celebrated Wonder Solo Cornets, etc. *Agents wanted everywhere.* Send for descriptive catalogue.

MANDOLINS and VIOLINS made by C. G. Conn, have the same superior degree of excellence that characterizes his famous band instruments. Unrivaled in tone-quality, scientifically constructed from carefully selected material, guaranteed superior to all others. Used by professionals everywhere.

...*Send for catalogue and prices...*

C. G. CONN, Manufacturer of Musical Instruments,
Elkhart, Indiana, and 23 E. 14th St., New York City.

2-81.
An advertisement for the "Double-Bell Wonder". *Courtesy of George F. Paul.*

2-82
A slightly later example of the "Wonder" using a metal bedplate and black japanned horns. Manufacture ceased after June 1898. *Courtesy of the Howard Hazelcorn Collection.*

2-83
Frank Seaman heavily promoted the Gramophone. This advertisement dates from December 1898. *Courtesy of George F. Paul.*

2-84
During the latter part of 1898, the "Improved Gramophone" was the only spring-driven disc talking machine available. It was occasionally sold with this all-brass "seamless" horn. *Courtesy of Norm and Janyne Smith.*

2-85
The Type "Q" Graphophone was available in a paper-covered pasteboard box for $6.50.

2-86
The Type "GG" ("Graphophone Grand"), introduced to the public a new type of record which became known as the "five-inch cylinder". This development was designed to increase volume and sound quality due to the correspondingly greater surface speed of a wider-diameter cylinder. In 1898 this machine was offered for a hefty $300.00. 5" "Columbia Grand" records sold for $5.00 each. *Courtesy of Norm and Janyne Smith.*

2-87
The Type "GG" was the only Graphophone to share with Edison the general design of the reproducer carriage, horizontal endgate and feed-screw on the same axis as the mandrel. *Courtesy of Norm and Janyne Smith.*

2-88
The feedscrew cover of Type "GG" serial No. 48 is lettered differently than other examples seen, and appears to have been hand-painted. *Courtesy of the Howard Hazelcorn Collection.*

2-89
Hawthorne and Sheble Manufacturing Company offered a
Columbia Type "B" Graphophone in this oak case with identify-
ing decal in 1898. *Courtesy of Robert T. Lomas.*

2-90
In 1898, the Talking Machine Company of Chicago (not to be
confused with the earlier Chicago Talking Machine Company)
announced an attachment for Phongraphs and Graphophones
known as the "Polyphone". By contriving two reproducers to track
in the same groove, it was claimed that volume would be doubled.
The $15.00 Polyphone attachment shown here is mounted to an
1898 Type "AT" Graphophone. *Courtesy of George F. Paul.*

2-91
A close-up of a "Polyphone" attachment mounted to a Columbia
"Eagle". *Courtesy of the Howard Hazelcorn Collection.*

2-92
Lt. Gianni Bettini offered a high-quality line of reproducing/recording attachments for Phonographs and Graphophones. This incandescent-motor Type "AI" Graphophone from 1898 is equipped with a "Bettini Attachment". *Courtesy of the Howard Hazelcorn Collection.*

2-93
A "Bettini Micro-Attachment" on an 1898 Edison "Standard". Bettini horns commonly had lightweight aluminum bells and red painted steel bodies, with a soldered metal elbow.

2-94
An Edison "Spring Motor" equipped with a Bettini recorder and rather unusual black Bettini horn. *Courtesy of Sam Sheena.*

2-95 (Opposite page)
A close-up of a Bettini reproducer, showing engraved trademark. *Courtesy of Sam Sheena.*

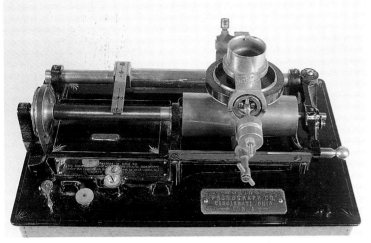

2-96
An early Edison "Spring Motor" with unusual identification plate for the Ohio Phonograph Company, equipped with a "Bettini Micro-Attachment". *Courtesy of Sam Sheena.*

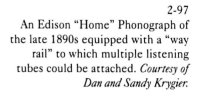

2-97
An Edison "Home" Phonograph of the late 1890s equipped with a "way rail" to which multiple listening tubes could be attached. *Courtesy of Dan and Sandy Krygier.*

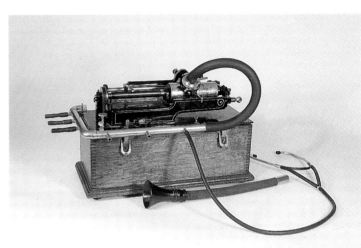

2-100
A circa 1898 interior shot of Berliner Gramophone facilities at 10th and Lombard in Washington, D.C. Note the dismantled "Montross Gramophone" and earlier metal-cased lever-wound Gramophone on the bench to the left. *Thanks to Raymond Wile, Courtesy of the late Robert Sanders.*

2-98
A rare 1898 cylinder box from a Japanese distributor of Edison Phonographs, showing the early "Standard". Records from this company appear to have been domestically recorded.

2-99
The "Oratiograph" was a quaint German-made cylinder machine of 1898 which used uniquely-sized records. The colorful graphics, manual fly-wheel mechanism and antic bend of the horn all suggest an instrument of novelty rather than musical value. *Courtesy of the Julien Anton Collection.*

2-101
The Berliner shipping department circa 1899, showing wrapped
horns like stalagmites on the floor and partially-assembled
Gramophones on the shelves to the right. *Thanks to Raymond Wile,
Courtesy of the late Robert Sanders.*

2-102
An 1899 Gramophone recording session in Europe, with engineer
William Sinkler Darby at the center. The accompanist and
rakishly-posed vocalist are unknown. The zinc master of this
performance could be rapidly processed by acid-etching and
auditioned on the "Improved Gramophone" atop the piano. *Thanks
to Raymond Wile, Courtesy of the late Robert Sanders.*

CHAPTER THREE:

THE TALKING MACHINE BECOMES AN INDUSTRY, 1899-1903

3-1
A.T. Armstrong's "Vitaphone" of 1899. This machine was offered for only $15.00, but had no effective sales organization. Columbia allowed the "Vitaphone" to wither while pursuing Frank Seaman's "Zonophone". *Courtesy of the Howard Hazelcorn Collection.*

The years leading up to 1899 witnessed activities which transformed the talking machine from a small machine-shop trade into a boiling cauldron of ambitious, litigious interests. From this explosive brew an industry would emerge, producing a bewildering variety of fascinating products. Of the talking machine's future, there was now no doubt. All that remained to be decided was which of the warring interests would survive.

-1899-

Edison's National Phonograph Company was enjoying steadily increasing sales of the $20.00 "Standard", $30.00 "Home", and the $75.00 "Spring-Motor" Phonographs. In February, Edison introduced two new models comprising both the cheapest and most expensive Phonographs now available. The Edison "Concert" Phonograph at $125.00 was a "Spring-Motor" with an enlarged playing mechanism to play the new 5" diameter cylinders. The Edison "Gem" was the smallest Edison Phonograph offered to the public, and cost only $7.50. Edison was finally competing with the popular Type "B" and Type "Q" Graphophones.

Columbia reduced the price of its "Graphophone Grand" from $300.00 to $150.00 in response to Edison's $125.00 "Concert" Phonograph. With an extensive line of cylinder Graphophones in place, Columbia prepared to break into the disc talking machine market using the Jones machine patent. As J.W. Jones tooled up to supply disc records, Columbia readied itself for disc machine manufacture.

In March 1899, Frank Seaman chartered a new corporation to replace his original National Gramophone Company. This new firm had an increased capitalization and a broader charter than before, and was known as the National Gramophone Corporation.

By July, Columbia had introduced its answer to Edison's $125.00 "Concert" Phonograph: the "Home Grand Graphophone", selling for $100.00. The Type "HG" used the same motor as the Type "AT" in an enlarged "AT"-style cabinet. Advertisements trumpeted the machine as:

> The Real Thing; not an Imitation.
> Made on the same Principle as the Graphophone Grand, by the Same Makers.
> Reproduces the Same Records with the Same Marvelous Effects.

Probably as a result of its preparations for building and marketing the "HG", as well as keeping pace with the phenomenal sales of its Type "B", "Q", and "AT" cylinder Graphophones, American Graphophone had encountered manufacturing difficulties in producing a disc talking machine. By mid-1899, Albert Armstrong had been forced to arrange for manufacture of machines with the International Stylophone Company of New Haven, Connecticut. The resultant disc talking machine was called the "Vitaphone". J.W. Jones was supplying discs in the form of "Red Process" records. These were stamped "American Talking Machine Record Disk", and were colored brick-red.

Protected by the Graphophone patents, the "Vitaphone" elicited immediate response from Seaman's National Gramophone Corporation:

> The recent appearance of circulars and advertisements put out by pirates who are endeavoring to break into the talking machine trade with an apparatus using 'hard flat indestructible' records, does not, in our judgment, render it necessary for us to add anything to what we have already said on the subject of infringing mechanisms.
>
> We will not insult your intelligence by any further exposé of these people. We have entire faith that your own business perspicacity, and the confidence which has grown out of dealing with us and in our goods, will certainly lead you to feel that so long as you confine your dealings in our style of talking machines to us, you are safe from all patent or legal complications.

NATIONAL GRAM-O-PHONE CORPORATION
November 10, 1899

While the "Vitaphone" was being launched, Seaman's Universal Talking Machine Company was preparing to produce its own disc machine, the Zonophone, under the patents of Louis Valiquet. In order to insure a supply of discs for it, Seaman had his workers drilling additional holes in Berliner records to accommodate the retractable record-securing pin found on the Zonophone turntable. Additionally, high-quality unlabeled pirate discs with Zonophone "depressions" (to accept the securing pin) on their reverse sides exist which are thought to have been made by Universal's John English at about this time.

In the fall of 1899, with his bets suitably hedged, Seaman made his final attempts to secure the Berliner Company's order for the Zonophone, supplied by Universal. The Zonophone's lower cost and higher quality could not overcome the Berliner group's covert financial ties to Johnson. Seaman presented another disc talking machine, this one designed by R.L. Gibson of Philadelphia, for Berliner Company approval. It was the same story: Seaman was warned not to handle any infringing goods. Presumably, Frank Seaman's patience had reached its limit.

In September, Edison lowered the price of the "Concert" Phonograph to $100.00, matching that of the Type "HG" Graphophone. Columbia had by this time made something of a reputation by undercutting Edison retail prices. Lowering the price of the "Concert" set the busy Thomas MacDonald to work once more, with results in time for Christmas.

3-2
Nipper and the "Improved Gramophone" as immortalized in "His Master's Voice." *Courtesy of George F. Paul.*

In late September 1899, artist Francis Barraud approached Managing Director William Barry Owen in the Gramophone Company offices at 31 Maiden Lane, London, and asked to borrow a brass horn for a painting he wished to modify. The artist explained that he had inherited a fox terrier from his late brother a decade earlier. In 1893 or 1894 Barraud had used the animal in a painting entitled "His Master's Voice." The faithful dog, Nipper, was depicted listening to a recording of the dead brother's voice being played on a British Edison-Bell "Commercial" Phonograph. Showing a penchant for the maudlin, Barraud pictured dog and Phonograph perched atop a casket. The Edison-Bell management had shown no interest in the picture at the time, and the painting had been gathering dust in Barraud's garret. Recently, a friend had suggested substituting a brass horn for the black one pictured on the Edison machine in order to brighten the picture. Owen offered to purchase the painting if Barraud substituted an "Improved Gramophone" for the Edison Phonograph. This was speedily done, and the painting served as a wall decoration for Owen's office.

Columbia was not yet manufacturing a disc product, but was receiving a royalty from Armstrong in return for its patent protection of the Connecticut-made "Vitaphone". This situation was not what the company had in mind. Accordingly, Columbia offered a hand-driven "Toy" disc Graphophone for the Christmas trade of 1899, probably using tools prepared under Armstrong's license. This machine was the first Disc Graphophone, and came supplied with vertically cut single-faced wax discs 3 3/8" in diameter which played from the center outward. Columbia's "Toy" Graphophone sold for $3.00 with five discs. It did poorly in the marketplace, even when the price was lowered to only $1.50.

Price of Toy Graphophone, including reproducer, horn and 5 disk records, $1.50
Price of disk records for the Toy, per set of five, 50 cents.

63

3-3
The 1899 Columbia "Toy" Disc Graphophone. This was the first disc machine manufactured by the Columbia forces. Despite its innocuous appearance and promotion as a child's plaything, the "Toy", with its small center-start brown wax discs, was an early test for Columbia's entry into the disc market. *Courtesy of George F. Paul.*

Columbia's other entries for the Christmas trade were the new MacDonald-designed "Columbia Grand" (Type "AG") and the redesigned Type "HG". The "Columbia Grand" was identical to the old "HG" except for the "AG" stamp on the ID plate and a $75.00 price tag. The new "HG" had a six-spring motor and a larger more ornate cabinet, while retaining the $100.00 price.

-1900-

This was an election year, and the talking machine participated in a small way. One of the primary points of debate was the question of converting the American monetary system from the "gold standard" to the "silver standard". Arguably the most notable campaign speech was Democrat William Jennings Bryan's "Cross of Gold" oration. Records of the speech sold well, although not always with the knowledge that Bryan himself did not make the recording. Republican candidate William McKinley felt that the talking machine lacked dignity, and like Bryan demurred from making recordings. Campaign songs for both candidates were offered. Republican songs included "One Good Term Deserves Another," "I'd Leave My Job To Vote For You" and "You Can't Keep McKinley From the Chair." Democratic campaign songs included "At the Polls," "Happy When We Get Him" and parody on "You'll Get All That Is Coming To You." The talking machine continued to reflect societal mores and tastes, as well as political ambitions.

3-4
The November 18, 1899, issue of *Judge* carried this lampoon of William Jennings Bryan, clearly enamored of the sound of his own voice! *Courtesy of George F. Paul.*

74

On March 5, 1900, Thomas Lambert incorporated a company in Chicago to mass-produce moulded celluloid cylinder records. By the summer, Lambert cylinders would reach the market in small numbers. Usually colored pink, these were the first moulded cylinders offered to the public. Lambert assigned 2/5 of his patent to Brian and Albert Philpot, whose names would re-emerge over a decade later.

Columbia was ever persistent in its effort to enter the disc talking machine trade. It had backed the "Wonder" and the "Vitaphone" as well as producing its little "Toy" Graphophone, without satisfactory financial or legal results. By late March of 1900, the mutually impatient forces of Columbia and Frank Seaman had found each other. The alliance of Seaman and Columbia had immediate, explosive results. On April 6, the American Graphophone Company licensed Frank Seaman to manufacture Zonophones under Graphophone patents. The machine line included the $25.00 Type "A" with glass panels in the cabinet, the $22.50 Type "B" and the $18.00 Type "C". All used the same mechanism, soundbox, and horn. Zonophone records were 7" diameter, and the words "Zon-o-phone Record - National Gram-o-phone Corp. - All Rights Reserved" were etched into the label area within a shield. This shield could well have symbolized the protection of the Columbia-held patents.

Albert Armstrong, financial backer of the American Talking Machine Company and marketer of the "Vitaphone" and its "Red Process" disc records, received a letter dated April 12, 1900, from the American Graphophone Company stating that it "...had decided to grant an exclusive license for machines of the Gramophone type to the Universal Talking Machine Co...This arrangement will not preclude your continuance in the manufacture of records, if it be advantageous to do so..."

Armstrong, suddenly deprived of Columbia's support for his Vitaphone, was anxious not to lose control of his disc record manufacturing as well. His would-be protection, the Jones application, seemed interminably mired in the U.S. Patent Office. In a probable state of panic, Armstrong appealed to Philip Mauro, Columbia's legal counsel, to expedite favorable action on the Jones application. It was completely re-written, only to be refused again.

Three thousand miles away, Emile Berliner was visiting the Gramophone Company's London offices when he noticed the Barraud painting of "His Master's Voice" hanging on the wall. With an evidently shrewder eye than Owen, Berliner brought a copy back to the U.S., trademarked the image, and used it on the last U.S. Berliner record catalogue issued in June, 1900.

On May 5, 1900, Seaman's National Gramophone Corporation dropped a bombshell. It accepted a consent decree admitting the infringement of Bell-Tainter patents by Berliner, thus enabling Columbia to terminate Berliner's Gramophone and record sales outlet through the National Gramophone Corporation. In addition, a permanent injunction was granted on June 25 prohibiting Berliner from selling merchandise to anyone other than Seaman. This action made the Zonophone the only disc talking machine which could be legally sold in America. Seaman had finally changed his allegiance: Columbia dealers began selling Zonophones and Zonophone records.

3-5
Disc competitors of 1900: Berliner, Vitaphone, Zonophone.
Courtesy of George F. Paul.

At the same time, recognizing the potential value of the Jones patent application for recording in wax, Columbia and attorney Philip Mauro exerted tremendous effort to obtain favorable action from the Patent Office. Claims were repeatedly re-written as they were rejected and returned.

In the midst of the fast-evolving disc market, Edison and Columbia took steps to make some of their cylinder machines more affordable. During June 1900, Edison lowered the price of the "Concert" Phonograph to

$75.00, and the "Spring-Motor" Phonograph to $50.00. True to form, Columbia discarded the aluminum bedplate of its $75.00 "AG", substituting black-painted cast iron and lowering the price to $50.00. Edison's "Concert" Phonograph was never offered for less than $75.00. Columbia continued to underprice comparable Edison products, but sometimes at the expense of quality. Columbia's use of injection-moulded "pot metal" alloy for certain Graphophone components may have been cost-effective at the time, but these parts would often fail over the passage of time.

The English Gramophone Company's success in Europe had been noted by the Zonophone management in America. Frederick M. Prescott was sent to Europe during this period to head a new sales organization for the Universal Talking Machine Company called the International Zonophone Company. Prescott's new organization would operate for only three years, but would make pioneering achievements in the field of recorded classical music. Beneath the blue labels of International Zonophone discs were the young voices of future operatic legends, notably Tetrazzini and Caruso.

3-6
The Lambert Typewriter, as marketed by the Gramophone and Typewriter Company of England. This particular typewriter was designed and used by Frank Lambert, who developed the incised lead recording machine of 1879, pictured in the first chapter. *Courtesy of the Aaron and Thea Cramer Collection.*

In London, William Barry Owen had reasoned that diversification of the Gramophone Company would be wise. To that end, the Company began selling Lambert (no relation to Thomas) typewriters and the Company's name was changed to the Gramophone and Typewriter Company.

Back in Camden, New Jersey, Eldridge Johnson had recently completed a new three-story factory which was turning out "Improved Gramophones" by the thousands. His precarious position in light of the Seaman/Colum-

bia threat had not escaped him. Both Johnson's and Berliner's enterprises were at risk, and needed legal sheltering. In June 1900, Philadelphian Charles Adamson issued a prospectus offering trust certificates in exchange for stock shares of the Berliner Gramophone Company, the U.S. Gramophone Company (holder of the Berliner patents) and the newly-formed Johnson Sound Recording Company (holder of the Johnson patents). The permanent injunction of June 25 brought orders for Gramophones to an abrupt halt. On July 7, the Consolidated Talking Machine Company of America was formed by Adamson. While litigation proceeded, Johnson continued his efforts to build a catalogue of new wax-recorded discs.

Faced with a $50,000-$60,000 debt on the factory and a large inventory of unsold "Improved Gramophones", Johnson was forced to go into talking machine retailing. Leon F. Douglass was brought in from Chicago to manage sales of Gramophones and records. Sales of Johnson's new products were conducted through Johnson's newly-established Consolidated Talking Machine Company (not to be confused with Adamson's patent-sheltering Consolidated Talking Machine Company of America). Johnson's new merchandise was notable in one important respect: the records. These Johnson discs were the first to use conventional paper labels (Patent No. 739,318 filed August 8, 1900), on which was printed: "IMPROVED GRAM-O-PHONE RECORD". Johnson had obtained the rights to use the "His Master's Voice" trademark, and it was used consistently by Johnson in his advertising and letterheads, but not yet on machines or records. The Johnson talking machines for 1900 comprised a $3.00 hand-driven "Toy" (which came with the first double-faced disc ever offered to the public), a $6.00 hand-driven Type "D", a $12.00 spring-driven Type "A", an $18.00 Type "B" (which was basically the old "Improved Gramophone"), and the $25.00 Type "C".

The fall of 1900 was a crucial period in Eldridge Johnson's career. In October, Frank Seaman and Columbia unleashed a massive legal attack on Johnson, claiming that his Consolidated Talking Machine Company was a thinly disguised front for the Berliner interest and therefore violated the permanent injunction of June 25. In addition, the Gramophone forces represented in Adamson's Consolidated Talking Machine Company of America took a dim view of Johnson's choice of "Consolidated" for the name of his sales agency. For both parties to survive, it was important to distance the Berliner interest from Johnson's enterprise (at least on paper). As a result, Johnson listed the name of his company simply as "Eldridge R. Johnson." Columbia sued Johnson in October on the grounds that his products infringed various claims of the Bell-Tainter patents. Johnson's position appeared so desperate that he approached Howard Hayes of Edison's legal staff to investigate the possibility of manufacturing the Johnson disc machines at the Edison Phonograph Works under its shop license obtained in the 1896 cross-licensing agreement with Columbia. Johnson's son later wrote that his father had loaded a wagon with record matrices and was preparing to hide them in the New Jersey countryside if Columbia should prevail in the courts. Johnson's star was on the rise, though he might not have known it, and Columbia was unable to obtain an injunction.

The word "Gramophone" was the property of Berliner, and in an attempt to appease Frank Seaman, the Consolidated Talking Machine Company of America forced Johnson to discontinue his use of the term. As a result, for approximately six weeks, Johnson's records were labeled "IMPROVED RECORD". For the moment, Johnson had succeeded in defending his enterprise. In December 1900, Johnson began labeling his records and (gradually) his talking machines as "VICTOR". Several stories surfaced over the years regarding Johnson's choice of "Victor" as a name. Possible reasons included his admiration of the "Victor" bicycle, and the wife of Leon Douglass, Victoria. Johnson family legend holds that "Victor" was chosen because it meant "winner." As the tumultuous year of 1900 drew to a close, "Victor" would inspire confidence and hope.

tor" and "Monarch" were marketing names: the 7" discs being called "Victors" and the 10" discs designated "Monarchs". Johnson applied these grades to his talking machines as well, introducing a $40.00 "Monarch" and, for a brief period, a $60.00 "Deluxe Monarch" with a heavily carved cabinet.

In February, all cabinets of the Edison Phonograph line were redesigned and referred to as "new style" cabinets. Up to this time, the only Edison Phonograph to carry a banner decal had been the "Home". With the introduction of the "new style" cabinets, all Edison Phonographs now had banners proclaiming their model name such as "Edison Gem Phonograph", and "Edison Concert Phonograph". The "Spring-Motor" Phonograph was rechristened the "Triumph".

3-8
Courtesy of George F. Paul.

3-7
To the left, an Eldridge Johnson "Consolidated" record of 1900: the first disc to carry a paper label. To the right, a "Climax" disc of 1901: the second paper-labeled disc. *Courtesy of George F. Paul*

-1901-

In January, Johnson introduced his first 10" diameter records, at first labeled "VICTOR TEN INCH RECORD". Within weeks the label was changed to "VICTOR MONARCH RECORD". At this point, "Vic-

In March, Seaman's Universal Talking Machine Company lost its chief record experimenter, John C. English, to the George Burt Company of Milburn, New Jersey. (This was the same Burt Company which had made Berliner test pressings for Frank Seaman three years earlier.) Burt established a subsidiary on August 1, 1901: the Globe Record Company. Within a short time, Globe was producing a satisfactory disc record known as the "Climax".

Emile Berliner had become aware of the repeated attempts to secure a favorable action on the Jones application, and had filed for a similar patent solely to protect himself from Columbia. On April 17, 1901, no doubt to the consternation of the Graphophone interests, the Jones application was placed in interference with that of Emile Berliner. This meant further delay for the impatient Columbia Phonograph Company.

Zonophone discs, like all others of the time except Victor "Monarchs", were 7" in diameter. In May 1901, a 9" Zonophone record called the "Superba" was introduced, using the familiar etched shield marking of the National Gramophone Corporation. The Zonophone catalogue offered this perspective:

> For more than a year we have been working upon a record with a larger sized capacity, sparing neither time, money nor inventive skill in the often baffling experiments through which it has finally been brought to complete success—the flat despair of rivals who have rushed upon the market a large sized record necessarily subject to all the very defects which alone our long experimenting, and our special process have finally overcome.

A "Concert Grand" Zonophone equipped with a 30" horn made its appearance for $40.00. In addition, a plain-looking Type "D" for $12.00 had also been added to the Universal catalogue.

Over the preceding nine months, Eldridge Johnson had built up a respectable business through sales of his existing stock and newly-designed machines. His recording procedure was based in wax, for which he had no patent protection. The Jones application was, no doubt, a major concern to Johnson.

The flurry of legal activities and advertising threats in this period created uncertainty on the part of dealers and customers regarding the Zonophone. The National Gramophone Corporation, financially drained and experiencing disappointing sales, applied for a voluntary dissolution in September of 1901.

America was shocked by the assassination of President William McKinley in September. Talking machine companies rushed to produce recordings of certain McKinley speeches, such as "McKinley's Inaugural Address" and "McKinley's Pan American Address." These were often described by salesmen, knowingly or unknowingly, as the actual voice of the dead President. In actuality, William McKinley maintained his antipathy for the talking machine and never spoke into a recording horn.

Columbia found that the patent interference with Berliner was proceeding favorably. Encouraged, the Graphophone management moved to invest in the Jones application. Columbia attorney Philip Mauro had dealt directly with Jones and had taken out an option under his own name. Albert T. Armstrong, the long-suffering benefactor of the Jones application, was not informed

of these maneuvers. Moreover, in the numerous revisions and rewritten claims Armstrong's name had disappeared. Columbia made necessary arrangements with the Burt Company, and was now prepared to handle the new "Climax" records supplied by the subsidiary Globe Record Company.

The all-consuming disc talking machine affairs of 1901 did not bring cylinder development to a halt. Columbia began superheated moulding of brown-wax cylinders, resulting in a harder surface, increased volume and the nearly limitless possibility of duplication. Edison also perfected a method of moulding black-wax cylinders using a gold-sputtering or vaporizing process, and began stockpiling an inventory. The end was in sight for the expensive, cumbersome 5" cylinders.

Columbia introduced a line of cylinder machines designed to play both the standard and 5" size cylinders. These were the $25.00 "AB", the $50.00 "AF", and the $75.00 "AD". In addition, Columbia introduced the Type "AA": a small, highly-nickeled machine in an ornate cabinet which played standard-sized cylinders. It used a motor closely based on the popular Type "B", and cost $18.00.

During October 1901, three noteworthy events in talking machine history took place. Eldridge Johnson, having come to terms with Emile Berliner and the Consolidated Talking Machine Company of America, reorganized his business on October 3. Johnson named his new firm the Victor Talking Machine Company. Confident of eventual victory, Columbia introduced its first spring-driven Disc Graphophones: the $40.00 "AH" and $20.00 "AJ". It supplied 7" and 10" paper-labeled "Climax" discs to play on them. Despite obvious infringements of Berliner and Johnson patents, Columbia felt secure that the Jones application was its "ace in the hole" by which its disc competition would be eliminated. The Universal Talking Machine Company, now deprived of its sales agent (the National Gramophone Corporation), was forced into a sale of assets on October 28. The production of Zonophones ceased while the company reorganized.

On December 10, 1901, after more than four years of effort, the Jones patent for recording in wax (No. 688,739) was issued. Columbia quickly purchased it from J.W. Jones for $25,000. This patent, in addition to the famous Bell-Tainter patents, gave Columbia a formidable legal position in the disc market.

The lines were now drawn for a legal battle between Victor and Columbia the likes of which would dwarf the struggles of 1900. For a young company like Victor, such a course could be ruinous. Eldridge Johnson and his sales manager Leon Douglass began to investigate a promising possibility in Milburn, New Jersey.

-1902-

During January, Victor began using the trademark "His Master's Voice" on its record labels. Nipper and his Gramophone were on their way to immortality. By mid-January 1902, Eldridge Johnson and Leon Douglass had made several visits to the Burt Company management in Milburn, New Jersey, and negotiated one of the most brilliant coups in talking machine history. While Columbia president Edward Easton was in California, Johnson and Douglass bought Burt's Globe Record Company for $10,000. Burt would be entitled to collect any unpaid bills due to Globe from Columbia, and would receive a lucrative pressing contract from Victor. In one decisive move, the tables had been turned on Columbia, which was now deprived of its only source of records for the new Disc Graphophones. Columbia had neither pressing plant nor personnel such as John English who could produce a satisfactory disc record. Globe's matrices were promptly shipped to Victor facilities in Philadelphia where they were marked "VTM".

Edward Easton's rage upon hearing this news can only be imagined. Squarely over a barrel, Easton began negotiations with his bitter rivals to re-acquire his disc record business. By mid-February, it had been agreed that Columbia would take possession of Globe for the same price Johnson and Douglass had paid, and would not be subject to suits alleging infringement of Berliner and Johnson patents. In turn, Easton would release Victor and the Gramophone interests from all impending suits against them.

Columbia was now firmly in the disc talking machine business, and Victor was, for the time being, safe from the Columbia patents, especially the almost-stillborn but now formidable Jones patent. This sleight-of-hand by Johnson and Douglass must have been a "bitter pill" for the Graphophone interest to swallow. To forestall any future complications, American Graphophone purchased the entire Burt Company and physically moved it to Bridgeport, Connecticut. Unfortunately for Columbia, these purchases did not include the able services of John C. English, whom Victor had lured into its fold. One wonders just how long English had been working for Johnson...

3-9
Courtesy of George F. Paul.

In February 1902, Edison released his first moulded black-wax cylinders. These produced volume equal to the 5" cylinders at less cost and with far greater ease of handling and storage. From this point on, 5" cylinders were available only by special order, and quietly disappeared from Edison catalogues five years later.

Columbia's efforts were clearly focused on the disc market, but one new cylinder model was introduced during 1902: the $30.00 "AO" in a highly ornate cabinet.

In February 1902, Fred and Will Gaisberg were sent to Milan, Italy, with instructions to record selections of Italian opera. At a performance of Franchetti's *Germania*, the Gaisbergs heard a young singer named Enrico Caruso. According to Fred Gaisberg's later account, they disregarded a cable from London forbidding them to pay Caruso 100 pounds for ten recordings. Fred paid Caruso out of his own pocket, recording ten arias on April 11. These first Caruso discs represent the beginning of a recording career which would make him a household name, help transform the field of serious music into a viable commodity for record companies and bring prosperity to Gramophone and Typewriter and its close affiliate the Victor Talking Machine Company. Other companies would soon preserve Caruso's vibrant tones on record, including Zonophone, the Anglo-Italian Commerce Company (cylinders) and Pathé (cylinders and discs), but none would enjoy a long-lasting relationship with Caruso like Gramophone/Victor. An early indication of the improving business climate was the Gramophone Company's move from Maiden Lane to a large, respectable building at No. 21 City Road in London.

In September 1902, Fred Gaisberg was sent on a long recording trip through India and the Far East. Gaisberg would not return until August of 1903. The Gramophone Company was pursuing ethnic and cultural music in a serious manner.

Back in the States, the Burt Company pressed records for Victor until October 1902, when Victor cancelled the arrangement due to allegedly faulty pressings. These Burt pressings are recognizable today by the presence of a "filled" Zonophone depression on the back and a small "B" printed on the label beneath and to the right of Nipper. The Burt Victors were transitional: the last repercussions of the clandestine, circuitous entry of Columbia into the disc record field.

The Universal Talking Machine *Manufacturing* Company, having been reorganized in December of 1901, began building new Zonophones in early 1902. The Universal Talking Machine Company became the sales agent for Zonophone. Louis Valiquet had designed an attractive line of machines including the "Parlor", "Home", "Concert", and "Concert Grand". Zonophone records of this period still lacked paper labels; the information on the record was incised and filled with white beneath a design of two crossed horns.

The Victor Talking Machine Company had disposed of the earlier Johnson machines and its line was now comprised of the $15.00 "Royal", the $25.00 "Monarch Junior", the $35.00 "Monarch", and the $45.00 "Monarch Special". All of these machines used the traditional support arm/traveling arm arrangement employed since the Kämmer & Reinhardt Gramophones of 1889.

3-10
Courtesy of George F. Paul.

On October 10, 1902, Victor shipped the first of a new type of disc talking machine. It was a "Monarch Special" equipped with a cast rear support upon which the horn was mounted. The soundbox was connected to the horn by a swinging tube of consistent diameter.

The steel needle was now subject only to the weight of the soundbox and the inertia of the hollow arm. The weight of the horn had been removed from the equation. Record wear was significantly diminished with the Victor tubular or "Rigid Arm".

-1903-

On March 9, 1903, Victor announced the availability in America of the Gramophone Company's European recordings of serious music. These discs were pressed in Camden, New Jersey, using Gramophone and Typewriter Company matrices, and carried red labels, or "Red Seals". At a time when regular 10" listings were $1.00 apiece, the "Red Seals" were $2.50. By the end of March, a recording studio had been set up in Carnegie Hall, and domestic recording of "Red Seal" discs was underway. The "Red Seals" were to lend to the disc talking machine an aura of respectability and refinement which would pay dividends far beyond their actual sales.

It did not take Columbia long to recognize the value of Victor's "Red Seal" catalogue. Columbia inaugurated its own "Grand Opera" series using red labels at first, reverting to black when Victor threatened litigation. The Columbia "Grand Opera" series was poorly recorded in comparison to Victor's "Red Seals". In addition, Columbia found that most high-ranking artists had already been secured by Victor.

Columbia's cylinder line, by contrast, was showing more activity at the lower end. During 1903, Columbia introduced the Type "AP" (a "premium" or giveaway machine), along with the $3.00 Type "AQ" and a second version of the enormously popular Type "Q".

On March 11, Victor announced the giant 14" "Deluxe" records. These were designed to play for five minutes due to the increased diameter and recommended slower speed of 60 rpm. By mid-1903, the 14" records had been rechristened "Deluxe Special Records". It would appear that the lesson of the fragile, cumbersome "Concert"/"Grand" cylinders had been lost on Victor. The 14" Victor disc lasted only until the end of 1904. Columbia offered its own 14" discs, with similar lackluster results. The 14" records represented one of the few "dead end" efforts of an otherwise burgeoning disc industry.

On April 13, 1903, Victor shipped a "Monarch Special" equipped with the new "Tapering Hollow Arm". This was a significant acoustical improvement over the tubular "Rigid" arm used for the previous six months. In addition, Johnson's patent (No. 814,786) for the tapering arm included what would become classic features of Victor machines for decades to come. The elbow-restraining clamp was used in virtually all rear-mount, external-horn Victors made from this point onward. The centering pivot for the tapering arm and the goose-neck soundbox tube would be used in Victor products for the next twenty-five years.

During the summer of 1903, the Auburn Button Works of Auburn, New York, made Zonophone test pressings in a brown material. The Universal Talking Machine Manufacturing Company approved the tests, and soon Auburn began pressing brown Zonophone records with green paper labels in 7" and 9" sizes.

Columbia had litigated Universal's recording method since 1900. Any method which used incising or engraving in wax was a clear infringement of the Bell-Tainter patents and the Jones patent controlled by Columbia. In 1903, Universal's chief recorder, George K. Cheney, finally revealed his secret. An apparatus had been devised which allowed an electric spark to arc between a charged wire and the recording stylus. This heated the stylus, allowing it to melt the recording wax rather than incise it.

In June, Prescott's International Zonophone Company was purchased by Deutschen Grammophon AG, the German subsidiary of Gramophone and Typewriter. Victor was planning litigation against Universal, but the June purchase of International Zonophone and the disclosure of Universal's hot-stylus recording method suggested another expedient. In September 1903, Victor purchased the Universal Talking Machine Manufacturing Company for $135,000. Once Universal was in Victor's hands, another cross-licensing arrangement was made with Columbia to avoid pending litigation. Such cross-licensing would occur on a regular basis for several years. Meanwhile, Victor would maintain Zonophone to produce low-cost machines and records, finally dissolving the subsidiary in June of 1912. Zonophone's one-time eminence was reduced to a "dime store" label status. Frank Seaman, in a final show of cheek, made a bid to his erstwhile opponent for Victor's lucrative advertising contract. Eldridge Johnson, having seen quite enough of Seaman for the past seven years, rebuffed the offer. For the redoubtable Frank Seaman, the talking machine business was over.

In October 1903, Victor introduced a 12" disc called the "Deluxe". Black-label popular issues on "Deluxe" records cost $1.50, while the Red Seal versions cost $3.00. Sales of the 14" "Deluxe Special" records had been disappointing; it was hoped that the new 12" format would represent an attractive combination of increased playing time without the weighty, unwieldy characteristics of the "Deluxe Special Records".

3-11
Victor discs showing 7", 10", 12", and 14" sizes. *Courtesy of George F. Paul.*

3-12
Columbia discs showing 7", 10", 12", and 14" sizes. *Courtesy of George F. Paul.*

The "Big Three," Edison, Victor, and Columbia, were now focused primarily on merchandising their products and competing with one another in the marketplace. Columbia adhered to its past policy of opening its own salesrooms and warehouses around the world, while Victor and Edison used already well-established commercial facilities to market their products. A store might feature both Edison and Victor products, and for many years these rivals would maintain a distant but mutually tolerant relationship. By the end of 1903, Columbia may have been aware that its industry status was slipping a bit, but chances are it went unnoticed. The talking machine industry settled into a war of merchandising, where the only losers were the small fry who would attempt to join the fray.

3-14
The Type "BS" Graphophone sold for $20.00 from its introduction in late 1898. Based on the popular Type "B" mechanism, it was carried in Columbia catalogues until 1905. This was the most popular coin-slot in Columbia's history as well as the least-expensive. *Courtesy of Allen Koenigsberg.*

3-13
An Edison advertising card which could be aptly titled: "Looking For A Trademark." *Courtesy of George F. Paul.*

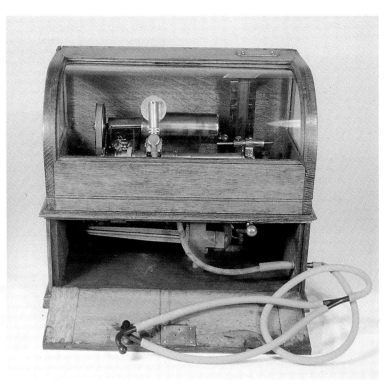

3-15
The Type "ES" coin-slot Graphophone shown here is a $65.00 variant of the more commonly found spring-driven Type "AS", which sold for $35.00. These machines used major components of the Type "A" Graphophone, and replaced the earlier Type "N" coin-slot introduced in 1896. *Courtesy of Sam Sheena.*

3-17
The Type "SG" ("Slot Grand") was offered in 1899 for $100.00 with a spring-driven motor in a floor-standing cabinet. This close-up shows the coin-slot to the lower right, as well as the upper works based on the "HG". This Type "SG" has a Lambert 5" cylinder in place. *Courtesy of Peter N. Dilg, Baldwin Antique Center.*

3-16
The 1899 Edison "H" coin-slot Phonograph was based on the "Home" upper works. This was Edison's first spring-driven coin-slot, selling for $50.00. *Courtesy of Sam Sheena.*

3-18
A three-cylinder pantograph from the former Columbia archives. This machine, when attached to a suitable motor, could make three cylinder duplicates (upper mandrels) from an original cylinder recording (lower mandrel). *Courtesy of the Howard Hazelcorn Collection.*

3-20
A Type "ERG" Graphophone, or "Continuous Running Graphophone". As stated in catalogues: "These instruments are especially desirable for use as store attractions, and at dinner and dancing parties, as the Graphophone, equipped with a 'continuous running' mechanism, will play the record over and over again, without attendance, as long as desired. Electric motor only is suitable for this instrument." The Type "ERG" sold for $125.00. *Courtesy of Sam Sheena.*

3-19
Another view of the three-cylinder Columbia pantograph. In actual use, this utilitarian machine would have been mounted on a bench rather than the decorative cast-iron base. A plate on the base reads: "Exhibit No. 31", suggesting that it was exhibited at Paris in 1900, or Buffalo in 1901. *Courtesy of the Howard Hazelcorn Collection.*

84

3-22
A Type "B" Graphophone made special by the addition of a Bettini attachment. This particular attachment is a European copy licensed by Bettini and sold through Columbia. Unlicensed imitations were also sold in Europe. *Courtesy of Sam Sheena.*

3-21
Although this Type "ERG" bears indications of being a prototype or "one-off," a close-up shows the "ER" stamp on the ID plate. Such oddities must certainly have sold in small numbers. *Courtesy of Sam Sheena.*

3-23
Polyphone attachments were available for Edison Phonographs in early 1899. This is an Edison "Standard" so equipped. The Polyphone attachments for Edison Phonographs were available separately for $15.00, including two horns. *Courtesy of Peter N. Dilg, Baldwin Antique Center.*

3-24

The Berliner "JS" Gramophone of 1899, Eldridge Johnson's "economy" model. Possibly he hoped to placate Frank Seaman, who had grown dissatisfied with the price of the Johnson-manufactured "Improved Gramophone" ($25.00). Seaman attempted to interest the Berliner Company in alternative Gramophone designs, as allowed by his contract, but the "JS" was Johnson's only (half-hearted) attempt to create a cheaper model. Berliner advertisements of 1899 occasionally mention a "New $18.00 Gramophone", which is undoubtedly the "JS". *Courtesy of the Howard Hazelcorn Collection.*

3-26

The Edison "Concert" Phonograph as introduced in February 1899, for $125.00. A 24" brass horn and stand were included.

3-25

A notice glued, of all places, to the turntable of a "JS" Gramophone. Spring-cases and soundboxes of these machines are marked "JS". It is interesting to speculate what the initials might have represented: perhaps "Johnson Special". *Courtesy of Allen Koenigsberg.*

3-27
An Edison "Concert" with a Polyphone attachment. *Courtesy of Sam Sheena.*

3-28
An Edison "Concert" Phonograph in a Hawthorne and Sheble cabinet. The "Concert" upper works were gold-plated and included a Polyphone attachment and repeater. *Courtesy of the Charles Hummel Collections.*

3-29
A close-up of the previous machine, showing details of the seldom-seen Edison ("Iris") repeating attachment. *Courtesy of the Charles Hummel Collections.*

3-30
A pair of "Grands": the Type "GG" ("Graphophone Grand") in the Columbia cabinet offered as "The Grand". Each drawer holds six 5" cylinders. The cabinet was offered in "black oak" for $50.00. *Courtesy of Norm and Janyne Smith.*

3-32
The Edison "Gem" Phonograph as introduced in February 1899, for $7.50. *Courtesy of the William Kocher Collection.*

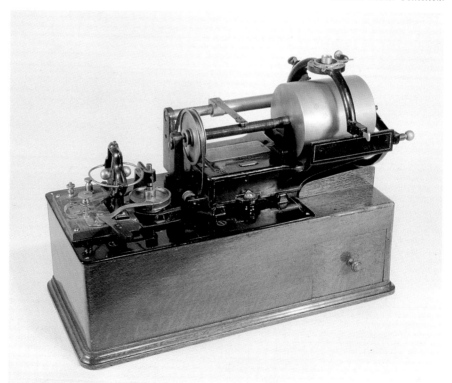

3-31
The 1899 Edison "Opera" Phonograph. Not to be confused with the much later model of the same name, this "Opera" was basically a Class "M" with a "Concert" upper works, selling for $85.00. The Edison "Oratorio" Phonograph was an identical machine with a 110-volt motor, selling for $100.00. *Courtesy of the Charles Hummel Collections.*

3-33
An early Edison "Gem" with a
Polyphone attachment. *Courtesy of the
Howard Hazelcorn Collection.*

3-34
An Edison "Spring-Motor" Phonograph with a mahogany cabinet and
nickel-plated upper works. *Courtesy of
Peter N. Dilg, Baldwin Antique Center.*

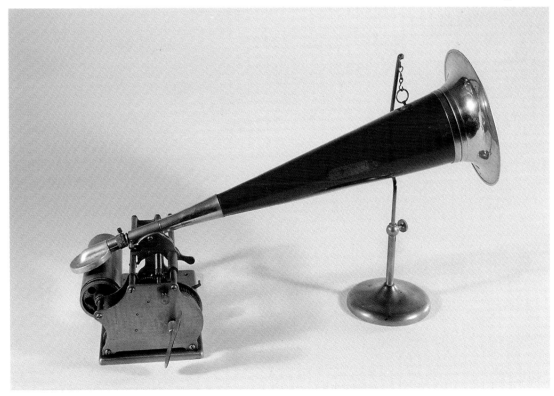

3-35
A Type "Q" Graphophone with the seldom-seen Columbia celluloid horn and stand. This "Q"
has been equipped with a later Type "D" reproducer. *Courtesy of the Charles Hummel Collections.*

3-36
A close-up of the Columbia celluloid horn showing the decal. *Courtesy of the Charles Hummel Collections.*

3-37
The 1899 "HG" (Home Grand") Graphophone allowed Columbia to offer a machine to play 5" cylinders for $100.00, underpricing Edison's "Concert" by $25.00. The motor was the same as used in the Type "AT". *Courtesy of George F. Paul.*

3-38
A Berliner "Improved Gramophone" of 1899. This machine, still selling for $25.00, was the standard by which others were measured. In certain respects, the "Improved Gramophone" would fall short of the emerging competition. *Courtesy of George F. Paul.*

3-39
A pasteboard box for holding fifty Gramophone Records. *Courtesy of George F. Paul.*

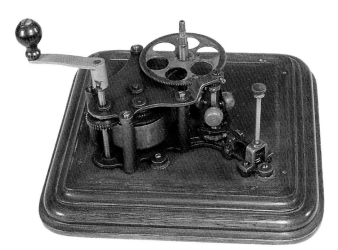

3-40
An unknown-make disc gramophone found in Philadelphia. The support arm bears strong resemblance to a "Vitaphone", but cabinet and motor are unique. *Courtesy of the Charles Hummel Collections.*

3-41
A close-up of the previous machine's motor shows a Columbia "look." *Courtesy of the Charles Hummel Collections.*

3-42
The Lioret Company of France produced this "Lioretgraph" No. 2 with seamless aluminum horn in 1899. The No. 2 mechanism proved highly adaptable to use with various horn combinations. *Courtesy of the Julien Anton Collection.*

3-43
A selection of Lambert cylinders.
The earliest are white, followed by
shades of brown, shades of pink, and
finally black. *Courtesy of Allen
Koenigsberg.*

3-44
The only piece of a Columbia "Multiplex Grand" known
to survive. This carriage carried its three reproducers
across a 14" long cylinder of 5" diameter. The mechanism
was driven by six mainsprings, housed in a massive
mahogany cabinet and played through three 56" brass
horns. The original was built for the Paris Exposition of
1900 and was sold to the Shah of Persia for $1000.00.
Columbia built at least one other which was exhibited at
the 1904 St. Louis World's Fair, of which this is probably a
part. It was the first talking machine capable of recording
and reproducing with stereophonic properties, since the
three tracks on the mammoth cylinder could be separately
recorded. *Courtesy of Allen Koenigsberg.*

3-45
A Type "A" Zonophone as offered in 1900 for
$25.00. Note early support arm placed toward
center of cabinet. Two beveled glass panels in the
cabinet allow the motor to be seen. *Courtesy of the
William Kocher Collection.*

3-46
Close-up of the earliest style Zonophone traveling arm: note its ovular cross-section. *Courtesy of the William Kocher Collection.*

3-47
A Type "A" Zonophone in an unusual cabinet with drawer. *Courtesy of the William Kocher Collection.*

3-48
A Type "B" Zonophone as offered in 1900 for $22.50. *Courtesy of Peter N. Dilg, Baldwin Antique Center.*

3-49
A Type "C" Zonophone as offered in
1900 for $18.00. Note early support
arm placement and squared end. The
soundbox is a 1901 "V Concert".
Courtesy of George F. Paul.

3-50
The Type "AG" ("Columbia Grand")
Graphophone of 1900. This model
was offered for $50.00, replacing the
earlier version with aluminum
bedplate.

3-51
The Type "HG" ("Home Grand")
Graphophone of 1900. This model features a
larger cabinet than the earlier "HG" and
added a six-mainspring motor, while retaining its $100.00 price.

The "Gramophone" as sold by Eldridge Johnson in the early fall of 1900. The celluloid plate replaces the Berliner decal on the cabinet. The horn on this example (No. 34983) is from a slightly later machine. *Courtesy of Dr. Jay Tartell.*

3-52
The nickeled six spring motor of the Type "HG" Graphophone.

3-54
Close-up of the celluloid plate on the previous machine. The "Gramophone" labelling would be prohibited after November, 1900. *Courtesy of Dr. Jay Tartell.*

3-55
The $3.00 "Toy" Gramophone with celluloid plate as sold by Eldridge Johnson in the August-November 1900 period. This hand-driven machine came with the first double-faced record ever offered to the public: A-490/A-491, "A Record For The Children." *Courtesy of Alan H. Mueller.*

3-56
The Type "D" Gramophone sold for $6.00 and was similar to the "Toy", but with a better soundbox and larger horn. This example lacks the celluloid plate, suggesting manufacture in late 1900. *Courtesy of Peter N. Dilg, Baldwin Antique Center.*

3-57
The Type "A" Gramophone was, at $12.00, the least expensive spring-driven machine offered by Johnson. This example carries a "Victor" plate, indicating manufacture in late 1900-early 1901. *Courtesy of the Howard Hazelcorn Collection.*

3-58
The 1901 Type "B" Victor was the direct descendant of the Berliner/Johnson "Improved Gramophone". With a decorative baseboard and an applied fleur-de-lis, the Type "B" still sold for only $18.00. *Courtesy of Dr. Jay Tartell.*

3-59
The 1901 Type "C" Victor used a new motor in which the crank (finally horizontal) did not revolve as the machine played. The columns on the cabinet were a portent of Victor style for years to come. *Courtesy of Norm and Janyne Smith.*

3-60
The 1901 Victor "Monarch" was a $40.00 machine "...especially designed for the 10 inch record." This example is No. 2406. *Courtesy of Dr. Jay Tartell.*

3-61
The rather bizarre Victor "Deluxe Monarch" was offered briefly in 1901 for $60.00. The mechanism was identical to the "Monarch". At least one family felt that it was worth the extra money, as this period photograph shows. *Courtesy of George F. Paul.*

3-62
Typical wooden needle boxes as supplied with disc talking machines throughout this period. *Courtesy of Dr. Jay Tartell.*

3-63
Unusual boxes for 7" disc records and a 16" horn. Early Victor letterheads were carefully cut out and pasted on these boxes by, in all likelihood, their enthusiastic owner. *Courtesy of the William Kocher Collection.*

3-64
An unmarked wooden cabinet for 7" disc records. *Courtesy of the Charles Hummel Collections.*

3-65
A rather elegant cabinet offered by
Columbia for 7" disc records. *Courtesy of the*
William Kocher Collection.

3-66
A "Lioretgraph" No. 2 of 1900 with "pleated"
horn and velvet-covered base, showing a
selection of Lioret celluloid cylinder records.
Courtesy of Sam Sheena.

3-67
The technical instrument
house of Mazo in Paris,
France, sold talking machines
including this ironically-
labelled Graphophone
"Eagle". The horn is a "cor-
de-chasse" or "hunting horn".

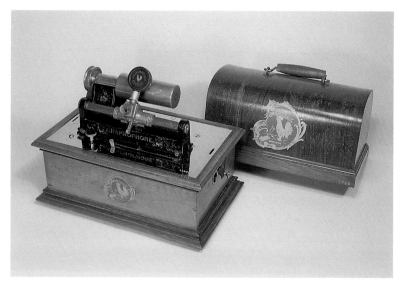

3-69
This Graphophone "AT" mechanism was sold in a special walnut cabinet by Pathé in 1900.

3-70
The Pathé "Duplex" of 1900 was a curiously-constructed instrument with detachable mandrels to play either regular or 5" cylinders (which were known as "Stentor" in France). Pathé followed Columbia's lead by making broad use of die-castings in machines such as this one. *Courtesy of Sam Sheena.*

3-68
In 1900, the Pathé Company introduced an inexpensive machine with cast-iron body, largely based on the first model of the Edison "Gem". With typical French élan, "Le Gaulois" was available painted in a variety of colors which included red, blue, green, black, and grey. Whereas many machines produced in Europe borrowed heavily from Graphophone designs, this is one of the few examples of the Edison influence.

3-71
The so-called "Lioret Clock". The clock mechanism bears no Lioret attribution, but employed a Lioretgraph inside. *Courtesy of Allen Koenigsberg.*

3-72
Hidden in the "Lioret Clock" was a "Le Merveilleux" mechanism which played a special cylinder. "Talking machine clocks" had been envisioned from the earliest days of Edison's Tinfoil machine. Many versions would be tried, including clocks that spoke the hours or merely used a record as an alarm (like this one). *Courtesy of the Julien Anton Collection.*

3-73
The "Idéal" talking machine was sold by the French religious publishing firm of Maison de la Bonne Presse. This company found it profitable to add talking machines and records to its printed offerings. The machine was available nickel-plated or in lacquered brass (shown). It featured a removable mandrel for the 5" cylinders, and an ebonite reproducer known as "Le Cahit".

3-74
An Edison "Gem" Phonograph of 1900-1901 with a "branded" cabinet. This was the second Edison Phonograph (since 1896, the "Home" came with a banner on its lid) to be given a decorative label. Original price was $10.00.

3-76
A 1901 Edison "Standard" Phonograph with New Style "banner" cabinet. Original price was $20.00.
Courtesy of Norm and Janyne Smith.

3-75
A 1902 Edison "Gem" Phonograph with a "banner" cabinet. This was far easier to read than the earlier "branded" version. The rest of the Edison line received "banner" labels on their New Style cabinets in 1901.
Courtesy of Norm and Janyne Smith.

3-77
A close-up of the previous "Standard", showing an unusual automatic stop mounted on the endgate. As the carrier-arm moves to the right, it pushes an adjustable screw, which in turn slowly presses a rubber wheel against the rim of the cylinder, thus stopping its rotation. *Courtesy of Norm and Janyne Smith.*

3-78
Another Edison "Standard" of the 1902-1905 period, nickel-plated and fitted with a Polyphone attachment. *Courtesy of the Howard Hazelcorn Collection.*

3-79
The Edison "Home" Phonograph of 1901 carried the familiar red-lettered banner now located on the front of the cabinet. Original price was $30.00. *Courtesy of Norm and Janyne Smith.*

3-80
The $50.00 Edison "Spring-Motor" Phonograph was re-named the "Triumph" in 1901, and supplied with an appropriate "banner" on its New Style cabinet. *Courtesy of George F. Paul.*

3-82
A 1901 Edison "Concert" Phonograph in its New Style cabinet. Original price was $75.00. *Courtesy of Norm and Janyne Smith.*

3-81
Another Edison "Triumph" of the 1901-1905 period, but gold-plated and in a mahogany cabinet. A 2/4-minute attachment was later fitted to this example. *Courtesy of the Charles Hummel Collections.*

3-83
A Hawthorne and Sheble cabinet No. 3a with an Edison "Standard" installed. This cabinet held 100 "P" or standard-sized cylinders. The lock on the upper drawer secures all five drawers. *Courtesy of Norm and Janyne Smith.*

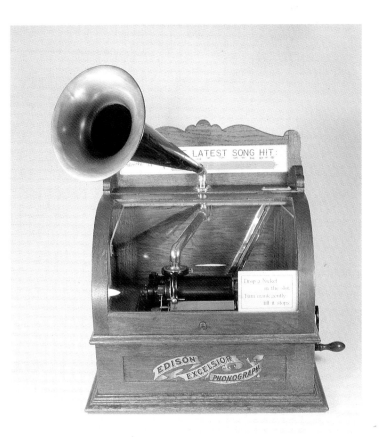

3-84
The 1901 Edison "Excelsior" Phonograph was a coin-slot machine based on the "Standard" mechanism. Original price was $50.00. *Courtesy of Alan H. Mueller.*

3-85
The 1901 Edison "Bijou" Phonograph was a coin-slot machine based on the "Gem" mechanism. Original price was $30.00. *Courtesy of Sam Sheena.*

3-86
The 1901 "Concert Grand" Zonophone was the top of the line at $40.00. The "V Concert" soundbox was standard equipment on this model. Beveled glass panels on two sides of the cabinet allowed the motor to be seen. *Courtesy of the William Kocher Collection.*

3-87
The Type "D" Zonophone was the least-expensive machine offered by Universal. The catalogue candidly stated: "Not so beautiful to look at—but a good all around substantial outfit." Original price was $12.00.

3-88
The Type "AA" Graphophone of 1901 reduced the charmingly ornate design of the larger Graphophones to diminutive proportions. Equipped with a 10" nickel-plated horn, it sold for $18.00.

3-89
The Type "AB" Graphophone was closely based on the Type "B". At $25.00, the "AB" was the least expensive American talking machine capable of playing 5" cylinders. A telescoping mandrel allowed standard-sized cylinders to be played as well. *Courtesy of George F. Paul.*

3-90
The Type "AD" Graphophone used a nickeled upper works and a six-spring motor in a Home Grand cabinet. It too was capable of playing both standard and 5" cylinders. The "AD" used two separate belts in the mechanism, and was originally offered for $75.00. *Courtesy of the William Kocher Collection.*

107

3-91
Another Type "AD" Graphophone, but with
Bettini attachment and horn. A Lambert 5"
cylinder is in position on the mandrel.
Courtesy of the Howard Hazelcorn Collection.

3-92
A close-up showing a Bettini horn and
cylinder boxes.

3-93
In October 1901, Columbia made a strong entry into the disc talking machine business with the introduction of two Disc Graphophones, of which the "AH" (shown) was the larger. It sold for $30.00. This example was equipped with extension and a larger horn at additional cost. *Courtesy of Norm and Janyne Smith.*

3-94
The Type "AJ" Disc Graphophone ($20.00), with vertical crank, was the smaller of the two Disc Graphophones introduced in 1901. This model used a 7" turntable. *Courtesy of Peter N. Dilg, Baldwin Antique Center.*

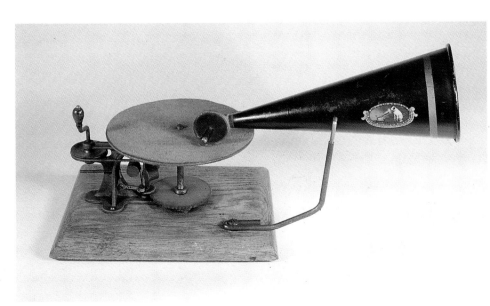

3-95
By the time this Victor "Toy" was built in 1901-1902, the catalogue referred to it as the "$3.00 Victor". The trademark decal on the horn is not usually seen on this model. *Courtesy of the Charles Hummel Collections.*

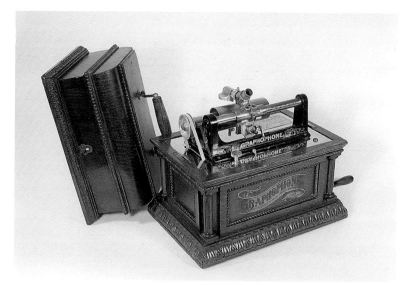

3-96
The Type "AO" Graphophone of 1902 sported an ornate cabinet, a 14" aluminum horn, and a powerful triple-spring motor. This machine originally sold for $30.00. *Courtesy of Lou Caruso.*

3-97
The "AO" was first offered with a conventional aluminum floating reproducer. Subsequently, an option was available for $5.00 to equip the machine with "...an entirely new form of reproducer, giving greater volume and perfection of tone." This reproducer was inspired by the soundbox used on Disc Graphophones. When sold with this reproducer, this machine was known as the "AW". *Courtesy of the Howard Hazelcorn Collection.*

3-98
A rather unusual Zonophone of 1902-1903 with a heavily ribbed cabinet. *Courtesy of Norm and Janyne Smith.*

3-99
A Zonophone "Grand Opera" of 1902-1903 was a top-of-the-line model with a beveled glass panel and powerful motor. (All Zonophone motors of this period were single-spring. Additional power was achieved by increasing the size of the spring.) Note the Universal Talking Machine Manufacturing Company decal.

3-100
In 1903, a back-mounted version of the Zonophone "Grand Opera" was offered, eliminating the glass panel in order to install the back bracket.
Courtesy of Peter N. Dilg, Baldwin Antique Center.

3-101
A Canadian Berliner Type "B" of 1903, which at first glance appears to be a replica of an American Victor "Monarch Junior". Closer examination of the traveling arm, soundbox, and motor will reveal differences. *Courtesy of Lou Caruso.*

3-102
A close-up of the typical Canadian Berliner stamped aluminum plate of the Type "B". *Courtesy of Lou Caruso.*

3-103
A Canadian Berliner Company tip tray.

3-104
A Victor "Royal" of 1902. This model
was equipped with a single main-
spring, 7" turntable, 16" horn, and
the "Exhibition Junior" soundbox.
Original price was $15.00. Later
"Royals" used a metal traveling arm.
Courtesy of George F. Paul.

3-105
A Victor "Monarch" of 1902. This
model featured a double-spring
motor, 10" turntable, the "Concert"
soundbox, and a 21" horn. Original
price was $35.00. *Courtesy of Norm and
Janyne Smith.*

3-106
A 1902 Victor "Monarch" equipped
with an optional 30" horn and
extension arms. These extra features
would have added an additional $6.00
to the "Monarch's" $35.00 price.
Courtesy of Lou Caruso.

3-107
The top-of-the-line Victor "Monarch Special" came with a triple-spring motor, 10" turntable, "Concert" soundbox, a 21" horn, and plenty of gingerbread for $45.00. *Courtesy of Peter N. Dilg, Baldwin Antique Center.*

3-108
A Victor "Monarch Special" equipped with the rear-mounted "Rigid Arm" as introduced in October 1902. In this configuration, the machine sold for $50.00 and was christened the Victor "IV". *Courtesy of Norm and Janyne Smith.*

3-109
When the Victor "Monarch Junior" was offered with the "Rigid Arm", it was called the Victor "II". Selling price was $30.00. (As can be surmised, a "Monarch" so equipped was called the Victor "III", selling for $40.00.) *Courtesy of Norm and Janyne Smith.*

3-111
A pressed-tin Victor dealer's sign of the period. *Courtesy of the Charles Hummel Collections.*

3-110
Even the little Victor "Royal" could be fitted with the "Rigid Arm", although it was apparently never catalogued this way. *Courtesy of Peter N. Dilg, Baldwin Antique Center.*

3-112
A 1902 Type "AK" Disc Graphophone. This machine featured a soundbox attached directly to the 16" horn, a single-spring motor, 7" turntable, and an original price of $15.00. *Courtesy of Norm and Janyne Smith.*

3-113
Another variation of the Type "AK" Disc Graphophone used the traditional traveling arm, and still sold for $15.00. This example is displayed with a shipping crate which is stamped on the back: "AK SMALL CAB". *Courtesy of George F. Paul.*

3-114
The 1903 model of the "AK" Disc Graphophone featured a dark oak fluted cabinet with mechanical features similar to earlier versions. Evidence strongly suggests that at least two versions of the "AK" were simultaneously available for a short time, giving the customer a choice of cabinets. *Courtesy of Norm and Janyne Smith.*

3-115
The Type "AJ" Disc Graphophone offered in 1903 featured a motor which was wound with a horizontal crank and a 10" turntable. The first examples of this model used leather elbows. *Courtesy of Norm and Janyne Smith.*

3-116
The Columbia Phonograph Company was the only American firm to exploit the inexpensive European "Puck"-type talking machine on a large scale. Although these string-driven, trivet-base devices were ubiquitous abroad, distribution was limited in the United States. Each "Puck" offered by Columbia carried a paper licensing label variously pasted on the mandrel or other parts of the machine.

3-117
The original box cover for a Columbia-sold "Puck" lists the instructions.

3-118
The Type "AP" Graphophone of 1903 was a "premium" or giveaway item used in a variety of sales promotions. There was no feedscrew; the grooves of the cylinder carried the reproducer. It was, in essence, an American version of the European "Puck", having a reproducer fixed to the end of the horn, and an adjustable screw keeps the machine level.

3-119
The Type "AQ" Graphophone was similar to the "AP", but with the addition of a feedscrew. When sold by Columbia in 1903, it cost $3.00 and used a conical horn identical to the "AP". Another version, pictured here, was sold by Sears in 1908 for $8.75 (including 24 cylinders) as the "Oxford, Jr"., and featured a squat, brass-belled horn.

3-120
The second series of the enormously popular Type "Q" Graphophone was introduced in 1903. A black cast base replaced the earlier one of steel, the governor was mounted entirely to the motor plate, and a filigreed key was provided in place of the earlier plain one. The "Q" remained available with or without a cabinet, and a choice of horns was offered. This example, with cabinet and 14" aluminum horn, was designated the "QA" and originally sold for $10.70. *Courtesy of George F. Paul.*

3-121
This Type "Q" Graphophone is equipped with a fancy cast base offered by the Talking Machine Company of Chicago and Sears, Roebuck & Company. *Courtesy of the Charles Hummel Collections.*

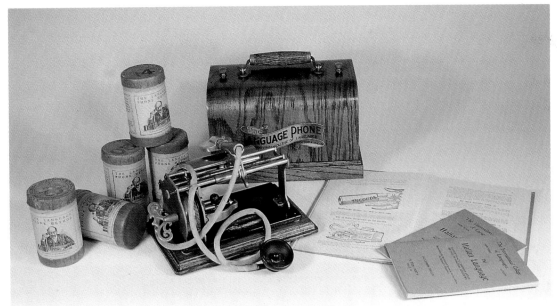

3-122
The versatile Type "Q" was sold as a "Languagephone" to play Rosenthal cylinders developed to teach a variety of languages. This example retains its original instruction books and cylinders. *Courtesy of Norm and Janyne Smith.*

3-124
The "Echophone" was a Swiss-manufactured cylinder machine based heavily on the Columbia "Eagle". This one, which carries a brass plate indicating it was sold in an Arabic country, used a Columbia-made floating reproducer.

3-123
The "Crown" talking machine was certainly manufactured in Europe, but sold inexpensively in the United States. It was one of the few machines in the American market of the "reversible" cabinet design. *Courtesy of Robert T. Lomas.*

3-125
The "Musica" was sold in France
circa 1903 in a variety of styles.
Although this one draws significantly
from the Columbia "Eagle", the
"reversible" cabinet is notable for its
marquetry. The graceful "hunting
horn" was a common accessory of
European talking machines. *Courtesy
Allen Koenigsberg.*

3-126
The Pathé Company's 1903-1904
line of cylinder machines included
this charming but unsophisticated
No. "0" ("Democratic"). It could
play either regular or "Intermediate"
cylinders.

3-127
Not unlike the Pathé "Democratic" was this "Au Sou BB de
1855", also sold under the
"Musica" brand by the Paris firm
of Dutreih.

3-128
The French mail-order firm of Girard offered this Pathé-manufactured "Le Ménestrel" in 1903. It was available the previous year in blue. It employed a single-spring motor which Pathé had copied from the Edison "Gem", and which found use in a variety of cylinder models.

3-129
The European "Midget Phonograph" of 1903 was about as simple as a talking machine could be. The collapsible horn was of stapled celluloid, and the miniature cylinder (with box shown) was driven by hand. *Courtesy of the Julien Anton Collection.*

3-130
M.O. Arnold's German talking doll which used a
cylinder mechanism. The Excelsior-made wax
cylinders were 100 tpi and would actually fit on a
conventional cylinder talking machine mandrel.
Courtesy of the Charles Hummel Collections.

3-131
The mechanism of the German
talking doll showing the horn which
directed sound through the head.
*Courtesy of the Charles Hummel
Collections.*

3-132
Gramophones based on Berliner's "Improved Gramophone" of 1897-1900 persisted in Europe until about 1904. Various slight modifications were made to cabinet and mechanism, but these low-priced machines retained unmistakable clues (most noticeably the vertical crank) to their origins. This Gramophone and Typewriter model is typical. *Courtesy of Alan H. Mueller.*

3-133
This machine, sold by Deutschen Grammophon AG, disguises its Berliner motor by turning it diagonally in the cabinet. The nickel-plated horn is typical of machines sold by Gramophone and Typewriter and its European branches. *Courtesy of Allen Koenigsberg.*

3-134
A 2 1/4" advertising mirror for the Hill Bicycle Store, which listed "Phonographs" among its various wares. By this time, many such stores balanced their inventories with "seasonal" items. Talking machines and records sold well during the winter, while bicycles and sporting goods were in demand during the warmer months. *Courtesy of George F. Paul.*

3-135
Unlike scenes of a decade earlier, many families now possessed their own talking machines. Holidays and celebrations often included recorded entertainment, and the pride felt by the patriarch on the right is evident. *Courtesy of Jim Kellish.*

3-136
An anachronism in 1903-1904 was the establishment of Burke and Rous in Brooklyn, New York. While advertising Talkophones and Universal Zonophones, Burke and Rous attempted to market its own brown wax cylinders in an environment dominated by Edison and Columbia molded cylinders. However brief and futile the effort, Burke and Rous along with many others enlivened the era with its plucky entrepreneurial spirit. *Courtesy of George F. Paul.*

3-137
Occasional examples of decorated trumpet-style horns, such as the example on the left, suggest a yearning to make the talking machine more decorative. As we have seen, talking machine cabinets became more ornate during this period, while horns merely grew in size. A noticeable change was about to occur in the talking machine industry: the glorification of the horn, as seen in the example on the right. The petalled, or "morning-glory" horn would come to symbolize the zenith of the external-horn talking machine, while the means of its demise simultaneously took root. *Courtesy of Norm and Janyne Smith.*

CHAPTER 4:

The Talking Machine Becomes a Household Word, 1904-1908

A BLOSSOMING BUSINESS

As the talking machine improved, competition increased between the disparate elements of the industry. New firms entered the race to put an instrument in every home. Like the cylinder record business prior to the limitations exerted by the introduction of the moulding process, the disc record trade now blossomed with many small manufacturers economically producing 78s. These firms lasted only as long as it took Victor or Columbia to sue them into oblivion, or until their capital ran out. The situation would become increasingly deadly for independents. In 1904, Victor and Columbia cross-liscensed each other and thereby added both power and concentration to their litigiousness. Yet, this period was rife with colorful little disc record operations.

The International Record Company of Auburn, New York, a subsidiary of the well-established Auburn Button Works, produced a panoply of brands headed by its own dazzling "International" label, 1903-1908. Included in this family of single-faced discs were "Buckeye", "Clico", "Clear Tone", "Vim" and many others. They even produced "generic" discs, with no brand name, only a space above the center hole for any seller's address to be rubber-stamped. The green label 7" and 9" brown Zonophone discs of 1903-1904 had been pressed in Auburn, encouraging the formation of the International label.

The Leeds family had been responsible for independent record endeavors since the 1890s, when Loring L. Leeds had tried cylinder manufacture. Despite constant litigation, which was to be expected, the Leeds name persisted on small disc brands beginning with the "Leeds" record of 1903, with its embossed gold foil label. By 1905, the Leeds and Catlin Company was producing single-faced discs under the "Imperial" house

brand, but also applying the labels of a variety of other small firms to its product. Later on, double-faced records were introduced. The October 28, 1905, issue of *The Music Trades* carried a story describing the company's move to a large factory in Middletown, Connecticut. Harry Leeds, Jr. was quoted as saying, "We have for some time past been so crowded for room...and business is growing so rapidly that I do not consider that our new plant will be any too large for us...We expect to employ about four hundred people...and, consequently, our output will be increased many times over..." The article also alludes to the firm's plans to get back into the cylinder business. However, in less than four years the unwanted attentions of Columbia would shutter Leeds and Catlin forever. Columbia succeeded in gaining a final ruling on damages in the fall of 1910. As reported in the September 15 issue of *Talking Machine World*, Leeds and Catlin, bankrupts, would be accountable for $81,250.85 in damages for infringement of the Jones patent. Columbia received thousands of disc records, which it disposed of through "client" brands.

The Talkophone Company of Toledo, Ohio, began by selling the 7" and 10" diameter single-faced "Monogram" disc in 1903, followed by a 9" diameter single-faced "Talkophone" record circa 1905, to accompany their line of disc machines. The company also distributed the gold labelled Leeds disc, for which it got credit on the label. It had begun as the Ohio Talking Machine Company, the brainchild of Winant Van Zant Pierce Bradley and backer Albert Irish. Bradley had been in the disc business for a few years, which is as long as discs had been a business. His associations, however, had been with men like Albert Armstrong, the "outlaws" of the group. This experience would serve him well for bucking the established forces in the industry.

Talkophones were well-made instruments, with Victor-inspired motors, attractive cabinets and very colorful decals. The company flourished between 1903 and 1909, at which time Talkophone succumbed to litigation and its unused wooden cabinets were assigned to Columbia to be fitted out and sold under that company's brand and a few others. In court, many small manufacturers asserted their machines had a "mechanical feed" device to escape litigation under Victor's patent No. 534,543 which governed the passage of the soundbox by use of the record groove. Talkophone made this claim, though no evidence has arisen to support it on machines other than court exhibits. In these cases, expert witnesses were brought in by Victor or Columbia to comment on the so-called feed devices. Usually, as with the Duplex Phonograph Company, the claim was dismissed as absurd, though certain brands (Sonora) really had a mechanical feed. Hawthorne and Sheble Manufacturing Company of Philadelphia tried it both ways, selling machines with a spurious feed (the "Yielding Pressure Arm") and a true one (the "Aretino" machine where the turntable tracked under a stationary soundbox).

The Duplex Phonograph Company of Kalamazoo, Michigan, sold a formidable double-horned disc machine by mail-order, 1905-1909. Although it took the normally safe road of buying motors and certain other parts from Columbia, this proved no defense against Victor, which sued the company in 1907 and won. A protracted bout of legal wrangling finally ended in the fall of 1910 when U.S. Circuit Court in Kalamazoo, Michigan, compelled Duplex to terminate any remaining affairs. As reported in the *Talking Machine World*: "The Duplex Phonograph Co. were doing a large business and were backed by wealthy men and had a strong financial rating until the Victor Talking Machine Co. secured an injunction in the circuit court restraining the Duplex Co. from infringing upon their patents, which was later made permanent." "Duplex" or "Kalamazoo" single-faced records were derived from the matrices of other firms, such as Columbia, International, and the American Record Company.

Hawthorne and Sheble remained a significant force in 1904. Its mid-decade activities rivalled anything it had done in an extremely colorful history. The firm already had run afoul of Edison and been black-listed by him. Soon, the wrath of Victor would descend when the disc market was explored by Hawthorne and Sheble. It operated the American Record Company with International Zonophone's F. M. Prescott, 1905-1906. American issued 7" and 10" single-faced discs in blue shellac. Some 10 5/8" records were also sold, conforming to the metric measurements of European "Odeons", a related brand. The label depicted an American Indian in whose pipe dreams appeared a talking machine. A surprising number of these discs survive under the "American" label and other brands (pressed in black shellac), considering the briefness of the endeavor. In 1907, Hawthorne and Sheble abandoned the enterprise in favor of its house brand "Star". These 10" and 12" single-faced discs were derived from Columbia, with the normally lengthy matrix number changed to four digits.

Hawthorne and Sheble began manufacturing client disc machines under the "Busy Bee", "Harmony", "Aretino", "Imperial", and "True Tone" brands in 1906. These were inexpensive front-mounted instruments with long panelled horns identical to the ones being sold by the manufacturer to fit cylinder phonographs. Along the same lines was a better-appointed model under its own "Star" brand. As well, a complete line of excellently-designed back-mounted "Star" disc machines appeared over the next few years, culminating in an imposing, floor-standing cabinet model known as the "Starola". These employed the "Yielding Pressure Feed", actually a coiled spring located inside the sound arm which exerted gentle force in the direction of play. This suggestion of mechanical feed failed to deter Victor, and Hawthorne and Sheble was forced to give up the manufacture of talking machines in 1909, including its one true mechanical feed model, sold as an "Aretino" and an "Imperial No. I" (patented by Leeds and Rumpf, September 1, 1908, No. 897,836). Much of the patent litigation against the independents trailed into 1910, and remnants of the firms clung to life. It is interesting to note that a patent (No. 968,483, August 23, 1910, Thomas Kraemer of Philadelphia) for a mechanically-fed (tracking turntable) disc talking machine with "back-mounted" external-horn was assigned to the Hawthorne and Sheble Manufacturing Company. The design bears strong similarities to a machine sold soon after as a Keenophone. The mahogany cabinet of this elaborate Keenophone was identical to one which had previously borne the "Star" emblem, although the basic mechanism also appeared in various internal-horn Keenophones.

4-2
A Zonophone "Parlor" of 1904. Brass horns such as this with permanently-attached elbows were offered in a range of sizes. *Courtesy of Norm and Janyne Smith.*

4-1
This Victor "MS" of 1904 had a fancy Victor oak horn added a few years later. *Courtesy of Norm and Janyne Smith.*

4-3
Following the Victor take-over in 1903, the final independently-designed Zonophone front-mounts such as this "Concert" continued to be sold. Soon, however, the look of the machines would begin to reflect Victor influences. This one is equipped with the smallest of the all-brass horns which characterized the brand. *Courtesy of Peter N. Dilg, Baldwin Antique Center.*

4-4
A Zonophone "C" in its last design
(1904) "dressed-up" with a fancy
support arm and 24" horn. Smaller
Zonophones of the later front-mount
period are found with all brass horns
up to 30" in length, which were
previous reserved for only the more
expensive models. *Courtesy of Peter N.
Dilg, Baldwin Antique Center.*

4-5
A 1904 Columbia "AH" Disc
Graphophone ($30.00) with original
carrying cases for horn and machine.
Courtesy of Alan H. Mueller.

4-6
The second cabinet design of the Columbia "AJ" Disc Graphophone, offered in 1904 at $22.50, conformed to the new curvy styling. This particular machine had extended arms and a larger than usual horn (at a slight increase in price). *Courtesy of Norm and Janyne Smith.*

4-7
The Columbia "AR" was an imposing mahogany machine, with 12" turntable and massive triple-spring mechanics based on the motor previously seen in the 1897 Type "C" and the 1898 "GG" cylinder machines. It was introduced in 1904 at $65.00. A larger horn was added to this one at increased cost. *Courtesy of the William Kocher Collection.*

4-8
The "AY" Disc Graphophone had a smaller (double spring) motor than the "AR" and a 10" turntable. It was offered in 1904 at $50.00. *Courtesy of Norm and Janyne Smith.*

4-9
A Pathé "Coquet" adapted and sold
by the French mail-order firm of
Girard. As equipped with "Système
Vérité", the horn and fixed reproducer "float" above the record, giving
ample lateral movement for proper
tracking.

4-10
A Talkophone "Ennis" model
(introduced in 1903 at $25.00).
*Courtesy of Peter N. Dilg, Baldwin Antique
Center.*

4-11
A Talkophone "Clark" model
(introduced at $45.00), displaying
the last version of the decal, with a
parrot "Learning Some New Ones."

4-12
A Talkophone "Brooke" (introduced at $20.00), a model which was near the bottom of the roster of Talkophones. This one features an early-style decal. *Courtesy of Norm and Janyne Smith.*

4-13
This mid-sized Talkophone of 1905 is interesting because its cabinet would later be used to make the Models "L" and "H" of the Standard Talking Machine Company of Chicago. Columbia, of course, was responsible for this, after they acquired the cabinets as the result of a court case. *Courtesy of Norm and Janyne Smith.*

4-14
The Talkophone "Sousa" (introduced at $75.00) was the top-of-the-line. It can be found with either gold-plated or nickeled fittings. *Courtesy of Peter N. Dilg, Baldwin Antique Center.*

Chicago was a beehive of activity in this period, hatching (pun intended) "Busy Bee" and a number of other small brands. Most were involved in premium or promotion schemes. Around 1904, when these firms began their activities, neither the talking machine nor the premium scheme was new to Chicago. Usually, promotional goods were utilitarian, like chinaware. In fact, one of the largest talking machine companies in Chicago started in dishes.

On October 11, 1901, the East Liverpool China Company was formed in Chicago. East Liverpool, Ohio, was a city noted for the earthenware it produced, used by the company which bore its name in promotional schemes. Around 1904, this firm began to distribute specially equipped Columbia disc machines and records under the name Standard Talking Machine Company. These were used as sales incentives, like the dishes. However, the advantage of the talking machine was that one instrument would create repeat sales of records—better for the distributor; better for the store running the promotion. To enforce this relationship, the turntable spindle of the "Standard" talking machine was enlarged to approximately 1/2" diameter, and discs were supplied with a corresponding aperture.

By 1906, a great many of the Standard "open works" disc Graphophones (Columbia's model "AU") were in circulation. A new style, known as the "X" was introduced, having the motor enclosed in a rather plain oak case. Soon, a dressed-up version ("X2") was offered, with a colorfully painted, panelled horn. The most popular model would be the well-proportioned little Model "A", a back-mount in the style of the Columbia "BN". Two larger models ("L" and "H") and two internal-horn models ("B" and "E") also would be introduced. Business in talking machines increased to the extent that the parent firm renamed itself the Great Northern Manufacturing Company in 1907, eliminating the reference to chinaware.

In 1907, Great Northern began to distribute "Harmony" brand disc machines and records, while Standard continued semi-autonomously. Distinguishing the "Harmony" was a spindle of approximately 3/4" diameter. While Standard chose the safe road and stuck to Columbia products throughout its lengthy existence, Great Northern took the risk of dealing with the Hawthorne and Sheble Manufacturing Company. Most front-mounted "Harmony" machines originated with that Philadelphia firm (whose plant, like Columbia, was in Bridgeport, Connecticut). Eventually, when the courts ruled these machines infringing, Great Northern would sell some front-mounted, a good many back-mounted and considerable internal-horn "Harmonies" purchased from Columbia. In 1911, another off-shoot of Great Northern appeared in the ironically-named United Talk-

ing Machine Company, which sold "Symphony" hornless machines and "United" records. Both were of Columbia origin. As if the market were not already a muddle of varying equipment, the spindle measurement of the United Company was approximately 1 1/2" diameter. Concurrently, all three branches of the original firm moved into shared offices in a multi-storied commercial building. Perhaps this explains the term "United".

In 1913, Standard, being the first and the most robust of the three, broke away to meet its fate alone. By 1916, the Consolidated Talking Machine Company of Chicago was calling itself the successor to the three Great Northern brands, selling off the remaining parts and records. This firm also sold its own "Consola" internal-horn instruments with a "regular" 1/4" spindle. The time for experimentation had passed.

Elsewhere in Chicago was Arthur J. O'Neill, a man with a plan. Why else would anyone have designed the "Aretino" machine? To begin his story, we must go back to Mr. O'Neill's origins as a commercial traveller and owner of a Chicago agency trading in "advertising specialties." This firm, the O'Neill-James Company (founded 1904), introduced the "Busy Bee" talking machines. "James" was Winifred B. James, and the final member of the staff was Sherwin N. Bisbee, who cleverly lent his name to the product. Under the "Busy Bee" brand O'Neill-James began distributing little Columbia "Q" Graphophones in 1904. These were specially equipped with a mandrel which was slightly larger than usual so that Edison or Columbia two-minute cylinders wouldn't fit it. Columbia supplied custom-made "Busy Bee" brand cylinders to go with the machines, thereby guaranteeing repeat sales. The Graphophones were distributed through in-store promotions where the public was encouraged to pay cash or clear up old charge accounts in order to receive credit toward them. O'Neill-James also issued catalogues of machines and records, making more of direct-to-customer sales than the Great Northern group.

In 1906, a "Busy Bee" disc machine was added, manufactured by Hawthorne and Sheble. O'Neill judiciously avoided the spindle-size muddle, but stuck to the basic idea by placing an additional lug on an otherwise "normal" turntable. The lug, located in the periphery of the label area, enforced the sale of "Busy Bee" discs, which were drilled to accept it. This allowed "Busy Bee" records, designed for the regular 1/4" spindle, to be used on any Victor, Columbia, or Zonophone talking machine. If this were tried with the records of the Great Northern group they would tend to get out of true as the small spindle worked about in the large hole. Home handimen could and did create adapters, and the knowledge of this was no doubt in Arthur J. O'Neill's mind when he created his masterpiece: the "Aretino".

Patent No. 874,985 was issued to Mr. O'Neill on December 31, 1907. In the text he gives a concise description of the nature of the talking machine business in Chicago: "In the sale of talking machine records, it is desirable that the record be shaped with special reference to the machine for which it is primarily intended in order that the manufacturer...may control the sale of records to be used therewith." However, a great number of lost sales were inherent to this situation, to wit: "United" records (1 1/2" hole) could be used on "Harmony" machines (3/4" spindle), but "Standard" discs (1/2" hole) wouldn't fit the "Symphony" (1 1/2" spindle). Why not create one disc which could be played on any or all machines—Victor, Columbia, Zonophone, the Great Northern group and even the "Busy Bee"? This would mean a record with the greatest-of-all-possible holes, with precious little room for any label at all. This would mean a virtual doughnut of a record, with a 3" aperture. This was how the "Aretino" record was designed. Through the use of adapters, this disc could be used on any other machine, though "Aretino" instruments with their huge center spindle would only accept records of their own brand. To quote further from O'Neill's patent:

> It is desirable, however, that records, peculiarly constructed for use on a particular machine, be usable on machines of different makes in order that the sale of records may be increased to the greatest possible extent. With this end in view, the object of the present invention consists in the provision of a record...which can be used on all machines without permitting standard (meaning conventional) records to be used upon the particular machine (that is, his "Aretino")...A supplemental disc or plate...is employed...to...entirely fill up the opening in the ring-shaped ("Aretino") record, thereby enabling such a record to be properly centered and used on a machine of ordinary make.

Clearly, the intent was to make the "Aretino" record playable on the thousands of major brand machines which were already in use, a concept which could certainly be extended to the instruments of the rival Great Northern group. This was the vision of Mr. O'Neill: the last, best disc in Chicago. In 1907, he started the Aretino Company, selling Hawthorne and Sheble front-mounted machines of the same style as the "Busy Bee", and discs drawn from Leeds and Catlin matrices. He named his instrument for a tenth century Benedictine monk, Guido Aretino, who originated the first notes in the musical scale.

The O'Neill story ends with shabby treatment by Victor and its subsidiary Zonophone, which had furnished many of the discs sold under the "Busy Bee" label. Eldridge Johnson, who was so bent on protecting the tony image of the Victor that he quit making a premium machine (the Victor "P"), somehow had allowed Zonophone to dispose of its overstock records to independents. Universal Talking Machine Manufacturing Company chief Belford Royal had developed a chummy relationship with O'Neill and his associates because of the considerable business they did together. This ended when Johnson suddenly decreed that contact with O'Neill be terminated, even though it represented a loss

4-15
The first machine offered by the Standard Talking Machine Company of Chicago in 1905, which was designated Style "AA". It was, in fact, Columbia's own Type "AU" Disc Graphophone with a modified turntable spindle. When sold by Columbia, the "AU" cost $12.00; Standard talking machines were distributed through retail promotions.

of revenue. What was really afoot was the beginning of an assault on the O'Neill companies for doing business with Hawthorne and Sheble.

A Victor agent was sent to Chicago to purchase a "Busy Bee" machine, to be used as evidence in the impending litigation. Then Victor set upon O'Neill-James and Aretino to enjoin them in the courts. As Hawthorne and Sheble machines were deemed infringing (notwithstanding the last-gasp mechanical feed "Aretino"), O'Neill was forced to go to Columbia to buy his goods, but not before being turned out like a beggar when he visited Camden to seek a settlement. After 1909, all

O'Neill-James "Yankee Prince" (an up-dated version of the "Busy Bee") and all "Aretino" (back-mounted) machines and records came from Columbia. In 1910, the two firms joined, after which only Aretino remained viable. Into 1913, O'Neill continued to distribute a "new hornless disc Graphophone" and a considerable catalogue of double-faced records including some 12". He announced his intention to place 100,000 of these "Aretino" machines that year. However, by 1916 the Consolidated Talking Machine Company was listing itself as the successor to both O'Neill firms.

4-16
A Standard Talking Machine Company Style "X2" of 1906. These can be found with horns painted blue, red, or black. *Courtesy of Lou Caruso.*

4-17
The "Queen Busy Bee" Graphophone of 1906 was a modified Columbia "BK". O'Neill-James Company offered these direct to the public for $27.50, with morning glory horn, stand, and six cylinders.

134

4-18
This "Englewood Musicalphone" of 1906 was another "client machine" made by Columbia. It is also seen with a brass-belled horn. *Courtesy of Robert Adams.*

4-19
A close-up shows the unusual horn elbow arrangement used with this type of "Musicalphone". As with the "Busy Bee"-style instruments made by Hawthorne and Sheble, the horn has been directly adapted from cylinder machine use. *Courtesy of Robert Adams.*

4-20
The "Harmony" (shown) and "Busy Bee" of 1906-1907 were similar machines which used blue and red horns, respectively. Whereas both were used in sales promotions, the "Busy Bee" could be purchased directly for $18.00.

4-21
A close-up of the "Harmony" with the turntable removed shows how the manufacturers, Hawthorne and Sheble, designed it to allow the most economical access to the motor.

4-22
The colorful decal of the "Busy Bee" disc machine. The same image was used on the record label, when the entrance to the hive becomes the spindle hole.

4-23
The "Aretino" machine of 1907 featured the largest diameter turntable spindle of any talking machine: 3". It was always sold with a green horn.

4-24
An advertisement for the "Aretino" from 1907 shows that it, like the other machines of the O'Neill group, could be purchased outright for $25.00.

4-25
Arthur J. O'Neill's patent (No. 874,985) in action: an "Aretino" adapter as sold in 1908. This simple device allowed "Artetino" discs (3" center hole) to be played on Victor, Columbia, Zonophone, or "Busy Bee" disc talking machines.

4-26
The "Yankee Prince" (1908) was a later version of the "Busy Bee". It featured an elaborate allegorical decal, and this style had a double-spring motor.

4-27
A detail showing the "Yielding Pressure Feed", which tried to suggest a mechanical feed device. The coiled internal spring (with partial white rubber sheathing) gently pushed the sound arm in the direction of play, but the needle was still guided by the record groove (an infringement of Victor-controlled patent No. 534,543).

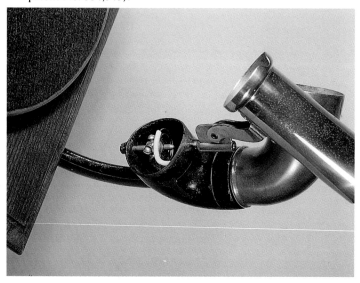

4-29
The "Imperial" was a "client" brand manufactured by Columbia after 1909. It was sold by the "D and R" ("Double and Reversible") Record Company of Chicago. This firm offered double-faced discs derived first from Leeds and Catlin, then from Columbia. *Courtesy of Norm and Janyne Smith.*

4-28
In this "Aretino" of 1909, Hawthorne and Sheble finally achieved in design what had been attempted by subterfuge until then: true mechanical feed. The turntable tracks under the fixed soundbox.

138

4-30
A "D and R" Record Company advertisement from 1909 illustrates two types of "Imperial" machine from the pre-Columbia period. These instruments were Hawthorne and Sheble products. The "Imperial No. I" on the right was the same real mechanical-feed model sold by Aretino. On the left, the "No. II" employs the "Yielding Pressure Feed" which was not a "feed" at all.

4-31
An assortment of independent labels from the 1903-1908 era. *Courtesy of George F. Paul.*

4-32
The "Type K Graphophone" of 1909 was a Columbia-built model ("BA") with a highly-decorative decal. *Courtesy of Norm and Janyne Smith.*

139

4-33
Hawthorne and Sheble's own "Star" brand talking machine of 1908 featured a cabinet with both square and serpentine elements. The "Yielding Pressure Arm" is present in a more substantial version which also featured a built-in volume control. *Courtesy of Norm and Janyne Smith.*

4-34
The "Harvard" was sold Ly Sears, Roebuck and Company of Chicago. This Columbia-made model ("3A", 1906-1908) featured an unique cabinet design. *Courtesy of Lou Caruso.*

4-35
The "Duplex", advertised here in 1908, was a machine of formidable appearance, though the motor was small compared to the size of the cabinet. The dual horns captured the air set in motion on both sides of the soundbox diaphragm (the "Duplex" had two diaphragms), as had the short-lived "Wonder" of 1898. *Courtesy of George F. Paul.*

4-36
This instrument, bearing the label of the Globe Talking Machine Company of Cleveland, Ohio, was manufactured by Talkophone, circa 1906. A related Cleveland firm, the Eagle Talking Machine Company, sold "Eagle" brand disc records, derived from Leeds and Catlin and International Record Company matrices. *Courtesy of George F. Paul.*

THE MAJOR FIRMS
SET THE PACE

Columbia continued its role as an innovator and risk-taker, putting before the public a number of technically interesting cylinder machines. The "AW" of 1904 used a reproducer modified from the "Analyzing" soundbox then sold on Columbia disc machines. This variation had first been seen as an option on the ornately-cased "AO" of 1902, but the "AW" took the same mechanics and put them into the earliest example of the "serpentine" cabinet design which would soon influence all Columbia models, cylinder and disc.

In 1905, the "AZ" was introduced. Though housed in the squared-off case of the later "AT", it employed the lyre-shaped reproducer carriage which would become standard equipment on Graphophones. This first version, however, had a counter-weighted reproducer, like an Edison. Even the second version had one, though the final "Lyric" reproducer, used after 1906, employed a spring tension design. A new "B" series of cylinder machines began with the huge "BC", launched with considerable fanfare. Its design addressed two important issues: increased volume and increased playing time. Dubbed the "Twentieth Century" or "Premier", it employed a friction amplification system. Resistance was created by the action of an ebonite shoe against a wheel of true amber. American Graphophone had purchased the rights to this invention from Daniel Higham, which he had briefly tried to market as the "Highamophone". The reproducer with its 4" diameter diaphragm was capable of stentorian volume, though many were rendered virtually mute over the years by the misguided efforts of their owners to oil the friction parts!

A new line of cylinders accompanied the introduction of the "BC": "Twentieth Century" or "Half Foot" records. As the name suggests, these were approximately two inches longer than regular 100 tpi cylinders, meaning they played approximately a minute longer. This was a revival of the Graphophone Company's original concept of the cylinder, since Bell-Tainter records (and thereafter all office cylinders) had been 6" long. It was also a variation of the "Busy Bee" gimmick, since one needed a Graphophone in the newly-initiated "Twentieth Century" series to play the new records (though ordinary records were usable on "Twentieth Century" machines). Unfortunately, the dearth of these records today suggests that the extra length was just enough to render the "Half Foot" cylinders unduly fragile.

In 1906, the "BE" ("Leader"), "BF" ("Peerless"), and "BG" ("Sovereign") were introduced, equipped with Lyric reproducers, and reflecting the new curvy cabinet design. The latter two machines were intended to play the new "Half Foot" records, and had correspondingly substantial motors. Retaining the older look of the "AZ" was the "BK" ("Jewel"), a cut-down version of the Lyric movement. An amalgam of the "BC" and "BG" was the "BM" ("Home Premier"), with a smaller (3" diameter) Higham reproducer in an imposing mahogany cabinet.

1907 brought the "BO" ("Invincible") and "BQ" ("Rex"), in which the positioning of the horn followed the same model it had with Columbia's disc Graphophones. A "back-mounted" bracket served as the pivot point for the sound arm and held the flower horn above the machine. Hereafter, the earlier style machines (like the "BK", "BE", "BF", and "BG") would be converted by the addition of a back-bracket. The "BV" ("Royal") was a small machine frequently made without a decal for "client sales." Sears, Roebuck and Company of Chicago did a good business in these, as well as the back-mounted or "tone arm" model of 1908, the "BVT". These modifications of the existing line (with the suffix "T" representing "tone arm") were among Columbia's last achievements in the cylinder business.

Among Disc Graphophones in 1904, the "AK", "AJ", and "AH" (well into production) were joined by the uncomplicated "AU" (called "open works" for its lack of a cabinet). The massive mahogany "AR" appeared that year, with its triple-spring motor the origins of which went back to the Type "C" ("Universal") Graphophone of 1897. A lesser version of this machine, with a smaller motor and turntable, was known as the "AY". Back-mounted forms of the "AR" and "AY" were introduced in 1905, known as "BD" ("Majestic") and "BJ" ("Imperial"), respectively. These were equipped with large nickel-plated, panelled horns and later wooden ones. 1906 brought a variety of machines, including many "client" instruments, such as those sold by the Great Northern group in Chicago, as well as "big-box-little-motor" styles based on the "BA" (straight horn) and "BAF" (panelled horn) which were sold as the "Englewood Musicalphone", "Type K Graphophone" and "Princeton", among others.

In 1905, the front-mounted "AH" (in its second, curvy design) received a back-bracket, aluminum tone arm and new flower horn, becoming the "BI" (Sterling). The "AJ" made a similar transformation in 1906, re-titled "BH" ("Champion"). 1907 brought the "BN" (later called the "New Champion" or "Improved Champion"), a lower-priced machine, and 1908 ushered in the lovely serpentine mahogany "BY" ("New Imperial").

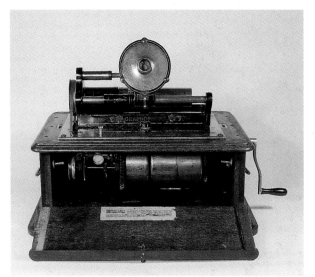

4-38
The "Twentieth Century" Graphophone ("BC") of 1905 was an imposing affair, with a sound-amplifying reproducer based on the patent of Daniel Higham, and triple-spring motor of the "Universal" Graphophone type (1897). The cabinet, too, was rather anachronistic with its hinged front panel and concealed lid fasteners such as Graphophones had used in the nineties. The "BC" sold for $100.00 without horn or stand. *Courtesy of Steve and Ellie Saccente.*

4-37
The Graphophone "AZ" (1905, $25.00) was the first of the "Lyric" reproducer machines. The initial version of the new reproducer (used here) employed a counter-weight design similar to Edison's. Later examples of the "Lyric" reproducer (from the "B" series Graphophones) would be known by the system substituted for the counter-weight: "Spring Tension". *Courtesy of Lou Caruso.*

4-39
This prototype "Highamophone" formed the basis upon which the Columbia "BC" and "BM" would be designed. *Courtesy of the Charles Hummel Collections.*

4-40
The Graphophone "BM" of 1906 ($75.00) employed a reduced-size version of the Higham reproducer.

4-41
The loud-speaking reproducer of the "BC" and "BM" (shown) worked on a principal of mechanical resistance. This was accomplished by an ebonite shoe bearing against a rotating wheel of amber. The brass shaft seen to the right of the diaphragm housing transferred power to run the amber wheel.

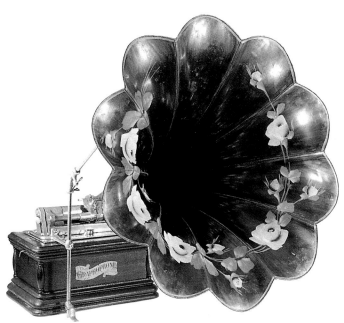

4-42
A Columbia "BG" equipped with unusual scalloped morning glory horn. The machine (1906, $50.00) was extensively nickel-plated, with a four spring motor. *Courtesy of Norm and Janyne Smith.*

4-43
A Columbia "BF" ($40.00) with "Twentieth Century" 6" long mandrel in fancy oak case, shown with both a "Half Foot" and a regular Columbia cylinder. *Courtesy of George F. Paul.*

4-44
The Columbia "BE" ($30.00) was the smaller of the two "serpentine" cabinet models introduced in 1906. *Courtesy of Norm and Janyne Smith.*

4-45
This machine appears to be a prototype for a final version of the Type "Q" Graphophone, considered by Columbia about 1906. It differs from the last production model most notably in the extended reproducer carriage (reproducer not in place). *Courtesy of the Howard Hazelcorn Collection.*

4-46
In 1905, Columbia introduced the elegant "BD" at $100.00. It retained the huge motor of the "AR", while adding a brightly-nickled tone arm assembly and horn (23 1/2" bell). This machine was sold with a smaller (two spring) motor as the "BJ" ($75.00). *Courtesy of Dan and Sandy Krygier.*

4-48
The "BN" Disc Graphophone appeared in this cabinet in 1908 ($25.00 with painted horn, $5.00 additional for the nickeled one shown). *Courtesy of Lou Caruso.*

4-47
The Columbia "BI" of 1905 ($45.00) shared the cabinet of the second-model "AH". In fact, the earliest examples retained the distinctive carrying handle of the front-mount machines. The "BI" remained in production over some seven years, during which various changes were made. The carrying handle was soon eliminated, as was, much later, the turntable dust ring. *Courtesy of Dan and Sandy Krygier.*

146

4-49
In 1908, the stylish "BY" in serpentine mahogany cabinet was offered by Columbia. It sold for $65.00 with nickeled morning glory horn. A year later, a "Symphony" spruce horn like the one shown could be purchased for $20.00. *Courtesy of Dan and Sandy Krygier.*

4-50
After Columbia began using up the wooden cabinets of the former Talkophone Company in 1909, machines like this appeared. The cabinet is from a Talkophone "Clarke" and tone arm parts show the refinements of the "Grafonola". The horn is the lesser of the two panelled oak models offered by Columbia, having no reinforcing around the edge (horn "No. 1", $7.50 separately). *Courtesy of David Werchen.*

4-51
The Graphophone "BO" (1907, $45.00) was the first "tone arm" cylinder machine to play the "Half Foot" records. It featured a cabinet with oval recesses, unlike any other Columbia. *Courtesy of Norm and Janyne Smith.*

4-52
A close-up of a Columbia "BQ" ($30.00) shows the "vertical" reproducer carriage which introduced the "tone arm" Graphophones in 1907. Soon, the carriage of this type of machine would revert to the normal "45 degree" design, as Columbia found it cost-effective to append back-brackets to existing stock. Thereupon, the "BQ" would be superseded by what it most resembled: the "BKT" ("T" = "Tone Arm").

4-53
The "BGT" Graphophone (1907) was just what the name implied, a "BG" tone arm machine. It sold for $70.00 with nickeled flower horn. The Columbia "No. 2" horn shown here was sold for $10.00 separately. *Courtesy of Dan and Sandy Krygier.*

148

4-54
The "BV" Graphophone of 1907 was sold with a decal by Columbia (as shown), or without one when sold by a "client" such as Sears, Roebuck and Company. The 10" nickel-plated horn is normal for the smaller Graphophones of this period. *Courtesy of Norm and Janyne Smith.*

4-55
This Graphophone "BVT" was sold by Sears in 1908 as the "new flexible arm Oxford" for $14.95. The back-bracket was hung from a yoke stretched across the rear of the bedplate. *Courtesy of Dan and Sandy Krygier.*

4-56
This sliver of a Columbia cylinder, with its equally low container, was called a "napkin-ring" record. They were sold, circa 1904, for the purposes of preparing 30 second audio "autographs". A photograph of the individual captured within was meant to be glued to the lid of the box. *Courtesy of George F. Paul.*

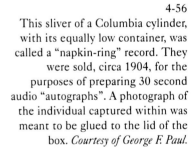

Edison's National Phonograph Company introduced revised models in 1905, designated model "B". The cabinets were slightly higher for the "Standard" and "Home", to accommodate a spring suspension system of the motor. The "Gem" gained a crank instead of a key, and the "Triumph" was re-housed in a sleeker cabinet, with raised panels on the front and back. The "green oak" finishes were replaced by "antique oak," a chocolaty brown color. At first, the banner cabinet decals carried over to the new models, but were soon replaced by the name "Edison" in simple cursive script. The "Concert" received a face-lift the following year when it was put into the new "Triumph" cabinet.

The model "B"s would not endure for long. Events were catching up to Edison which would soon precipitate a rapid escalation of model designations. Firstly, an adverse court decision forced Edison to abandon several design features, minor at first but most notably the hinged endgate which supported the mandrel, and the built-in shaver. In early 1908, the model "C" machines were introduced (initially in New York State only, due to the action of the court) which would prove the immediate precursors of the "four-minute" instruments to appear later that year.

The limited playing time of the 100 tpi cylinder (approximately two minutes) had become a significant issue by 1908. 12" disc records had been on the market for five years, and now could accommodate a performance of about four minutes duration on two sides. Columbia's response was the "Twentieth Century" cylinder, which proved extremely fragile at only three minutes playing time. Cylinders with finer grooves had long been envisioned (the Bell-Tainter cylinders had 160 tpi, which carried over into the 150 tpi of office machines), yet it fell to The Edison Company to design and market the first 200 tpi record. The Edison four-minute "Amberol" records should have been a stunning coup for the great inventor. However, a streak of nasty luck marred the event.

Edison had years before planned to introduce cylinders made of durable celluloid. He was granted a patent for such a process, No. 713,209, on November 11, 1902. Yet, rather than immediately introduce the improved records, National Phonograph sued Thomas Lambert to eliminate the competition. The Lambert Company had been making celluloid cylinders since 1900. The unexpected result of these efforts to brush Lambert aside was that the court declared the Edison patent void due to prior publication, a technicality. No other celluloid patents would be available to Edison for some time. This meant that when National Phonograph came to introduce the 200 tpi cylinder, it was moulded of a harder but far more brittle version of the same metallic soap material of the two-minute cylinders.

Though not nearly as bad as the reputation it has acquired over the years, the new "Amberol" was not the strong, wear-resistant record it should have been. In October 1908, the four-minute records and a new "D" series of machines were introduced. Immediately, National Phonograph fell to the task of offering packages to re-equip its older models so that more customers could enjoy the new cylinders. Even the earliest machines, like "Spring-Motors" or "Concerts" can be found converted, attesting to the success of the program. After this, the Edison two-minute wax cylinder would sell for 35 cents, and four-minute for 50 cents.

Other firms would introduce four-minute gearing to their cylinder machines, most notably Columbia. Whereas Edison offered interchangeable reproducers with specially shaped styli to play two or four-minute records, Columbia settled the issue with a sapphire sized midway between the two. The later Lyric reproducers equipped in this way are recognizable by their fluted, black-painted copper diaphragms, with counterpoise flaps occasionally painted black as well. Columbia was not much concerned with the problem of record wear caused by the slightly inexact stylus. It intended its machines to play Columbia cylinders, and it had plucked the brass ring which had eluded Edison's grasp: Columbia cylinders were now made of celluloid.

This is how it happened. After the failure of Edison's litigation versus the Lambert Company in 1905, a void had occurred in the American celluloid cylinder market. Whereas Britain and Europe had "Lioret", "Lambert", "Edison-Bell", "International Indestructible" and others, the Lambert Company had been the only American manufacturer of such records. Lacking the capital and distribution network to properly exploit the product, and no doubt weakened by legal expenses, the Lambert Company drifted into bankruptcy despite its success against Edison. In July 1906, the Indestructible Record Company was formed to exploit the languishing Lambert patents. Commonly known as "Albany Indestructibles" because of the location of the factory in New York State, they were sold in the two-minute and later four-minute format. They are easily identifiable by the steel re-inforcing rings inside both ends, and their cardboard cores.

In 1908, Columbia began purchasing the entire output of the Indestructible Company, to be boxed under its own name (two-minute 35 cents, four-minute 50 cents: a better record for the same price as Edison). This they would do until they exited the cylinder business in 1912, after which the Albany Indestructibles continued to be sold in boxes usually marked "Everlasting Indestructible" (not to be confused with "U.S. Everlasting throughout the 'teens.

4-57
An Edison "tin" dealer's sign from about 1904. *Courtesy of Peter N. Dilg, Baldwin Antique Center.*

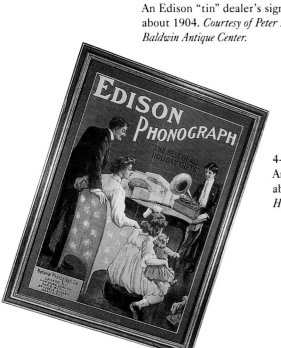

4-58
An Edison publicity poster from about 1906. *Courtesy of the Charles Hummel Collections.*

4-59
After experimenting with a trademark showing a little boy about to dismember a Phonograph while "Looking for the Band," the Edison Company settled upon this memorable but mawkish painting by Italian artist Pompeo Massani to use in advertising during the last half of the century's first decade. *Courtesy of George F. Paul.*

4-60
This unusually well-preserved Edison "Standard" Model "B" (introduced 1905) still has the original price sticker on the upper right corner of the cabinet ($20.00). *Courtesy of Peter N. Dilg, Baldwin Antique Center.*

4-61
A close-up of a Model "B" Edison "Home" Phonograph ($30.00) which has factory decoration in the style of the Model "D" machines that were to follow (1908). This may be a later version of the "special decoration" listed in the catalogue at $8.00 extra. *Courtesy of Peter N. Dilg, Baldwin Antique Center.*

4-62
This Model "B" Edison "Triumph" ($50.00) displays the optional "special decoration" of flowers and gold stripes ($8.00 extra). In addition, it has a mahogany cabinet ($10.00 extra) and a "Weber" repeating mechanism (briefly offered on "Triumph and "Home" machines). *Courtesy of Robert and Marilyn Laboda.*

4-63
A close-up of the "special decoration Triumph" shows what $8.00 could buy. *Courtesy of Robert and Marilyn Laboda.*

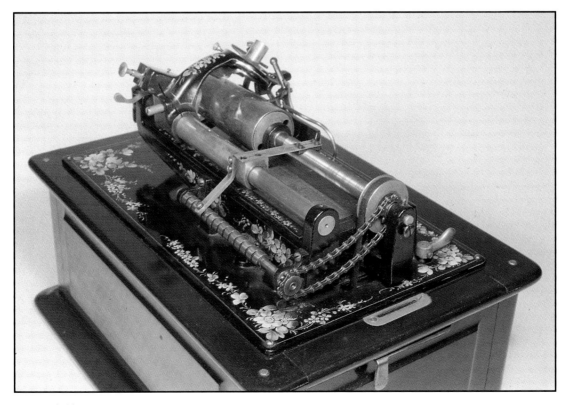

4-64
A close-up of the "Triumph" showing the "Weber" repeater with its interesting chain drive off the pulley. The later (called Model "D") repeater would put the coarse return screw on the front of the upper casting. *Courtesy of Robert and Marilyn Laboda.*

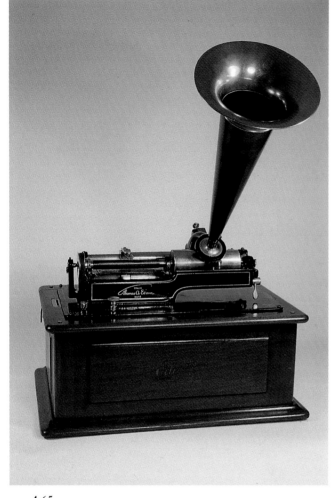

4-65
An Edison "Triumph" Model "B" in mahogany case ($10.00 extra) with 14" horn as it was sold in 1906. *Courtesy of Norm and Janyne Smith.*

4-66
Also available for Edison Phonographs was complete nickel-plating of the upper works. This "Triumph" Model "B" was nickeled at $25.00 extra, a significant cost at the time. After 1910, it was "Amberolized" (to play the new four-minute records) and given a Model "O" reproducer in a later-style carriage (also nickeled). *Courtesy of the Charles Hummel Collections.*

4-67
An Edison "Ideal" Phonograph ($125.00) made in the first two months of production (1907) before the name was changed to "Idealia". After 1910, it had a Model "O" reproducer and "Amberol" attachment added. The "oxidized" finish of the metal parts was an interesting convention of the day, appearing on some of the very cheapest and some of the most expensive talking machines. *Courtesy of Norm and Janyne Smith.*

154

4-68
An Edison "Universal" shaving machine from 1905. This was primarily for office use (note the 6" long mandrel—Edison did not make an entertainment record of this length) and cost $35.00. *Courtesy of Norm and Janyne Smith.*

4-69
The Edison "Gem" Phonograph was the model least affected by the Model "C" design changes of early-1908. However, it did receive more complicated decoration, as shown. The horn is one subsequently purchased from a talking machine dealer. An Edison-made black, 19" panelled horn was also available for this model. *Machine Courtesy of Robert T. Lomas.*

4-70
If the Edison four-minute "Amberol" cylinder of 1908 had been what it was claimed, it would have been a far better product. Denied the use of durable celluloid by legal entanglements, the Edison Company relied on the metallic soap with which it was making the two-minute ("wax") cylinders. The resulting "Amberols" were extremely well-recorded, but prone to become brittle and worn over time. *Courtesy of George F. Paul.*

155

The Victor company gained steadily in power and prestige during this period. 1904 was a watershed year between the old front-mounted styles and the new back-mounted or "Tapering Arm" models (which improved upon and replaced the "Rigid Arm" design). As a shift began from letter to number model designations, some interesting transitions occurred. The Victor "E" or "Monarch Junior" ($25.00) got a back-mounted "tapering" arm and horn, an 8" turntable and started to be called the "Improved Victor II" ($30.00). The "Monarch" ($35.00) received the same treatment and became the "Improved Victor III" ($40.00). The ornate "Monarch Special" ($45.00), when fitted with the tapering arm became the "Improved Victor IV" ($50.00). Finally, the big Victor "D", a back-mounted, 12" turntable version of the "MS", began to be known as the "Improved Victor V" ($60.00). All this was in preparation of further changes to the line, and the serial-plates of these machines did not have time to reflect their transitional designations.

The new line needed a *ne plus ultra*, which it got later in 1904 with the introduction of the Victor "VI", with mahogany cabinet, gold-plated hardware and $100.00 price tag. The "D" soon received an entirely redesigned cabinet, the gingerbread giving way to the stately bulk which would become the final look of the Victor "V". The "MS"/ "Improved Victor IV" followed suit, getting a new oak cabinet with rounded pillars and plain molding in 1906. Soon, the motor was up-dated, the wood was changed to mahogany, and the ID plate finally amended to read "IV". The rest of the numbers were filled in as convenient.

In 1905, the diminutive and affordable Victor "I" ($22.00) took over the slot formerly held by the "Rigid Arm" "Royal", the Victor "II" got its own cabinet and a new motor, the "III" was slightly enlarged and equipped with the new mechanics and the "IV" and "V" evolved as previously noted. Last to join would be the small mahogany "0" ($17.50, 1908) destined to outlast some of its larger brethren when the external-horn Victors became low-priced alternatives to cabinet models in the next decade.

The "Z" was just what the name implied, intended to be the last of the Victor front-mounts, offered in 1905 at $17.00 (an obvious replacement of the $15.00 front-mount "Royal"). In fact, the "Junior" would be the final front-mounted machine. It was introduced in 1909 at the inexpensive price of $10.00, which helps to explain why it would enjoy healthy production though a technical anachronism. Now in place was a solid line of talking machines which would carry Victor into the 'teens.

In 1906, the company introduced its first internal-horn floor model, the "VTLA" (standing for "Victrola"). It was intended as an elite model, with a sobering price-tag of $200.00. The mahogany cabinet was initially designed and produced by the Pooley Furniture Company of Philadelphia, but was replaced within a year by a Victor-built cabinet whose shape would define the look of internal-horn machines for nearly twenty years.

After 1903, the Universal Talking Machine Company became a subsidiary of Victor and followed the parent's trend by offering a new series of back-mounted Zonophones, while continuing to maintain a couple of inexpensive front-mounts. The cheapest of the newer models, with a clever back-mounted sound arm which snapped in and out of the resting position, was the oak "Parlor" ($30.00). The most expensive was the mahogany, triple-spring "Royal Grand" ($75.00). Though some former features carried over, it was from this point that Zonophones began to use more and more Victor parts. Even the nomenclature was shared, as in, "The New Tapering Arm Zon-o-phones are the best." Front-mounted machines, cost-reduced versions of earlier models, continued to be offered until 1909, as Zonophones were promoted as a cheaper alternative to Victors.

The talking machine was about to enter a period of transition. Not the least of the many changes which would occur was the steady shift from external to internal-horn machines—but why? The new cabinet models offered no improvement in sound. In fact, technical merit was put aside while the visual elements were worked out. The cramped and boxy sound passage in an early Victrola "XVI"; the mouth of the Victrola "XII" internal-horn nothing more than a slit; the complete lack of any substantial internal-horn structure in the lesser Victrolas, where the sound bounced around the sides of the motor; all these meant *poorer* sound reproduction. So, why did the world give up quality for a "look"?

A good case can be made against the physically cumbersome external-horn. It "got in the way." It needed to be dusted. It could get dented or scratched or even misplaced. The cabinet model represented a self-contained unit. Moreover, it did not remind people about how the sounds came out, which, for the young consumers of 1908, was essentially unchanged since the days of their parents in the 1890s. The music emerged from a beautiful piece of furniture, and all the "wonderful improvements" could be therein imagined. So, the talking machine buyer embraced the inescapably modern idea of the Victrola.

4-71
The Victor "P" of 1904 was promotionally distributed, not sold direct to customers. This one used the same motor as a "Royal", though with a bigger cabinet, turntable (10"), and horn. *Courtesy of Norm and Janyne Smith.*

4-72
The motor of this Victor "P3" from 1906 would serve a number of inexpensive machines over a long period, including the Victor "Junior" and various Zonophones. *Courtesy of Norm and Janyne Smith.*

4-73
This Victor "Z" of 1905 was a low-priced successor to the "Royal". Extended arms and a larger horn were added to this one at an increased cost (regular price $17.00). It used the same cabinet and motor as a Victor "I". *Courtesy of Norm and Janyne Smith.*

157

4-74
The Victor "E" in its "Improved Victor II" form of 1904. Soon the cabinet and tone arm parts would be somewhat enlarged and the serial-plate amended to read Victor "II". *Courtesy of Norm and Janyne Smith.*

4-76
The Victor II of 1905 had a new, simplified motor, but a cabinet based on the "E" ("Monarch Junior") from which it had evolved. The smaller Victor wood horn (shown), which was an option on the "I", "II", and "IV" (in mahogany), was available from 1909. *Courtesy of George F. Paul.*

4-75
The Victor "I", with the same cabinet and motor as the "Z", featured a tapering arm and brass-belled horn in 1905. This example has been given an elbow extension to allow it to accept the horn of a Victor "II". *Courtesy of George F. Paul.*

158

4-77
A Victor "III" of 1906 with an optional brass "morning glory" horn, purchased from a talking machine dealer. *Courtesy of Norm and Janyne Smith.*

4-78
This Victor "ms" of 1907 sits atop a record storage cabinet with special molding to accept it. The common black Victor panelled horn is shown. *Courtesy of Norm and Janyne Smith.*

4-79
The Victor "III" could also be had with a wooden horn. This is the larger of the two models made, with fancy design (commonly called "spear-tip"). Sold separately, the horn cost $10.00.*Courtesy of Lou Caruso.*

4-80

A Victor "IV" from 1906 with optional wood-grained morning glory horn manufactured by Hawthorne and Sheble, which had a thriving talking machine accessory business. The record storage cabinet reflects the same design as the machine. *Courtesy of Norm and Janyne Smith.*

4-81
A Victor "V" of 1905, with a brass-belled horn of the type available on the first "Tapering Arm" machines. *Courtesy of Norm and Janyne Smith.*

4-82
The Victor "VI", introduced in 1904, was to long remain the firm's premier external-horn machine. Gold-plated hardware and a nickel-plated triple-spring motor were among the amenities which $100.00 bought. At first, it was supplied with a shiny black fiber horn (shown). Over the years, a variety of horns, metal and wood, were offered. *Courtesy of Norm and Janyne Smith.*

4-83
This custom "Douglas" mahogany cabinet houses the mechanism of a Victor "D" (1905). The better models could be specially equipped in this way for discerning customers. The horn is typical of an "optional" morning glory available from various manufacturers. *Courtesy of Peter N. Dilg, Baldwin Antique Center.*

4-84
Another "Douglas" cabinet, this one floor-standing, with Victor mechanism and spruce wood horn, circa 1908. The doors open to reveal record storage. *Courtesy of the Charles Hummel Collections.*

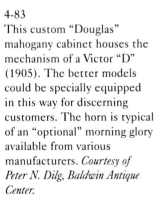

4-85
The Victor "Auxetophone" was a very sophisticated piece of loud-speaking equipment offered in 1906. The compressed-air amplification system it used was invented by C.A. Parsons in England, where the machine had already been put on sale by the Gramophone Company. The bottom compartment of the cabinet houses an air-compressor. The special soundbox is shown in its storage box. At $500.00, it was aimed at institutional more than home use. *Courtesy of Norm and Janyne Smith.*

161

4-86
The very first (Pooley) design of the "VTLA" ("Victrola") of 1906. It sold for $200.00. *Courtesy of Dr. Jay Tartell.*

4-88
Interior of the "Pooley Victrola". *Courtesy of Dr. Jay Tartell.*

4-87
The "Pooley Victrola" in its awe-inspiring open position. *Courtesy of Dr. Jay Tartell.*

4-89
When Victor began to manufacture its own cabinets, late in 1907, the design of the "VTLA" was changed as shown. The price, for mahogany cabinet, was kept at $200.00. In this form it became the Victrola "XVI" (commonly known as the "L-door XVI"). *Courtesy of Norm and Janyne Smith.*

4-90
The open "VTLA/XVI" gives a grand appearance, but the sound chamber is boxy and small, no improvement of external-horn technology. *Courtesy of Norm and Janyne Smith.*

4-91
The interior of the "VTLA/XVI" shows that the mounting board, controls, and motor of a Victor "VI" were dropped in with no modification. *Courtesy of Norm and Janyne Smith.*

4-92
This Zonophone "Grand Opera" of 1906 ($60.00) was designed to suggest the earlier model of the same name. However, the cabinet has been simplified and many parts borrowed from Victor machines, though the all-brass horn, back-bracket, and brake are still characteristically Zonophone. This machine cost dealers $36.00, allowing them a $24.00 profit, not including freight. *Courtesy of Norm and Janyne Smith.*

4-93
The "Royal Grand" Zonophone was the top-of-the-line in 1908 ($75.00). The horn, with its shallowly scalloped edge, was grained to match the mahogany cabinet. Wholesale price: $45.00. *Courtesy of Norm and Janyne Smith.*

4-94
The Zonophone "Eclipse" is a machine about which little is known. The cabinet and works suggest it was connected with models sold by the International Zonophone Company in Europe, circa 1905. Like Victor *vis a vis* the British and European branches of the Gramophone Company, U.S. Zonophone shared technology with its foreign associate. *Courtesy of Peter N. Dilg, Baldwin Antique Center.*

4-95
The horn of the Zonophone "Eclipse" was made by Hawthorne and Sheble, and received the "silk finish" exterior for which that firm was known. Except for the company name, the emblem shown here is identical to the ones with which Hawthorne and Sheble marked such horns in its own name. *Courtesy of Peter N. Dilg, Baldwin Antique Center.*

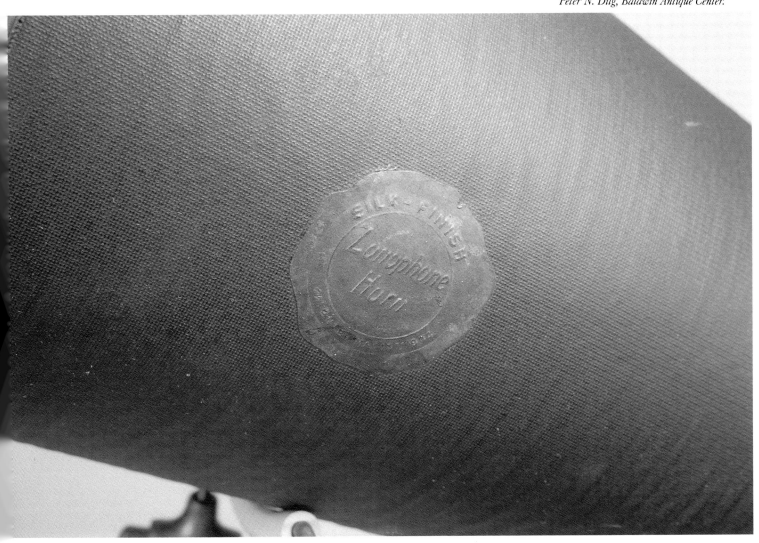

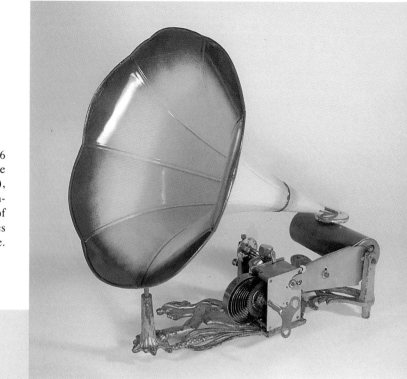

4-96
The "Mermaid" or "Siren" talking machine (in the unsophisticated "Puck" category), circa 1905, combined diminutive mechanics with graceful design. This model was of French manufacture, though most varieties of "Puck" were German-made.

4-97
The "Biophone" was an odd sort of Puck sold in Britain (made in Germany). Conventional Puck works, slightly rearranged, are disguised by the stylish metal housing.

4-98
This variety of Puck retains the marginal mechanics, but combines them with a tapering tone arm (no fear of Victor's lawyers in Germany) and a horn in the shape of a blossom, surmounted by an elf! *Courtesy of the Julien Anton Collection.*

4-99
This Puck was sold in a wooden cabinet, circa 1905. The fancy cast bedplate and support arm based on front-mount disc machines distinguished it, though the motor (as always) was the same. *Courtesy of Dan and Sandy Krygier.*

4-100
The "Skylark" was another variety of German-made Puck sold in Britain. The *art nouveau* pretensions of the bedplate make it unusual. *Courtesy of Dan and Sandy Krygier.*

4-101
This "Lambertphone" was sold in Britain circa 1906. As in the U.S., the Lambert Company manufactured celluloid cylinders, but only in Britain were the six-inch "Imperial" records available. The machine was equipped with a longer mandrel in the manner of Columbia's "Twentieth Century" models. *Courtesy of Allen Koenigsberg.*

167

4-102
This Pathé "Coq" (rooster) of 1904 was known as a "reversible" model. The lid of the box, to which the machine was screwed, could be inverted for storage. The horn is a European style, also manufactured for use on Pucks. The machine was equipped with a removable mandrel to play the mid-sized (3 1/2" diameter) Pathé "Intermediate" cylinders. To change between the regular and "Inter" records required an adapter for the reproducer.

4-103
The problem of adapters to reposition the reproducer was solved when Pathé introduced a "floating horn" design: a refinement of the Girard Company's "Système Vérité". Built into this pretty Pathé "Royal" from 1905 is the ability to play either type of record without removing the reproducer. *Courtesy of Lou Caruso.*

4-104
The Pathé "2" of 1906 had a well-designed double-spring motor and decorative walnut case. Pathé had begun to construct its machines with die-cast parts, which have proved to be of better quality than most produced in the U.S.

4-105
The Pathé "4" was capable of playing the three sizes of Pathé cylinder available in France: "regular" (Edison/Columbia size), "Inter" (called "Salon" in Britain), and 5" diameter (called "Stentor" in France).

4-106
A selection of Pathé cylinders. At the rear: the immense "Le Celeste", which played on a machine of equally grand proportions. In front, left to right: a "regular" cylinder, an "Intermediate", and a "Stentor".

4-107
A selection of British and European cylinders, which frequently were housed in very decorative containers. *Courtesy of Allen Koenigsberg.*

4-108
In 1906, Pathé introduced a line of disc talking machines in France. This upper-range Model "D" was first offered with a front-mounted aluminum horn, later equipped with fanciful bracket and arm as shown.

4-109
The Pathé Model "D" came with a stylish-looking dust cover for the turntable, decorated with the image of a cylinder machine.

4-110
This Pathé Model "P" disc machine, circa 1907, suggests the earliest design features. The cabinets were often rather low and plain (this one has been dressed-up with pillars), and made of a light-colored walnut. The motor was activated by a "push-pull" lever at the top of the front panel. The decal was the same used on Pathé's cylinder models: depicting a rooster before a cylinder talking machine.

4-112
The "Wizard" phonograph of 1911 was made by the International Phonograph Company of Newark, New Jersey, and sold for several years. The design, like the name of the firm, suggests European origins: the works are "reversible" in the cabinet (stored upside-down) and the horn is a variation of the "cor-de-chasse" or "hunting horn" common on talking machines in France. It was available in oak with a black horn (shown) or mahogany finish with a red horn. *Courtesy of Dan and Sandy Krygier.*

4-111
This Pathé "No. 4" disc machine from 1908 illustrates the changes which occurred in the later disc models. The cabinets were given decorative molding, the motor was most frequently activated by a sturdy lever at the top of the front panel which moved side-to-side and the decal depicted a muscular gentleman in the pose of a discus thrower about to hurl a Pathé disc record. *Courtesy of Alan H. Mueller.*

171

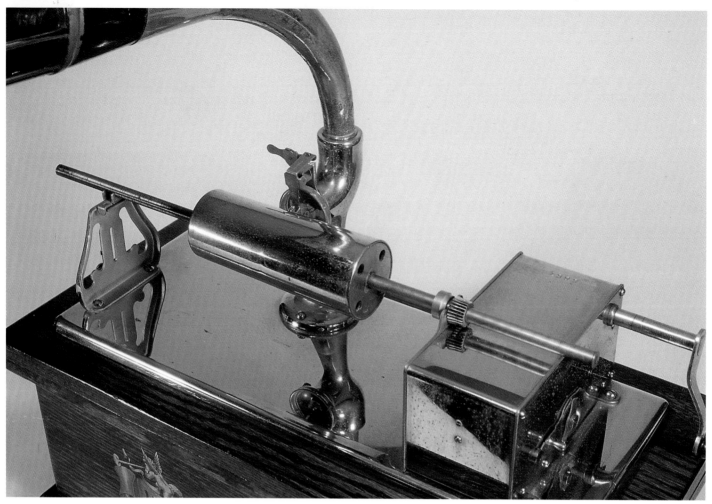

4-113
The works of the "Wizard" (invented by the exotically named
Pliny Catucci) also show an odd combination of design elements.
The mandrel tracks under a stationary reproducer which is fixed to
a post that supports the horn (as seen in the Edison "Opera").
However, the mandrel was completely detachable, in a manner not
employed since the old Bell-Tainter Graphophones. *Courtesy of Dan
and Sandy Krygier.*

4-114
The "Rectorphone" of 1906 was an unusual
cylinder machine carried by a number of
small distributors. One such outlet was the
Baird-North Company, a mail-order firm
specializing in domestic items. Enoch J.
Rector of Parkersburg, West Virginia, had
envisioned his machine (patented August 15,
1905, No. 797,020) as an accessory for the
treadle-powered sewing machines which
were popular throughout the U.S. A friction
wheel would run the phonograph right off
the sewing machine belt. The production
model, however, employed a typical talking
machine motor with mainspring. Mounted to
a simple wooden plank (oak or mahogany
finish), it sold for $3.50.

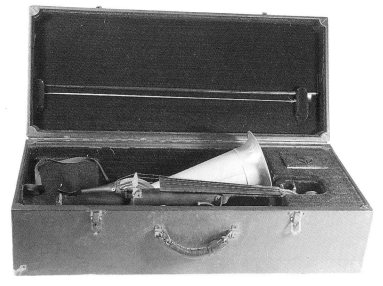

4-115

The "Stroh" violin was an instrument developed specifically for recording purposes. A metal horn amplified the sound of a violin bereft of the familiar wooden body. In this way, the tones of the instrument could be better focused for acoustical recording. The instruments were made by George Evans and Company of London, England. *Courtesy of Norm and Janyne Smith.*

4-116

The "Cailophone" of 1906 employed the works of an Edison Phonograph activated by a coin. The cabinet style reflected a design frequently seen in other coin-op talking machines of the period, including Edison's own line. *Courtesy of the Howard Hazelcorn Collection.*

4-117

This coin-operated Columbia "AZ" Graphophone, circa 1906, was produced by the Rosenfield Manufacturing Company of New York City. Rosenfield offered various coin machines, including one which displayed illuminated views as a record played (the "Illustrated Song Machine"). Listening-tubes were most frequently used with coin-ops, where the machines might be grouped to allow a choice of selections (one record to a machine). During this same period, Edison's floor-standing slot Phonographs were housed in very similar oak cabinets with rectangular, glass-panelled lids and ball-and-claw legs.

4-118
A charming selection of talking machine horns from the 1906 period.

4-119
4-120
Courtesy of Norm and Janyne Smith.

4-121
Courtesy of Norm and Janyne Smith.

CHAPTER 5:

THE TALKING MACHINE IN TRANSITION, 1909-1914

THE TALKING MACHINE IN AMERICAN LIFE

This period began with attrition. Numerous small manufacturers disappeared, leaving the power of Victor, Columbia, and Edison unrivalled. The business depression of 1908 hadn't helped anyone, but the bigger firms were able to endure. Within the industry, a steady drift away from cylinder records left Edison the least viable and started him seeking a way to enter the disc market. This was a route peppered with the patents of others.

Some independent talking machine firms struggled on into the century's second decade without benefit of protection from the Victor or Columbia patents. The Sonora Phonograph Company of New York City fought a long and costly struggle with Victor regarding the authenticity of the Sonora mechanical feed device. At this time, Sonoras were produced primarily by the Swiss firm of Paillard. They were fitted with a self-tracking soundbox, but among the nuances of patent litigation this was ruled infringing by Judge Hough in U.S. Circuit Court on December 12, 1910. He concluded, "...the assertions made by the defendant's expert are not borne out by evidence; the reproducer is not positively driven by the feed across the face of the record..." While appealing this decision, Sonora pursued another thrust. It argued that due to certain technicalities, the basic Berliner patent under which Sonora had been prosecuted, No. 534,543, was actually due to expire in February of 1911, a full year ahead of schedule. Here was a tiny chink in the Victor armor, but one which portended greater ruptures!

On February 25, 1911, the same Judge Hough who previously had ruled against Sonora decided that the crucial Berliner patent had indeed expired. To emphasize this determination, Sonora immediately began to sell instruments with "conventional" tone-arms (no

mechanical feed). It was Victor's turn to appeal, but with only a year remaining in the life of the Berliner patent by even the most favorable reckoning, the path was cleared for independents to consider the manufacture of talking machines without mechanical feed clap-trap or ruses. Aware of the hopelessness of its situation, the Victor Company issued a statement to the *Talking Machine World* on March 9, 1911, in which it listed its "other" patents. It added, "The Victor Co., therefore, as we believe, notwithstanding the eventual expiration of the term of the Berliner patent, is abundantly protected and will be able to control the disc machines and records of a commercial, practical type for a number of years to come..." In truth, it could no longer keep smaller firms out of the machine business, though it (and Columbia) retained control of the lateral cut record. During the 'teens and into the twenties, the high-quality Sonora line would be a potent force in the market.

The talking machine had already proved it could mimic real events. Subjects like Spanish American War battles, the San Francisco earthquake, and the last speech of President McKinley (imitated by Len Spencer) intrigued the public in a day before newsreels, and long before radio or TV. Soon enough the cinema would give stirring testimony to world events, but the ability of the talking machine to inspire the imagination with sound was unique indeed. All the record companies added "descriptive specialties" to their repertoire. Everything from "The Shelling Of The Forts At Port Arthur" (during the Russo-Japanese War) to "Sleigh-Ride Party" was tried. The talking machine record really fulfilled its promise, however, when it preserved the voices of the famous and infamous. Great singers like Nellie Melba and Enrico Caruso had been captured forever on shellac for the delectation of millions.

The voices of important political figures, too, were now saved, not as impersonations but the real thing.

During the 1908 U.S. Presidential campaign, opponents William Jennings Bryan (Democrat) and William Howard Taft (Republican and the hand-picked candidate of incumbent Theodore Roosevelt) had been invited to record a series of speeches on current issues by Edison (two-minute wax), Victor, and Columbia (discs and two-minute wax).

These records proved very successful, and when Theodore Roosevelt challenged Taft for the 1912 Republican nomination a series of Roosevelt speeches appeared on Edison "Amberol" cylinders and Victor 12" discs. Though he had successfully supported Taft to replace him, Roosevelt was unhappy with the way things were being run. When Taft won the Republican candidacy, Roosevelt formed a third party, the "Progressive". On Edison "Amberol" No. 1146, "The Progressive Covenant with the People," he speaks with more animation than any of the other three "Amberols" he recorded. Roosevelt recalled his betrayal by his own party, and the final line, "We stand at Armaggedon and we battle for the Lord" is unforgettable. It's a shame that this was the one speech not re-issued on celluloid.

Modern listeners, whose brash image of Teddy Roosevelt may have been drawn from recent representations like "Arsenic and Old Lace," might be surprised by the cultured, patrician voice (with a slight hesitation) which emerges from the talking machine horn. Though Roosevelt received a large portion of the vote, the net effect of having two *de facto* Republican candidates was the election of the Democrat, Woodrow Wilson, whose speeches appeared on 12" Victors.

Average Americans could finally hear the words of important candidates in their own homes, a great step toward a truly informed choice. The record companies seemed to realize the importance of what they had done and rushed to offer special recordings by Polar explorers Byrd and Shakleton. Edison himself would record only once for public consumption. "Let Us Not Forget" gave his thoughts on the contributions of America's allies during World War I. Issued on four-minute ("Blue Amberol") cylinder No. 3756 (and "Diamond Disc" No. 50509) following the Armistice, its message soon paled before the fame of the voice which carried it.

CHANGES IN THE EDISON CAMP

The Amberola "1A" of 1909 was the first internal-horn Edison cylinder machine, and was introduced at the lofty price of $200.00, following the example of the expensive models which had initiated the Victor Victrola and Columbia Grafonola cabinet instruments. The first Amberola was the only one of the series to play both two and four-minute cylinders. Those to follow, beginning with the slightly modified "1B", would be exclusively four-minute machines.

Edison ceased production of two-minute cylinders in 1912. A quick succession of Amberola models began that year; a progression which would start with substance and end with fluff. The Amberola "III" (1912), "IV", "V", "VI", and "VIII" (all 1913) came flying out of West Orange, each one getting flimsier as the company endeavored to use up existing parts of the external-horn models, most notably the "Fireside". This had proved a very popular instrument when introduced in July of 1909 (at $22.00 to occupy the slot formerly held by the "Standard" prior to its price increase to $30.00).

Edison "Firesides" would continue to be sold into 1914, but their about-to-be-redundant mechanisms were used up in the Amberolas. The Edison Company had been lured by the siren of economy into degrading its line. Finally, parts from the humble "Gem" appeared in the Amberola "X" (1913), completing Edison's journey from the sublime to the ridiculous. In one year, the price of an Amberola had gone from $80.00 (for the solidly-built "V") to $30.00 (for the hodge-podge "X"). Despite the savings, the customer was not well-served.

In 1910, the Phonograph Division of the newly reorganized Thomas A. Edison, Inc. had begun experimenting with discs. Steering clear of the Victor patents which had only recently eliminated so much of the disc talking machine competition, however, was a thorny task. The Edison company decided to explore only vertical cut recording, a system in which Edison firmly believed as well as one not threatened by the patents of other disc manufacturers. This recording process would become the refuge of firms which would dare the disc market in the 'teens. Edison was haunted, too, by the old issue of mechanical feed, which had figured so prominently in the court battles of the previous decade. At least the feed concept could be proved essential to the system which the Edison Company would devise: a fine-grooved record played by a heavy-weighted reproducer.

Care had to be taken to avoid key cabinet model features already patented by Victor and others. By this point, the internal-horn Victrola was well off the ground, with a complete line of cabinet machines soon to be released following the success of the "VTLA". Although external-horn talking machines of various makes were still being sold in strong numbers, the trend toward cabinet styles was clear. Edison originally envisioned a low priced external-horn model of his "Disc Phonograph", but none ever came to market. In fact, the line would suffer from the failure to offer more affordable models, partly due to the elaborate constraints placed upon design by the fear of litigation.

The disc record itself would prove a serious technical achievement: the first disc carefully developed, not haphazardly evolved like the "78". A compressed wood-flour core was given a skin of Condensite, a phenolic resin. The resulting disc was thick (1/4") but perfectly flat (if stored properly); well-suited to be recorded at 150 tpi (finer grooves than a lateral disc). The reproducer employed a diamond stylus and a substantial counter-weight, technology which was borrowed from the Amberola cylinder reproducers introduced in 1909 and perfected after the introduction of Edison's celluloid cylinder in 1912. A mechanical feed device moved both the reproducer and the internal-horn together, eliminating the problem of sound loss through the moveable joints which plagued the "78" machines.

The Edison Company was carving itself an unique but costly position. Good sense speaks to the efficacy of making one's products adaptable, but Edison decided, soon after his disc machine entered the market, to discourage efforts to modify his instruments to play regular "78s". Of course, many, many convertors were offered by other firms to allow cross-over in both directions, but the Edison Company was determined to make it on its own. With its now customary paternalism it would force upon its dealers and the public the superiority of the complicated and expensive system.

During 1912, the first Edison discs (which we shall call "Diamond Discs", ignoring a host of changes in nomenclature) went on sale (expensive at $1.50 and up). A limited line of internal-horn machines was offered for which the price was indicated by the model number. The "A60", a table model in an oak-grained metal cabinet, was the cheapest. Another table model, the "A80", came next, followed by several floor models ascending to the "A250" which shared the heavily-built cabinet of the Amberola "1B" cylinder Phonograph. The immediately-apparent problems of record quality and mechanical reliability (especially in the table models) would be the focus of the Edison Company's efforts for the following few years. The next significantly different models would come slowly.

In October 1913, the Edison Company announced an end to its external-horn phonographs. By that time, the "Standard" and "Triumph" had reached a venerable old age (both reached model "G"), while the "Home" ran to model "F", and the "Gem" to "E". The "Fireside" would conclude with model "B", a four-minute-only machine. Model "A" was commonly equipped with the same deep red, panelled horn used on the "Gem" "D" and "E". The "Fireside B" is most often found with a "cygnet" ("swan's neck") horn of the type introduced in September 1909. These black, panelled horns with their long, graceful elbows were Edison's response to the success other firms had en-joyed in getting the horn over the top of the machine, not out in front of it.

The Edison "Opera" phonograph, introduced in November 1911, coupled the sophisticated mechanism of the Amberola "1B" with a stylish cabinet and a wooden-belled horn inspired by the cygnets. It was expensive ($90.00 mahogany, $85.00 oak) but sold well. Today, it frequently represents the finest cylinder machine commonly available to collectors, though there were equal or more expensive models at the time, such as the electric-motored "Alva" ($80.00 to $100.00 depending on equipment) or the top-of-the-line "Idelia" ($125.00).

It is impossible to imagine that the Edison Company could have sustained its line of four-minute cylinder phonographs if a replacement of the unsatisfactory Amberol records had not been developed. It has been suggested that Edison did not consider the surface of celluloid smooth enough to produce a record which would satisfy him. Yet, surely he would have been exploiting his own celluloid patent by this time, if the court had not found it invalid.

Edison, at last, bought the rights to a celluloid record process from Englishman Brian F. Philpot, and introduced his "Blue Amberol" cylinders in 1912 (50 cents each). He did indeed have to improve the smoothness of the commercial celluloid he bought, but the result was a medium able to record much more information than could be got out of it by contemporary equipment. These sturdy records, with their ribbed plaster cores and rich cobalt celluloid skins, would endure into the following decade—and the one beyond that if you count a special educational series!

5-1
The ability to make amateur records had always been an important selling factor of the cylinder talking machine. Even in the "four-minute" era attachments were sold to allow home recording. *Courtesy of George F. Paul.*

5-2
The Edison "Fireside" Model "A" was introduced in July of 1909 at $22.00. It was meant as a successor to the "Standard", which it very much resembled but which had grown in price and importance in the Edison line over the years. Its simplified redefinition of the "Standard" turned out to be a significant improvement, and the machine was popular. The red, panelled horn was regular equipment. *Courtesy of Dan and Sandy Krygier.*

5-3
The Edison "Gem" Model "D" of 1909 shared the same style of red horn with the "Fireside". In fact, the horns were all marked "Fireside" regardless of where they were used. By this point, the price of the "Gem" had risen to $15.00. Although kits had been made available to "Amberolize" earlier, two-minute "Gems", the results had been marginal due to the weakness of the motor. In the Model "D", the spring was strengthened to give puissance to the factory two-and-four-minute gearing. The color of the body was changed to a rich maroon, and the enhanced decoration of the Model "C" carried over. *Courtesy of Dan and Sandy Krygier.*

5-4
The Model "E" was the last of the Edison "Gems", introduced in October of 1912 and officially discontinued one year later. This was a four-minute-only machine, and a large-diameter carriage arm was substituted to hold a Model "N" (four-minute sapphire) reproducer. The same red horn was used. *Courtesy of Robert T. Lomas.*

5-5
This "Fireside" Model "A" was fitted with the ten-panel "cygnet" (swan's neck) horn which was introduced in September of 1909. Equipped this way, it cost $27.00. The cygnet horn would carry over to the Model "B" (introduced 1912), though the reproducer carriage was changed to a vertical design to accept either the four-minute "N" or "Diamond B" reproducers, or Model "O" with dual styli. *Courtesy of Norm and Janyne Smith.*

5-7
This Edison "Home" Model "B" was "Amberolized" and fitted with a No. 10 cygnet horn after September 1909. *Courtesy of Norm and Janyne Smith.*

5-6
This Edison "Standard" Model "D" was equipped after August 1910 with an oak "Music Master" cygnet horn (by Sheip and Vandegrift of Philadelphia). It is fitted with a Model "S" reproducer, essentially a Model "K" (dual styli) with a larger diaphragm for increased volume. *Courtesy of Norm and Janyne Smith.*

5-8
This Edison "Triumph" Model "B" was refitted with a two- and four-minute attachment, Model "O" reproducer, and oak cygnet horn after August 1910. *Courtesy of Dan and Sandy Krygier.*

5-9
A close-up of the "Triumph" shows an unusual starting and stopping device fitted to it, patented July 16, 1907, by Charles H. Wilkes and Howard Lyke. *Courtesy of Dan and Sandy Krygier.*

5-11
The "Triumph" Model "F" was introduced in November of 1911. The motor was significantly altered from the venerable "Triton" which had been designed by Frank Capps some sixteen years earlier. Note the nickeled starting lever protruding straight up from the left of the upper casting, resembling a "Home". *Courtesy of Terry Paul Baer.*

5-10
Another Edison "Triumph" Model "B" fitted with a cygnet horn: this time, a No. 11 (eleven panels) in oak wood-grained finish to match the cabinet. *Courtesy of Lou Caruso.*

5-12
The redesigned "Triumph" motor, this time in a Model "G" (introduced October 1912, $75.00 with oak cygnet horn). The same motor had been used in the Amberola "I" and "III", as well as the "Opera". *Courtesy of Terry Paul Baer.*

181

5-13
This Edison "Idelia" Model "D2" (introduced September 1909, $125.00 with metal cygnet horn) was later fitted with a mahogany "Music Master" cygnet. Edison Phonographs didn't get much fancier than this. *Courtesy of the Aaron and Thea Cramer Collection.*

5-14
The Edison "Opera" (introduced November 1911, $90.00 mahogany) employed the same mechanically advanced works originated in the Amberola "IB" of the previous year. The cabinet was distinctive: carrying handles were mounted on either side since the cover did not latch in place. It was also available in oak (for $5.00 less) in a cabinet shared with the last "Triumphs". *Courtesy of Dan and Sandy Krygier.*

5-16
Edison introduced the Amberola (indicating internal-horn) Phonograph in December 1909, at $200.00 in oak or mahogany (shown). The earliest cabinets, like this one, were built by Herzog, but the Edison Company's dissatisfaction led to the contract being given to the Pooley Furniture Company from early 1910 onward. Four drawers in the cupboard below held cylinders. This example is serial No. 48. *Courtesy of Norm and Janyne Smith.*

5-15
The Edison "School" Phonograph (introduced December 1912, $75.00) was an all-metal, black-enamelled version of the "Opera" on a stand which held boxes of cylinders. Intended for educational sales, the machine arrived late in the life of Edison's external-horn machines and did not do well. *Courtesy of the William Kocher Collection.*

5-17
The interior of the earliest Amberola, showing the maroon-painted works, with gold-plated and oxidized bronze features. The mandrel tracked under a stationary reproducer, in a redefinition of Edison's original concept of the Phonograph. This Amberola was geared for both two- and four-minute cylinders. *Courtesy of Norm and Janyne Smith.*

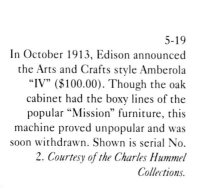

5-18
The Edison Amberola became known as the "I" when other internal-horn models were contemplated. Upon the introduction of a four-minute-only works (November, 1911), it was designated the Amberola "IB" and the two- and four-minute version came to be called the "IA". A number of cabinet variations began soon after the machine was introduced, due to hurried preparation and change of manufacturers. Here we see a Herzog-style cabinet with the later Pooley-designed "rococo" grille. *Courtesy of Lou Caruso.*

5-19
In October 1913, Edison announced the Arts and Crafts style Amberola "IV" ($100.00). Though the oak cabinet had the boxy lines of the popular "Mission" furniture, this machine proved unpopular and was soon withdrawn. Shown is serial No. 2. *Courtesy of the Charles Hummel Collections.*

5-20
The works of the Amberola "IV" combined a "Standard" Model "G" top with a "Home" Model "F" motor. Edison had begun to use up existing parts to complete the Amberola line, a policy which would compromise its integrity. *Courtesy of the Charles Hummel Collections.*

5-21
The Amberola "V" was announced at the end of 1912 ($80.00) and was the first table model of the internal-horn line. The sturdy cabinet housed a direct-geared mechanism of considerable substance which shared some design elements with the "Opera". *Courtesy of Norm and Janyne Smith.*

5-22 (Above left)
By October of 1913 when the Amberola "VIII" was released at $45.00, the Edison Company was using modified "Fireside" mechanisms in order to control costs and make the internal-horn line more affordable. This, unfortunately, was a major step backward from the earlier (more expensive) direct-geared models. *Courtesy of Dan and Sandy Krygier.*

5-23 (Left)
The Edison "Disc Phonograph", generally known as the "Diamond Disc", was introduced in fits and starts in 1912, after a considerable publicity build-up. The initial "A" models experienced various mechanical problems, which contributed to the acceleration of a "B" series (begun a year later) of which this "B-80" was a member. The prominent speed control lever, seen to the left of the winding crank, appears to be a customized feature. The "B-80", at $80.00, was a lower-range model, which indicates how top-heavy in terms of price the "Disc" line was. This particular machine is missing its round feet. *Courtesy of Norm and Janyne Smith.*

5-24 (Above)
The Edison "Disc Phonograph" Model "B-250" ($250.00, late 1914) inhabited the same cabinet as the "A-250" (1912), but used the new "standardized" works which had been developed by the Edison Company in an effort to control costs. This was a familiar design, first seen in the Amberola "1A" (and "B") after 1910. *Courtesy of George F. Paul.*

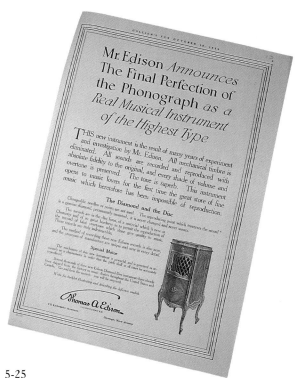

5-25
An early advertisement for the Edison "Disc Phonograph" claims much more than could be achieved in the first years of trial and error. Pictured is the expensive Louis XV model, which sold for $375.00 in mahogany or $425.00 in Circassian walnut. *Courtesy of George F. Paul.*

The Edison Company, during this period, was very much concerned with the activities of the U.S. Phonograph Company of Cleveland, Ohio. This firm, which got underway in May of 1910, after a couple of years of planning, combined the patents of Harry McNulty and Thomas Towell for a complex two-and-four-minute talking machine with the patent of Varian Harris for a cylinder record consisting of a thin celluloid skin over a composition core. The resources of the Babcock-Bishop-Becker Company (a soda-fountain manufacturer) were used to create an interesting line of instruments and well-recorded cylinders in both two and four-minute formats.

The more expensive U.S. Phonograph models ("Junior", "Banner", "Opera", and "Peerless", priced $30.00 to $200.00) used an enormous "double" reproducer, full of complicated die-castings, as well as two feed screws (one for each type of cylinder). Smaller internal-horn models like the "Rex" ($25.00) and later models, both internal and external-horn, featured a single reproducer with an "in-between" stylus such as Columbia had used. U.S. machines and records were supplied to the mail-order firm of Montgomery-Ward to be sold under the "Lakeside" brand.

The high quality of the U.S. "Everlasting" cylinders (two-minute 35 cents, four-minute 50 cents) seemed to irk Edison at a time when his inferior wax "Amberol" records were most embarrassing. According to an article in the November 15, 1910, issue of *Talking Machine World*, "U.S. Everlasting Record No. 223, Peter Piper March (xylophone) by Albert Benzler...was placed in a penny arcade last March, where it remained on a machine equipped with an ordinary reproducing sapphire until the middle of October. During that time it was played 40,444 times by automatic count, and earned for the proprietor of the arcade $404.44. The record cost 35 cents... It is in perfect condition, the company claims, to be played 50,000 times more..." Edison's former instrumentalist Albert Benzler had defected to become Everlasting's musical director, and the two company's catalogues shared many of the same artists. Edison sued repeatedly, actually employing the smarmy services of an industrial spy, Joseph McCoy. Exhausted by the fight, the Everlasting Company succumbed by the end of 1913, though Edison had failed to enjoin it. Thus ended some of the most clever talking machine technology ever put on the American market.

5-26
This "Lakeside" machine, sold by the Montgomery-Ward catalogue house of Chicago was really a U.S. Phonograph Company "Banner" model ($45.00, circa 1911). Clearly featured are the articulated sound arm and wide, oval reproducer housing. Two separate diaphragms were used to achieve reproduction in either the two- or four-minute format.

5-27
Another "Lakeside" machine, this time an inexpensive model also sold as a U.S. "Rex". The small but plucky two- and four-minute mechanism employed a conventional reproducer with a single spike-shaped stylus, which could play either 100 or 200 tpi celluloid cylinders. The cabinet, which is primarily empty, is only there to give stature to the works. A lid was not sold with this machine. *Courtesy of Norm and Janyne Smith.*

5-28
The U.S. Company sold the "Rex" mechanism in this internal-horn cabinet for $25.00. *Courtesy of Norm and Janyne Smith.*

5-29
Another "Lakeside" manufactured by the U.S. Phonograph Company of Cleveland, Ohio. Sold as a U.S. "Royal" ($50.00) it can be found with either a double-diaphragm reproducer or conventional one (shown).

COLUMBIA AND VICTOR AT A CROSSROADS

Columbia was practically out of the cylinder machine business by 1909, though it continued to sell celluloid cylinder records until 1912. In 1909, it dropped the price of the remaining stock of wax two-minute records from an already low 25 cents to an unheard-of 15 cents. Surely, this move aggravated Edison who had only wax cylinders to sell at much more expensive prices (two-minute 35 cents, four-minute 50 cents). The November 1909 Columbia record supplement states, "CLOSING OUT! Gold Moulded Records...while they last...This is the first chance in your life to buy phonograph records at a cut price—and it will probably be the last...It could never happen except that the Columbia Indestructible Cylinder Record has put the gold-moulded wax record completely out of business." (The ad copy failed to mention that Sears, Roebuck and Company of Chicago had already been selling the Columbia wax cylinder at only 18 cents!)

The reasonably priced "BKT" ($35.00) was retained in the catalogues, even as Disc Graphophones began to give way to internal-horn Grafonolas. Still available in the early 'teens, though squeezed by an ever growing number of Grafonolas, were external-horn machines like the "BNW" ("Improved Royal") and "BII" ("Improved Sterling"). The latter, introduced in 1909 at $50.00, was made over a long period with slight modifications. It proved so popular that it continued to be adapted, receiving modified Grafonola tone arm parts and finally a virtually unaltered Grafonola motor as it reached its last incarnation: the "60H" with oak horn ($60.00) of the mid-teens.

Meanwhile, the company continued to evolve the internal-horn machines, from the popular table models with their distinctive louvres such as the "Eclipse" ($20.00) and the "Jewel" ($35.00) to the elegant "DeLuxe" ($200.00) with its carved lion's heads.

Victor, too, maintained certain external-horn models in limited numbers well into the Victrola era. Versions of the "0", "II", "III" and "V" were available until 1920 and occasionally beyond. As the 'teens wore on, they were fitted out with the motors, tone arms, brakes, and various controls of Victrolas. The culmination of this progression was the last of the "V"s: mahogany cabinet, automatic stop, and quaduruple-spring motor right out of a Victrola "XVI".

At first, the expanding line of Victrolas borrowed heavily from Victor external-horn machines, though not at the sacrifice of quality such as the Edison Amberolas had experienced. From 1910 to 1913, nearly everything from motors to crank escutcheons was shared. The tone arm of the earliest Victrola "IV" was the same as a Victor "II". The motor in the table model versions of the "X" or "XI" was that of a Victor "III". The turntables matched. The ubiquitous "Exhibition" soundbox produced the same sound, carried up through the customary black, panelled external-horn or down inside the cabinet and out through the little front doors which served to control the volume of Victrolas.

Zonophones were allowed to fade by Victor. The name that had wreaked such havoc in the early years was gone after 1912. The last of them were sold through clients like Montgomery-Ward and Sears, cost-reduced and bearing hardly an identifiable Zonophone feature. Some even shared the cabinet and motor of the Victor "Junior".

In 1912, the latest legal assault on the Universal Talking Machine Company by American Graphophone was successful. The court directed that all Zonophone record matrices be destroyed. This finally convinced Victor to drop the line. With the reasonably-priced Zonophone record gone, it would be nearly ten years before another 50 cent 10" disc appeared. The name

Zonophone lived on in Britain and Europe, where the only internal-horn machines appeared, and the brand persisted on records ("Regal Zonophone") for many years.

This period ended with America in the grips of a dance craze. Interest in social dancing was abounding, and everywhere talking machine records both reflected and facilitated it. Ballroom dancers Vernon and Irene Castle became national figures, admired and imitated from Boston to Biloxi. In 1914, the duo danced for the movies, and the Victor company put out a booklet of dance instruction using still frames from the film to illustrate various steps. The pair were shown traipsing in front of a Victrola, with the top doors spread wide to suggest a Victor record had set their feet in motion. Included were descriptions of the famous "Castle Walk," the "Hesitation Waltz" and various types of tango. The latter, with its uneven, throbbing sensuality seemed an unusual fad for the unsophisticated American people, who had not yet experienced the cultural displacement of a World War. The sweeter, perhaps, to breach their inhibitions at "Tango Teas" and other such social functions or in their own living rooms, in front of the talking machine.

5-31
Delightful, if heavy-handed, allegory on the cover of this listing of Columbia disc and cylinder machines from 1909, offered by a famous American catalogue house.

5-30
A Columbia advertisement from 1909 showing the disc record in the ascendant. Late in 1908 both Victor and Columbia had introduced double-faced records. *Courtesy of George F. Paul.*

5-32
A sign featuring the "profile" logo which Columbia used on its Disc Graphophones during the post-1909 era. *Courtesy of the Charles Hummel Collections.*

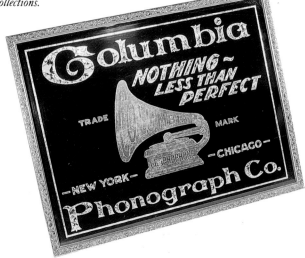

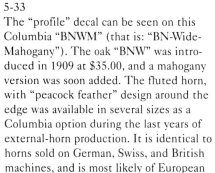

5-33
The "profile" decal can be seen on this Columbia "BNWM" (that is: "BN-Wide-Mahogany"). The oak "BNW" was introduced in 1909 at $35.00, and a mahogany version was soon added. The fluted horn, with "peacock feather" design around the edge was available in several sizes as a Columbia option during the last years of external-horn production. It is identical to horns sold on German, Swiss, and British machines, and is most likely of European origin. *Courtesy of Robert and Marilyn Laboda.*

5-35
The Columbia Grafonola "DeLuxe" of 1909 ($200.00) furthered the pricey image of the internal-horn talking machine. To be sure, it was an elegant example of cabinet design (here seen in quartered oak), but the day of the cheap table model Grafonola was coming. *Courtesy of Dan and Sandy Krygier.*

5-34
The Columbia "BII" was offered in 1909 for $50.00 (with nickeled, panelled horn). An additional $5.00 bought the "No. 2" oak horn shown. For $60.00 it could be purchased with the smooth Columbia "Symphony" oak horn. The use of wooden horns to dress up external-horn machines increased as sales decreased in favor of "Victrolas". *Courtesy of Norm and Janyne Smith.*

5-36
The Grafonola "Eclipse" (introduced 1912, $20.00) was the kind of machine that replaced the "old-fashioned," brightly-decorated external-horn talking machine in the front rooms of America. To the present-day observer, it may seem a puzzling change. *Courtesy of Lou Caruso.*

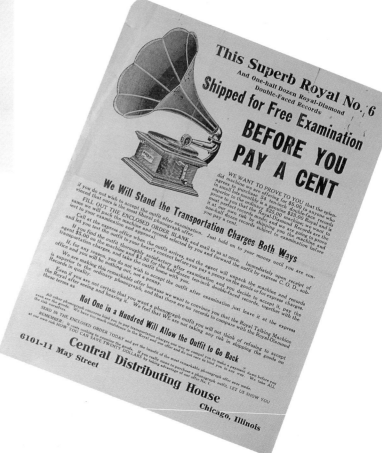

5-38
The "Royal" (circa 1910) was produced by Columbia incorporating the oak cabinets of the popular Talkophone "Brooke" model which had been acquired as part of a court settlement.

5-37
The "Marvel" was manufactured by Columbia and used as a premium circa 1912. With the patent wars of the 1907-1909 period over, Columbia settled comfortably into its role of being very nearly the only supplier of "client" brand disc talking machines in the U.S. *Courtesy of Lou Caruso.*

5-39
The Standard Disc Talking Machine Model "L" of 1910 combined a cabinet of Talkophone origin with Columbia mechanical parts. It had a single-spring motor and black back-bracket. The "Standard" Model "H" used a double-spring motor and larger, nickel-plated bracket. *Courtesy of Norm and Janyne Smith.*

5-40
A "Harmony" with characteristic blue, petalled horn and Byzantine-inspired pillars, offered by Chicago's Great Northern group in 1909. *Courtesy of Norm and Janyne Smith.*

5-42
1911 brought cost-cutting in the Great Northern camp. This Columbia-made "Standard" Model "B" used the same cabinet as the 1911 Model "A" external-horn machine, but with decorative perforations in the front panel to allow the sound to escape. When sold with back-bracket and horn as a Model "A", the cabinet looked rather too high, putting it in the "big-box-little-motor" category.

5-41
Arthur J. O'Neill's "Yankee Prince" of 1910 featured an allegorical decal emphasizing hard-working American (as opposed to decadent European) values. It was the last machine equipped with a lug on the turntable to conform to the "Busy Bee" discs.

5-43
Looking expectedly Columbia-like is this "Harmony" from 1911.

5-44

In 1911, Standard Disc and Harmony got another sibling in the United Talking Machine Company of Chicago, and they all moved into the same suite of offices. United offered the "Symphony" internal-horn machine and United 10" double-faced discs (all of Columbia origin) through in-store retail promotions. No external-horn "Symphony" was ever produced.

5-45

A rare glimpse into the sales schemes employed by the Chicago "odd-spindle" companies and the life of a commercial traveller is provided by this United salesman's kit. Included was a sample machine, along with pages of testimonials, an example of an advertising placard, and an order book.

5-46
The internal-horn "Aretino" of 1913 which Arthur J. O'Neill's catalogue predicted would be distributed in great numbers. The rareness of this machine today indicates that just the opposite was true.

5-47
The ignominious end of the rival Great Northern and O'Neill factions of Chicago was to be listed together as defunct on the Consolidated Talking Machine Company order form of 1916.

5-48
This odd-looking fellow is a Vitaphone (known at various times as Type "No.15", $15.00, or Type "F", $17.50), made by the Vitaphone Company of Plainfield, New Jersey. This company was in business around 1912-14, selling a truly unusual product. The best description of it can be quoted directly from a catalogue: "...the patented WOODEN ARM...carries all the sound waves from the delicate needle to the patented STATIONARY SOUND BOX which is not swaying with the wave of the record." This arm (of "violin wood") was held by a metal superstructure pivoted at the rear. The connection between the arm and the mica diaphragm was of cat-gut. Because it transferred any type of vibration to the diaphragm, there was no need to re-orient the arm to change between lateral and vertical cut formats. With the correct stylus, Edison "Diamond Discs" or Pathé records could be easily played.

5-49
The Vitaphone could also be purchased with this "Baby" oak horn manufactured by Sheip and Vandegrift ("Music Master"). The identical horn, equipped with a hanger, was available in music stores to be fitted to cylinder talking machines. The single-spring motor of the smaller Vitaphones was virtually indistinguishable from that of a Victor "II", suggesting it could have only been used under contract.

5-50
A Vitaphone Type "No. 50" ($50.00) in "Mission" style. A full line of machines was catalogued. The horns of the larger table models and floor models were contained in the lid of the cabinet, a conceit also used by the Keenophone Company around the same time. There was a Canadian branch of the Vitaphone Company which sold a similar line.

5-51
The Keen Company of Philadelphia dealt in talking machines during the century's first decade. Morris Keen was an inventor and entrepreneur who sought to establish his own brand. In 1911, the "Keenophone" machines were introduced in a variety of styles, including at least one external-horn model. Initially, they were equipped with a stationary soundbox under which the turntable tracked (like Hawthorne and Sheble had previously manufactured), but conventional mechanisms were soon substituted as the expiration of the "Berliner patent" made mechanical feeds unnecessary. In this model, no attempt was made to disguise the horn as a lid. *Courtesy of Robert and Marilyn Laboda.*

5-53
The Regina Company of Rahway, New Jersey, had been a well-known maker of disc music boxes for many years when they produced this coin-operated "Hexaphone" in 1914. Intended to play (six selective) Edison "Blue Amberol" cylinders, it was reliable and enjoyed considerable popularity. Regina had made coin-op cylinder machines since about 1907, beginning with two-minute models. The firm had co-operated with Columbia to produce a line of "Reginaphones" (music box/disc talking machine combinations). The "Hexaphone" was also something of a joint effort, with reproducers made by the Indestructible Record Company and Music Master wooden horns. *Courtesy of Norm and Janyne Smith.*

5-52
The simplest Keenophone floor model (1912-1914) much resembled a talking machine missing its sides! In fact, this style was also available with an enclosed bottom half containing a Pooley (automatic selecting) record cabinet. Contemporary Keenophone advertising suggests that well-respected Pooley was the source of its cabinets. *Courtesy of Norm and Janyne Smith.*

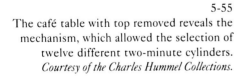

5-54
This coin-operated French café table offered customers a place to sip espresso and listen to recorded music, circa 1910. *Courtesy of the Charles Hummel Collections.*

5-55
The café table with top removed reveals the mechanism, which allowed the selection of twelve different two-minute cylinders. *Courtesy of the Charles Hummel Collections.*

5-56
The Victor "Junior" was the last of the "old style" Victors, and a very late addition in 1909. First introduced with a plain, black horn in the manner of the former Victor "Royal", it sold for only $10.00. *Courtesy of Norm and Janyne Smith.*

5-57
The "Junior" was later offered with a small, petalled horn painted a translucent red color.

5-58
The Victor "0" (meaning "zero") was introduced late 1908 at $17.50. To today's ear the term "zero" has a pejorative sound, but it was frequently used at the turn-of-the-century to begin a numerical series of commercial items. So, this machine was intended to precede the Victor "I" in order of importance. The mustard-colored, petalled horn with rose highlights was the only other Victor horn besides the "Junior's" to have any dash.

5-59
Bailey's Music Rooms of Rochester, New York, Spring of 1912.
Courtesy of Alan H. Mueller.

5-60
The interior of Bailey's store, showing the Victrola department. The lone example of an external-horn machine is a Victor "0": inexpensive and pretty.
Courtesy of Alan H. Mueller.

5-61
An advertisement from late 1910 shows the early table model versions of the Victrola "X" and "XI", and the first cabinet design of the "XIV".
Courtesy of George F. Paul.

5-62
This double-sided trade card from 1912 gives equal attention to the external-horn Victor and the Victrola. Here, a family is enthralled by a Victor "V".

5-63
The opposite side of the trade card pictures a Victrola "XIV". Usually, internal-horn machines were the primary focus of advertising at this time.

5-64
A Victrola "XVI" from 1913 in Circassian walnut ($250.00). The artistic effect of the carefully selected veneer is extraordinary. *Courtesy of George F. Paul.*

5-65
An oak Victrola "XIV". Introduced in 1910 at $150.00, this slightly modified version was available after August of 1912. *Courtesy of Lou Caruso.*

5-67
The "VV-VI", at $25.00, was the next sized model in the Victrola line. Introduced slightly after the "VV-IV" in 1911, the first version had a 10" turntable. A 12" turntable was soon supplied, and the machine could be ordered in oak (shown) or mahogany. *Courtesy of Lou Caruso.*

5-66
The "VV-IV", smallest member of the Victrola clan, was introduced in 1911 at $15.00. This is the first design, using a stamped metal louvered grille. A cost-reduced version of the "Exhibition" soundbox (with partially-enclosed face plate) commonly identified with the Victor "0" was also used on this machine. It was only available in oak.

5-68
An advertisement for Victrolas from late 1912 including the Queen Anne design of the "VV-X" which followed the table model (introduced September 1910) and preceded the full floor-standing cabinet (July 1913). *Courtesy of George F. Paul.*

5-69
The Queen Anne Victrola "X", which proved unpopular and was soon redesigned with enclosed sides. It sold for $75.00. *Courtesy of Norm and Janyne Smith.*

5-70
A Zonophone "Concert" from the later (1909) period. They were typically sold with these "morning glory" horns painted in blue, green, or red.

5-71
The Zonophone in its final incarnation: an unmarked "mahogany finish" machine with Music Master horn sold by Sears, Roebuck and Company from Fall 1910 for $39.35. Stocks must have remained after Victor's 1912 decision to discontinue Zonophones, since this machine lasted in the Sears catalogue until Fall of 1913. This model, known as the "Oxford" Type "BW", was the larger of two, the lesser being the "AW" with oak case and horn ($27.50). *Courtesy of Dan and Sandy Krygier.*

5-72
This "Klingsor" is a German-made machine from the 1912 period (sold heavily in England) with a fascinating harmonic premise. The strings of the harp which served as the mouth of the horn were meant to be specifically tuned. It was suggested that they would resonate with the notes of the music. Beyond this difficult-to-prove gimmick, the "Klingsor" was visually arresting. This model was fitted as a coin-op, with low coin drawer at the left rear. The "Klingsor" was manufactured for a long time, lasting all through the 'teens and into the twenties.

5-73
America's dance craze of the 'teens had
wide-spread repercussions, eventually
inspiring a toy circa 1920; "The Magnetic
Dancers", also known as the "Tango Two".
This charming talking machine novelty
operated as the record played. Its three
cams produced the amusing simulation of
different dance steps. Also shown in this
illustration is a "Repeatograph", a
peculiarly-designed record repeater.

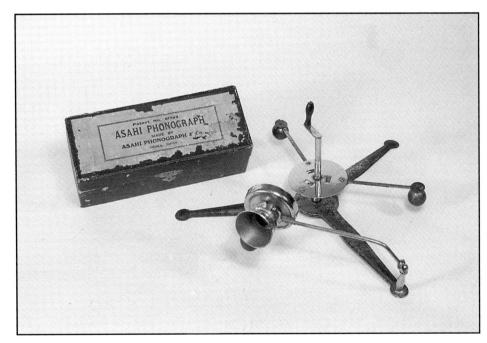

5-74
The Asahi Phonograph was sold in Japan, and
prefigured the Japanese penchant for technological
miniaturization. The simple movement is turned by
hand, and fits into the unimposing box shown. *Courtesy
of the Charles Hummel Collections.*

CHAPTER 6:

THE VICTROLA ERA, 1915-1920

THE VERTICAL CUT RECORD ASCENDS

During the 'teens, palpable tensions existed within the talking machine industry. The principal conflict was that of lateral versus vertical recording, or rather the attempts of the vertical format to make a dent in the market. By now, a familiar theme had begun to recur: what would begin with defiant assertions of innovation and independence would end in a roll of the legal dice.

Victor and Columbia had succeeded in bringing to heel practically all other manufacturers of lateral machines or records; just in time, too, since the valuable patents they shared were expiring. In February of 1912, that sledge-hammer of jurisprudence the Berliner patent No. 534,543 officially ran out, but not before Victor had used it to sweep the market clear of practically all competition. While Victor exploited the exclusivity of its products, Columbia would press discs or supply machines under anyone's label. This helped a feeble secondary market to stay alive, just barely. Examples are the "Royal" talking machine of Chicago, an inexpensive external-horn instrument in the big-box-little-motor style, and "Silvertone" records sold by Sears, Roebuck and Company.

In 1915, the market was deadlocked by seemingly insurmountable odds in favor of the major forces. However, the success of the vertical cut recording system in France, and Edison's promotion of it under his name (the "Diamond Disc Phonograph") suggested an avenue of commerce not sown with problems.

In 1914-1916, a number of independent vertical cut record labels appeared, a movement which was further encouraged by Columbia's decision to stop pressing client records around this same time. The Pathé Company, with its operations firmly in place in France, set up the Pathé Frères Phonograph Company in the U.S. It began issuing vertical cut discs in various metric sizes which were identical to the products it sold in Europe and Britain. These had etched title information, filled with white paint, and played from the center outward. Pathé discs of this type had enjoyed great popularity abroad for nearly ten years.

Relatively soon, however, the American Pathé Company replaced its European-style records with edge-start, paper-label discs, though still vertical cut. The labels had a colored field to denote the category (and price) of the selections, as Victor had done, but ever-present was the red Pathé rooster. This bird, contentious and tenacious, was often used by the French to represent themselves, and made a striking mascot for the company. During the 'teens, Pathé records were distributed by the Brunswick-Balke-Collender Company, a pool table manufacturer and producer of the "Brunswick" talking machine line. One important feature of the "Brunswick" was its ability to play all types of record (even "Diamond Discs"). Later, the firm would introduce a lateral cut label under its own name, a brand which would last for decades under various ownership.

Pathé also sold a complete line of internal-horn talking machines, from the simplest oak table model to the grandest mahogany upright with electric motor (typically priced $15.00 to $200.00). Though external-horn machines persisted in Europe for years to come, and even Victor offered them at this time, Pathé never catalogued anything but internal-horn models in the U.S. It is interesting to note that the last enterprise of that Chicago go-getter Arthur J. O'Neill was the State Street Pathéphone Company, in that city. Just before his untimely death in 1916, O'Neill, recently of the Aretino Company, had recognized the beginning of a trend.

At first, the Pathé soundbox, which reproduced with a sapphire ball, was fixed in the frontal (vertical) position. It was normally attached to the sound arm by a length of rubber, a carry-over from the external-horn machines. Pathé advertising made much of the jewel stylus, crowing, "NO NEEDLES TO CHANGE!", but even the earliest catalogues mention that lateral discs can be played (by detaching the vertical head and installing another as was common practice with Sonora). Discretion, however, being the better part of self-promotion, the company soon modified the arm to allow the soundbox to swivel easily into the lateral position. This accommodation would be found frequently in independently produced disc machines of the 'teens and early twenties, a simple bit of good sense which Edison had rejected. In truth, it no longer mattered where or how you put the arm and the soundbox. The patents which had brought a generation of independents to grief had run out. However, you still couldn't make lateral cut records, at least to hear Victor and Columbia tell it. That was to come next.

Victor Emerson, a highly experienced recording engineer who had worked for Columbia since the nineties, left to form his own firm in 1916. At first he sold cheap 6" single-faced discs (10 cents) with a label identifying them as vertical cut. What Emerson really intended to do, however, was to break into the lateral market through the side door.

Emerson had a process he claimed would allow a record to be played effectively on either system. To quote a contemporary record sleeve, "These records...can be played on any disc talking machine without an attachment (except the Edison). Either a needle or an Emerson sapphire (25 cents) may be used. A sapphire is preferred, as it does not have to be changed, it wears out less, and insures a longer life for the record." Emerson's 25 cent double-faced 7" disc with its combination cut made an immediate impact on the market. He also offered a rather peculiar-looking front-mount external-horn talking machine for $3.00 (or slightly more depending on finish). With its all-black flared horn it very much resembled something out of the nineties. However, its soundbox could swivel to play either vertical or lateral: the only external-horn machine besides the "Keenophone" to do this.

Needless to say, lawyers rained down upon the Emerson Company, and its cheek in flouting Victor and Columbia would precipitate the resolution of the vertical/lateral mess altogether. Late in 1918, Emerson won an important court decision against Columbia upholding the claim that the "Universal Cut" record was genuine and not an infringement. The following year, Victor's luck would run out.

The major appeal of the "Emerson" and a number of other small diameter vertical cut discs of this period was price. Certainly, the content was no particular attraction, as the material could be had by the same or better artists on lateral records. Columbia-pressed "Little Wonder" single-faced 5 1/2" discs (1914-1923) were lateral cut snippets of adult music (not kiddie records) sold for only 10 cents. A Columbia or Victor 10" disc from 1915 brought 65 or 75 cents, respectively. The vertical brands saw a market for lesser-priced records, though it was not until 1920 that the standard of the industry, the 10" disc, would be sold at a cut-rate, when Emerson introduced its "Regal" record at 50 cents.

The Emerson "Universal Cut" was by no means the only variation in the independent field. Certain small-diameter verticals like "Operaphone" (8", 35 cents) and "Par-o-ket" (7", 25 cents) were meant to be played with a steel needle (thereby eliminating one of the advantages of the system). On the other hand, "Rex", which had been around since before Pathé commenced its operations in the U.S., used the jewel-point design in the machines and records it sold. Added to the list of vertical brands, of which most required a sapphire, were "Okeh", "Aeolian-Vocalion", "Starr", "Paramount", and "Lyric".

The July 18, 1917, issue of the trade publication *The Phonograph* contained the following item:

> "$100,000 Company At Albany Absorbs Old 'Indestructible' Property...In the incorporation at Albany last week of the Federal Record Corporation...was the first apparently large enterprise to embark in the production of lateral-cut records that the talking machine trade has known for some years. The concern is understood to have taken over the patents, matrices, plant and equipment of the old Indestructible (cylinder) Record Co...The Federal company has originated an indestructible lateral-cut record that is first to be made in 10-inch diameter...a large number of artists have been contracted with and...record-pressing will be commenced very shortly."

Despite these sunny predictions, actual production of the lateral disc was stalled by the same legal barriers all the independents had experienced. In the meantime, manufacture of the "Indestructible" cylinder continued for several years, to a declining market in which Edison was the only competition. The Federal disc was offered in 1919 (made of ordinary "destructible" shellac), and the company pressed records for Sears, Roebuck and Company.

As the second decade of the century progressed, more and more firms began to assemble disc talking machines, frequently using commonly purchased parts such as Heineman motors. Many of these companies were furniture manufacturers (such as Pooley, which offered its own upright machine for a time) with existing facilities to make cabinets. The instruments sold under a plethora of "-phones" and "-olas". The November 15, 1916, issue of *Talking Machine World* lists a directory of fifty-eight manufacturers, compiled from its pages over the previous six months. There were many others not listed. The same periodical lists eighteen disc record makers, compiled the same way. Of these, most were independent vertical cut firms.

6-1
The Royal Talking Machine Company of Chicago sold this Columbia-made disc machine during the mid-teens. The cabinet was much larger than was needed to house the relatively small motor. *Courtesy of Robert and Marilyn Laboda.*

6-2
This unmarked Columbia "client" machine used a mahogany-finished version of the "Royal" cabinet, which had been designed large enough to accommodate an internal-horn. The United Talking Machine Company of Chicago sold this model (modified with a 1 1/2" turntable spindle) during its last days (circa 1914). *Courtesy of Lou Caruso.*

6-3
The "Brooks Automatic" talking machine was one of many independents which sprouted up in the 'teens. Its cabinet design owes much to Victor's Victrola. *Courtesy of Norm and Janyne Smith.*

6-4
A close-up of the "Brooks" shows the unusual repeating mechanism, and construction of the solid wood (rather than typically veneered) lid. *Courtesy of Norm and Janyne Smith.*

6-5
Haywood-Wakefield, a manufacturer of wicker furniture, sold internal-horn talking machines in both table and floor models. A feature unique to these machines was a soundbox completely sheathed-over in rubber to cut down on rattle. *Courtesy of Dan and Sandy Krygier.*

6-6
The "Kurtzmann", produced in Buffalo, New York, was constructed largely of plate glass—even the turntable! *Courtesy of Robert and Marilyn Laboda.*

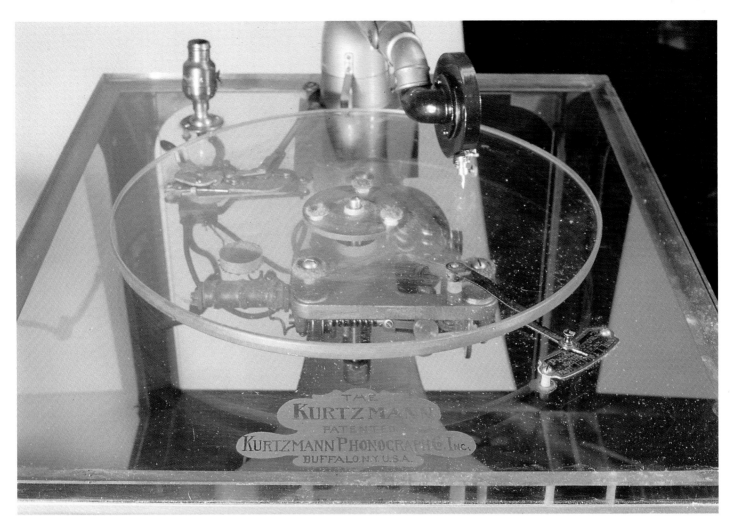

6-7
A close-up of the "Kurtzmann" shows
details of the mechanism, powered by
an electric motor. *Courtesy of Robert and
Marilyn Laboda.*

6-8
The "Modernola" did indeed look more
like something out of the fifties than the
'teens! The cabinet was perfectly round,
and usually surmounted by a lamp. This
style appears to be the only floor model
the company made (it produced an
unusual portable), but was available in a
variety of finishes, including painted
decoration in Oriental and other motifs.
"Modernolas" were frequently equipped
with electric motors. *Courtesy of Dan and
Sandy Krygier.*

213

The "Carola" was not a child's machine. It was an inexpensive ($15.00) talking machine for adults produced by the Carola Company of Cleveland, Ohio. A 1916 advertisement states that, "One winding plays one 12-inch record or two 10-inch records or three 8-inch records...Cabinet body is made entirely of acoustic metal with exquisite mahogany finish." It belongs to a class of "resonator" talking machines which utilized part of the cabinet (in this case, the lid) instead of a conventional internal-horn.

6-10
This "Qualityphone" in a custom carrying case was also sold under the name "Trumpet Tone". It had a remarkably stout imported motor (typical of independent brands of the 'teens), but a rather inadequate external-horn.

6-11
The "Stewart" sold in 1916 for only $6.50. It was available in a variety of colors and finishes including wood-grain. *Courtesy of Lou Caruso.*

214

6-12
Another small, all-metal table model was the "Madison", in which the cabinet was also the horn. *Courtesy of Lou Caruso.*

6-13
The cabinet of the "Orpheus", manufactured in Newark, New Jersey, was made from two finely finished blocks of mahogany joined together by screws. *Courtesy of Alan H. Mueller.*

6-14
The "Universal" was characteristic of many cast-iron talking machines of the teens. *Courtesy of Lou Caruso.*

6-15
The "Little Wonder" talking machine was a machine designed to play the many brands of small-diameter discs produced during the 'teens (nearly all of which were vertical cut). It had nothing whatsoever to do with the popular 5 1/2" "Little Wonder" disc record (which was a Columbia product). *Courtesy of Norm and Janyne Smith.*

6-17
The sleeve of a 6" record of 1916 illustrates the "Emerson" talking machine; a veritable anachronism in an age of Victrolas.

6-16
The "Emerson" talking machine, which sold for only $3.00 in 1916, existed solely to promote the sale of Emerson discs.

6-18
An American Pathé catalogue of 1916 pictures the famous brothers who had made the talking machine a significant industry in France. Shown to the right are views of the Pathé facilities, largely in Europe.

6-20
A Pathé "Reflex" which utilized the lid as a resonator. This example has been adapted to play lateral cut discs. *Courtesy of Dan and Sandy Krygier.*

6-19
A Pathé display rooster featuring the motto: "No Needles To Change."

6-21
A Pathephone Model "15" from 1916 was the least expensive member of the early line at $15.00. *Courtesy of Lou Caruso.*

THE VERTICAL CUT RECORD DIES, BUT FOR EDISON

Despite the success enjoyed by companies like Pathé and Emerson, the vertical field was too limited and full of variations to satisfy a real businessman. What needed to be done was to crack the lateral market and gain access to the customers Victor and Columbia were hoarding. Consequently, Okeh and a group of independents supporting Starr ("Gennett") allied in a court case versus Victor.

In 1919, Victor's legal resources finally failed. Most of its patent ammunition was blank by this time, and it was handed an adverse judgment. The door to the lateral market must have bumped pretty hard as it flew open. Not surprisingly, all the vertical manufacturers still in business went over to the lateral system, not counting those who had already deserted in anticipation of a victory. Even Pathé, whose entire business over about 14 years had been built on sapphire disc reproduction, introduced the lateral "Actuelle"

6-22
By the mid-teens, Edison was the only company still manufacturing cylinder talking machines. This glass advertising sign echoes Pathé's slogan. *Courtesy of the Charles Hummel Collections.*

("up-to-date") record in 1920. Only one firm, not a party to the assault on the lateral battlements, continued to hold fast to the vertical system: Edison.

The withering array of patched-together Amberola machines which the Edison Company had churned out in 1913 and 1914 was wisely reduced and standardized in 1915 with the introduction of three models whose designations would (at least temporarily) reflect their prices. This simplified line, with gradual degradations of quality, would last until the later twenties. A devastating fire at the Edison plant in December1914 had helped bring about an end to the old models, destroying existing stocks of parts and making the way clear toward the new styles.

The Edison Amberola "30" was a small, oak table model with a domed lid, as the "X" had been. The single-spring motor had the direct gear drive of the best members of the former line. The reproducer, called a "Diamond C", was an obvious refinement of the "Diamond B", which had given fine service over three years. The Amberola "50", a larger table model available in oak or mahogany, had a double-spring motor and slightly larger internal-horn. Finally, a floor model of paltry styling, the "75", came in oak or mahogany. It had a cupboard door behind which three trays could hold cylinders.

Although these models, with improved mechanics, were a much-needed relief from the tangle of styles which had preceded them, they were disappointing as Edison products. The cabinets were cheaply made, and would get cheaper. The horns were small, complimenting neither the well-recorded "Blue Amberols" nor the excellent diamond reproducer. Today's collector is most likely to find them cute. However, even the record quality of which the Edison Company had been so proud would be compromised for expediency. After November1914 "Blue Amberols" began to be dubbed from "Diamond Discs", so that one disc master of any particular selection could serve both formats. This was done with varying degrees of success, and today one may hear the hissing of the disc player as it kicks in prior to the start of a great many "Blue Amberols".

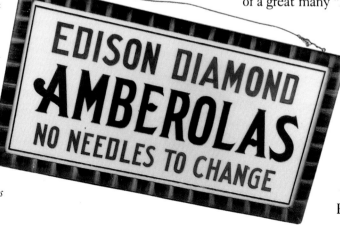

Edison Company treatment of the cylinder line suggested a secondary position, something which could not have been lost on dealers, despite continued floggings with the formidable Edison reputation.

The cylinder would be promoted for rural areas; the "Discs" were high-class entertainment. Even the introduction of the "Royal Purple Amberols" in 1918, with their eye-catching violet color and serious vocal content, did not do much to rescue the cylinder from its "country bumpkin" status. The "Royal Purples", intended to compete with the prestige records of other brands, ran to nearly 80 releases but were dropped in the summer of 1921. They had been no bargain at one selection for $1.50. Even if certain Victor "Red Seal" discs chose to be single-sided, it wasn't because they *couldn't* have two selections. The Edison Company seemed resigned to the down-grading of the cylinder catalogue.

Edison was intently focused on the "Disc" machine. In 1915, new models were introduced which were to incorporate simplified and improved design, hard earned during the first years of trial and error. Among this group were two of the strongest sellers the company would produce. First came the "C-250" (introduced at $250.00, increasing slowly thereafter) which would prove enormously popular despite (or perhaps because of) the odd combination of Chinese and Gothic elements in a cabinet known as "Chippendale". This model is frequently called the "Laboratory Model" because of the medallion it carried, but that term was applied to a number of the larger "Disc" machines. Next, the "C-150", or "Sheraton", (introduced at $150.00; $175.00 by September 1918) would sell briskly in both its original design and the one into which it evolved some four years later ("S-19", $195.00).

The Edison machines and records would sell well all through the World War I period. "OUR TROOPS MUST HAVE PHONOGRAPHS" demanded an editorial in the July 25, 1917, issue of *The Phonograph*, after America had become involved in the European war. A military model of the Edison "Disc" machine (painted olive drab for the Army or blue for the Navy and built like a battleship) was offered at virtually no profit to the company. These were carried abroad by the armed forces, and no doubt introduced many service people to the "Diamond Disc". Perhaps this was not done to the best advantage, since a war shortage of phenol, essential to a smooth surface, hurt the discs' already inconsistent quality. When the war ended, the records improved, but other forces hampered the success they enjoyed.

Edison himself insisted on personal supervision of the talent. His stodgy tastes kept the catalogue mired in out-of-date material and repetitive, unimaginative arrangements. Who else could have released a solo banjo version of the "Poet and Peasant Overture" (No. 51523)! This was a situation which could only worsen as Mr. Edison grew more curmudgeonly and popular music progressed.

The merits of the catalogue aside, the Edison Company spotlighted the "fidelity" of the "Discs" in a long series of "Tone Tests". Edison artists gave appearances during which their performances alternated between live and recorded. This was done artfully, of course, with lights and scenery to disguise or hide the changes. Yet, the many credulous testimonials which claimed the artist could not be distinguished from the record may seem far-fetched to us. We must remember that the audience was listening with less sophisticated ears, the records were specially prepared to make them free of surface-noise and the reproducing equipment was brand new. In truth, most of the audience had probably come with a firm belief in Mr. Edison as something like a god, and the theatrical setting alienated them from normal reality, as it does with a play. This is not to impugn the Edison system—it was good. In fact, only the advent of electrical recording would put as much information into the grooves of a disc record as did Edison. It's a shame that the catalogue and the failure to produce a low-priced machine would keep them out of so many hands.

6-23
In 1915, the Edison Company standardized the formerly confusing line of Amberola cylinder machines. This Amberola "75" ($75.00) was the largest of the three models introduced at that time. All three featured improved direct-gear mechanisms. *Courtesy of Dan and Sandy Krygier.*

The smallest of the new Edison cylinder Phonographs was the Amberola "30" ($30.00), a table model, shown here enclosed in a special cabinet sold only through the Babson Brothers mail-order firm of Chicago. F.K. Babson was a tireless promoter of the Edison Phonograph, and his advertising reached a wide audience through magazines and newspapers. *Courtesy of Robert and Marilyn Laboda.*

6-24
The mid-sized Amberola of the 1915 series: the "50" ($50.00). At first, the reproducers were nickeled (shown), in traditional Edison fashion. Black anodizing was substituted as the Company almost immediately began to cheapen these models.

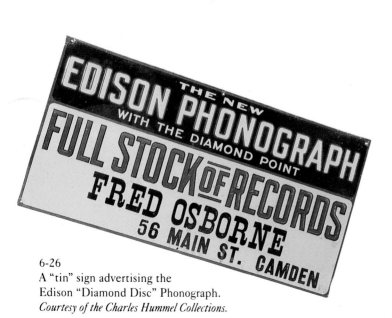

6-26
A "tin" sign advertising the Edison "Diamond Disc" Phonograph.
Courtesy of the Charles Hummel Collections.

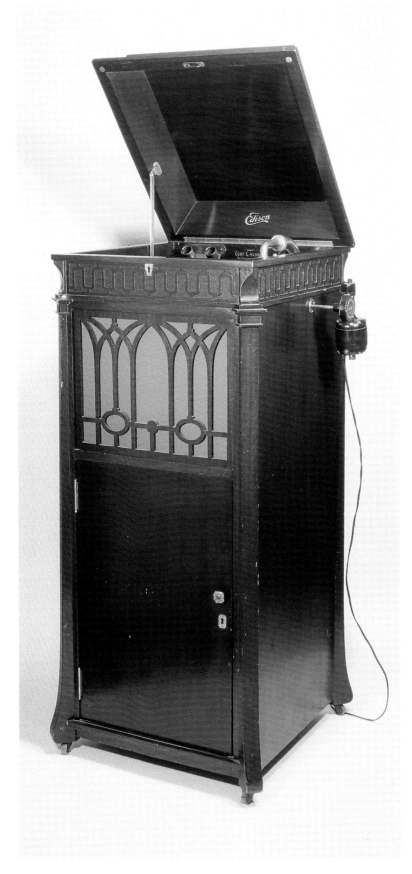

6-27
One of the most popular Edison "Disc Phonograph" models proved to be the "C-250" (introduced in December 1915 at $250.00). People loved the unusual combination of design elements which uneasily co-existed in a cabinet designated as "Chippendale", and the high price was no deterrent. *Courtesy of George F. Paul.*

6-28
An Edison "Diamond Disc" Model "W-250" ("William and Mary"). This machine was introduced in September 1917 at $250.00, but the price rose rapidly thereafter due to the wartime economy. *Courtesy of Dan and Sandy Krygier.*

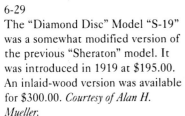

6-29
The "Diamond Disc" Model "S-19"
was a somewhat modified version of
the previous "Sheraton" model. It
was introduced in 1919 at $195.00.
An inlaid-wood version was available
for $300.00. *Courtesy of Alan H.
Mueller.*

6-30
A close-up of an "S-19", showing the
seldom-seen "Horn Gauge" as it
would have been used by an Edison
dealer to set the height of the
reproducer. *Courtesy of Alan H. Mueller.*

THE VICTROLA, A SUCCESS IN FEAR OF CHANGE

The Victor Company continued to refine the numerical series of Victrolas it had evolved in the early 'teens. Remaining pre-Victrola parts disappeared from these models, replaced by improved mechanics. Although external-horn machines were still sold, the focus was on the Victrolas, with the $300.00 "XVIII" at the head. This prestige model, with artfully matched veneers, lasted only a year and a half, disappearing after Christmas 1916. It was supplanted by a somewhat simplified version at $250.00 designated the "XVII". This would remain the most expensive Victrola without special art case or decoration through the war years. In 1921, the price of this machine reached $350.00 when Victor worked it into its slightly modified line under the title "130".

The 1921 catalogue of Victrolas, given Arabic rather than roman numeric designations, made no effort to depart from familiar (or maudlin?) Victor styling. This was more a convenience for the company than the customer, who was beginning to yearn for something new. In a short time public apathy toward the Victrola would become evident, though Victor's initial attempts to overcome customer ennui would fail, as we shall see. We remain in awe of the Victor name and the famous fox terrier who represented it. It seems the company rode a formidable wave of success practically from its inception. To be sure, it prevailed both in the courts and the front rooms of America. Yet, Victor was not invulnerable, a fact which it sometimes forgot. Witness the reversal in the lateral record litigation of 1919.

Furthermore, on April 4, 1921, a court of appeals decision declared John B. Browning, a former Victor employee, to be the real inventor of the Victrola. Eldridge Johnson was judged to have stolen the idea from him. Browning claimed that his 1897 sketches were shown to Johnson and others at the company, and subsequently appeared as Johnson's patent No. 774,435 for a "Cabinet for Talking Machines". Victor pursued appeals unsuccessfully for years, though the only damage done was to Johnson's image. Still, Victor's millions could not protect it from adverse court or bad business decisions.

During the late 'teens, the federal government had been investigating Victor and Edison for anti-trust violations. The August 8, 1917, issue of *The Phonograph* carried this item:

> "The Victor Talking Machine Company, on July 31, filed its answer to the complaint of the Federal Trade Commission calling upon the company to show cause why an order should not be issued forbidding it to continue the practice of selling its machines under the license system pronounced illegal by the Supreme Court...In its reply the company states it has voluntarily ceased to do the acts set forth in the complaint...and is no longer disposing of its machines with the proviso they should be used only as set forth by the company."

Victor, in its enormous conceit, had tried to control its Victrolas even after the sale. Edison had been almost as overbearing. In 1918, presented with overwhelming evidence of the paternalism and bullying that they had heaped upon their dealers and the public (nearly turning the talking machine business into a feudal state), both firms signed consent decrees and paid assessments. While self-righteously denying the charges, they admitted their guilt: a neat trick. To quote the Government from Victor's decree, May 3, 1918, "For many years the defendant had systematically made contracts and engaged in a conspiracy in restraint of that trade." Enough said.

6-32
The Victrola "XI", here shown in oak, was the best-selling instrument in Victor's history. It sold for $100.00 until the war economy forced the price slowly upward, eventually reaching $130.00.
Courtesy of Alan H. Mueller.

6-31
This jigsaw puzzle was used by dealers to promote Victor's famous stable of classical artists. *Courtesy of the William Kocher Collection.*

6-33
The top-of-the-line Victrola "XVIII" was offered during 1915-1916 for $300.00. It was soon to be replaced by the Victrola "XVII", in a somewhat simplified cabinet. *Courtesy of Dr. Jay Tartell.*

6-34
A Victrola "XVI" with Oriental finish, featuring inlaid mother-of-pearl. Such decorated talking machines were popular during this period and even lesser models could be enhanced in this way. *Courtesy of Norm and Janyne Smith.*

6-35
The interior color of these Oriental Victrolas could be ordered in a number of pastel shades, including blue, green, and red. *Courtesy of Norm and Janyne Smith.*

6-36
The Victor/Victrola "XXV" enjoyed a long production life as an instrument designed for school and institutional use. During the World War I period, the price rose from $67.50 in 1915 to $115.00 by 1920. *Courtesy of Norm and Janyne Smith.*

Columbia developed its own special look for the internal-horn Grafonolas it sold through the 'teens. The volume-controlling louvers, Queen Anne legs, and flat-topped lids made them as instantly recognizable as Victrolas. Yet, this was really no more than a personalized form of copy-cat styling. It was with its "furniture" pieces that Columbia really distinguished itself.

A series of Grafonolas disguised as or suggesting other objects was offered all through the second decade of the century. The very first Columbia internal-horn machine had been the "Symphony Grand" (1907, $200.00), in the image of an upright piano complete with fallboard. The "Grand" ($500.00, later $350.00), introduced in 1912, was a figurative grand piano, with gold-plating and electric motor. Following were the "Regent" ($200.00), a desk, "Regent, Jr" ($150.00), a library table, "Colonial" ($150.00), a round table, "Baby Regent" ($100.00), a Queen Anne table, and "Princess" ($75.00), an end table.

World War I had a profound effect on the talking machine, both in practical and popular realms. In Europe and Britain, where the war lasted over twice as long as it did for the U.S., the physical disruptions of population and commerce were catastrophic. Germany had been a major supplier of talking machines, records, and supplies the world over. The least effect of this was felt in the U.S., where fully-assembled German machines were not sold. However, German-owned businesses in the U.S. were strongly disrupted. During America's participation in the war, these firms were confiscated by the government and re-organized. This is what happened to the Otto Heineman Phonograph Supply Company, which made vertical "Okeh" discs. Heineman was the U.S. agent of the German record empire of Carl Lindstrom. Re-organized as the General Phonograph Corporation, the firm continued to sell "Okehs" after the war, switching to lateral when everybody else did.

On the popular front, the mood of the American people may be sampled by the songs to which they listened on record. At the beginning of the European conflict songs like "I Didn't Raise My Boy To Be A Soldier" left no doubt of a strong isolationist sentiment. As events began to persuade that intervention was necessary, songs like "Lusitania (When the Lusitania Went Down)" argued the case. With war declared, no more stirring anthem of anticipation and assurance could be found than George M. Cohan's "Over There." "Good-bye Broadway, Hello France" was the quintessential Tin Pan Alley contribution. As the war progressed for Americans, songs spoke of lonely soldiers and forlorn families. "Rose Of No Man's Land" is a tribute to the valiant Red Cross nurse, as was "Don't Forget the Salvation Army" dedicated to the "doughnut girls" who gave coffee and comfort to the weary soldiers. By the time that song came out, the war was over and the survivors of the American Expeditionary Force were returning home. Inevitably, songs reflected the upheaval in their lives, most giving it a humorous twist, like "How Ya Gonna Keep Em Down On the Farm (After They've Seen Paree?)." The war had been a watershed in the lives of people everywhere, and tragedy had marched right along with triumph. The twenties would bring great changes. The talking machine, too, needed to change.

6-37
One of the last of Columbia's external-horn disc talking machines was the "60H", introduced in 1915 (with the model number denoting its price). Columbia placed an unaltered Grafonola motor into a cabinet based on the former "BII", and added an inverted Grafonola tone-arm and wooden horn to create this machine. It is shown here with a panelled rather than smooth wooden horn.

6-38
Columbia distinguished itself in the category of "talking machines as furniture." Beginning in 1911 (this advertisement dates from 1912) and continuing through the 'teens, Columbia sold a varied line of instruments disguised as tables or desks. *Courtesy of George F. Paul.*

6-39
This unusual Grafonola was disguised as an Empire gaming table. *Courtesy of Norm and Janyne Smith.*

6-40
A view of the gaming table in the open position reveals a conventional Grafonola mechanism. *Courtesy of Norm and Janyne Smith.*

227

6-41
A colorful Columbia catalogue cover from 1919.

6-42
A rarely-seen talking machine toy from 1916 depicting Uncle Sam chasing Pancho Villa. This was manufactured by the National Toy Company of Boston, Massachusetts, which sold a variety of dancing, fighting, and topical novelty figures. *Courtesy of the Aaron and Thea Cramer Collection.*

6-43
An assortment of turntable toys, left to right: National's "The Boxers", National's "Dancing Rastus", National's "Uncle Sam Kicks the Kaiser", and a dancing scarecrow of unknown manufacture. *Courtesy of Norm and Janyne Smith.*

6-44
During World War I, Columbia sold a disc recording of President Woodrow Wilson's daughter, Margaret, whose royalty was donated to the American Red Cross. It's a pity that altruism and talent are not always balanced. An original 22" x 28" dealer's poster. *Courtesy of George F. Paul.*

CHAPTER SEVEN:

STAGNATION AND INNOVATION, 1921-1929

After a postwar boom that witnessed record-breaking sales of talking machines and records in 1920, including the birth of numerous small manufacturers, the industry lost ground during the business recession of 1921. Victor had managed to show growth during 1921: sales of $51,000,000, which was a scant $1,000,000 over 1920. Columbia, on the other hand, showed 1921 sales of $19,000,000, down from $47,000,000 the year before. In order to preserve capital, Columbia's bondholders accepted a voluntary adjustment in interest payments. Wall Street responded predictably and Columbia stock fell from 65 to 1 5/8. Desperate attempts were made to bail out the Company by selling the British branch in December 1922 and the Dictaphone branch in March 1923. By October 1923 nothing more could be done. One of the industry's oldest companies went into receivership with liabilities of $21,000,000 and assets of $19,000,000.

A relative newcomer to the talking machine industry, the Brunswick-Balke-Collender Company, had enjoyed steadily increasing sales of its machines since 1916. In 1921, Brunswick surpassed Edison Phonograph production, thus becoming one of the "big three" in the long-standing U.S. talking machine industry triumvirate. That Brunswick, with a mere five years of machine sales behind it, could have successfully outstripped Edison suggests the volatility of the market at that time. Only Victor, looking down on struggling Columbia and the brash newcomer Brunswick, seemed unassailable in its position.

PRESSURES FROM MARKET TRENDS

Yet Victor had troubles of its own. The inauguration of regular radio broadcasts and alarming growth in the number of radio receivers around the country threatened sales, and the products of the Victor Talking Machine Company were virtually indistinguishable from those of a decade earlier. Victor Victrolas were becoming passé, yet creative ideas were not welcome at Camden. Even when pressured by retailers to conform to the current public liking for console or "low-boy" talking machines, Victor smugly declined. Only in 1922 did Victor appear to relent, introducing a series of new console models. Retailers' rejoicing was short-lived when they found that the new instruments had the familiar domed Victrola lid insolently mounted at the center of the cabinet. Eldridge Johnson had come a long way from the eager, earnest mechanic working on a spring motor to make the Gramophone a success. He deigned now to dictate to the public what it could have, and like Thomas Edison before him, would suffer the consequences. The new Victrolas were derisively called "humpbacks", and were not popular. By 1924, Victor's sales had shrunk to only $37,000,000, down from $51,000,000 three years earlier.

The fledgling Radio Corporation of America (RCA) had, by contrast, shown a *profit* (not sales) of $54,848,131 in 1924, up from its profit of $26,394,790 in 1923. Brunswick began selling RCA Radiolas in its phonographs. Sonora introduced its "Sonoradio" combination.

Yet, the word "radio" was discouraged from use at Victor and Thomas A. Edison, Incorporated. The two foremost proponents of the talking machine in the 20th Century maintained the attitude of an ostrich insofar as radio was concerned. In 1923, when Victor finally abandoned the anachronistic Victrola lid, it began to include in its flat-topped cabinets an empty compartment where the customer could place a radio. Thus did Victor begrudgingly acknowledge radio's existence.

EDISON LEFT BEHIND

If Victor was warming the bench in the evolving talking machine game, Thomas A. Edison, Incorporated wasn't even playing. Its "Disc Phonographs", like Victrolas, had not changed significantly in a decade, except that the cabinets had become generally smaller, plainer, and cheaper. Twenty years after paper record labels had come into use, the Edison Company finally adopted them for its "Diamond Discs". The musical repertoire lagged similarly twenty years behind the competition. One could find multiple renditions of "I'll Take You Home Again, Kathleen" in the Edison catalogue, but only a few rather stilted jazz records. The cylinder line was equally bereft of life, and was increasingly relegated to rural areas where its homespun offerings could still find a following. Business for the Edison line became so bad in 1924, that the company sent a special disc record to dealers in order to bolster their sagging morale. Titled "Holiday Greetings From The bunch At Orange," the disc contained brief messages from top management, assuring Edison dealers that better times were coming. Art Walsh, advertising manager, promised, "A lot of good old 'Tone Tests'" apparently missing the point that few cared to listen anymore. With accidental candor, Walsh added, "I pick the hits, so I'm going to beat it before you hit me." Venerable Walter Miller, manager of the Recording Division, and a loyal Edison man since the nineties, promised that, "The records will be better still, next year." Jeff Buchanan, manager of the Record Manufacturing Division jokingly asserted that, "I make 'white-

7-1
In 1923, the Victrola "215" was available in mahogany or walnut (shown) for $150.00. A double-spring motor, 12" turntable, and the Victrola No. 2 soundbox were standard equipment. Though the "console" design seemed to enjoy a brief resurgence in the mid-twenties after a bout of popularity in the 'teens, Victor's "lowboy" experiment was short-lived. *Courtesy of Lou Caruso.*

7-2
Edison dealers, strapped for business in 1924, were barely achieving the title of this "Diamond Disc" record. A paper advertisement approx. 10" long.

label' records. I never had anything to do with 'black-label' records." The spectre of the noisy "etched-label" Edison discs still haunted West Orange. Charles Edison, chairman of the Board and son of the great inventor, confidently stated that, "The midnight oil still burns in the Edison Laboratory." The comparatively few remaining Edison dealers might well have asked: "To what end?" Finally, Thomas Edison himself, seventy-seven years old and functionally deaf, assured the listeners that, "I'll see that they do what they say." Edison didn't know that revolutionary changes were indeed in the offing, although they came from outside the talking machine industry.

DEVELOPMENT AND REPERCUSSIONS OF ELECTRICAL RECORDING

In 1919, the Bell Telephone Laboratories and Western Electric had begun exhaustive research into sound reproduction and electromagnetic recording. Under the supervision of Joseph P. Maxwell, the Western Electric engineers developed an electromagnetic recording head and an improved acoustic talking machine designed by Henry C. Harrison. Harrison used the electrical theory of matched impedance to create a horn of precise relative length, rate of taper, and size of opening. This "exponential" horn was then folded within a cabinet of commercially-viable size. In early 1924, the Bell Laboratories shed their cloak of secrecy and demonstrated the new electrical recording/acoustic reproducing system to Victor. Officials at Camden vacillated. For the rest of 1924, Victor left Maxfield and Harrison hanging, unable to decide if the mighty Victrola really needed help from these upstarts.

Meanwhile, the Pathé pressing plant in Brooklyn had been processing the Bell Laboratories' electrically-recorded masters into test pressings. Frank Capps, who had designed the famous "Triton" spring motor in 1895, was visiting Russell Hunting, manager of the Pathé plant and himself a veteran recorder of the nineties. When Capps heard the electrically-recorded pressings in December 1924, he had some extra copies sent abroad to Louis Sterling, who now headed English Columbia. Sterling, not afflicted with Victor's lethargy, immediately sailed for New York and met with officials of the re-organized Columbia Phonograph Company and Western Electric. Sterling purchased the financially-strapped American Columbia Company for $2,500,0

upon Western Electric licensed it (for $50,000 plus royalties) to use the new electrical recording/acoustic reproducing method. Sterling's English Columbia was licensed as an affiliate of American Columbia.

Victor had finally come to the inescapable conclusion that it must do business with Western Electric. Another demonstration was scheduled for February 1925, and a contract was signed in March, a few weeks after Columbia signed. Had Victor been the brash, decisive company it had been in January 1902, it might again have deprived its old rival, Columbia, of the means to use a revolutionary recording system. As it happened, Victor itself was fortunate to avoid that fate.

Victor released its first electrically-recorded disc quietly during May 1925, in order that stocks of acoustically-recorded records would continue to sell. November 2, 1925, was denoted "Victor Day," the day on which the new "Orthophonic" Victrola (using the exponential horn) would be formally unveiled. Columbia released its first electrical record in June 1925, and introduced its own exponential horn machine called the "Viva-Tonal". Victor had even begun selling Victrolas equipped with RCA Radiolas in late 1925. Brunswick introduced the first all-electric radio/record player called the "Panatrope" in October, along with Brunswick electrically-recorded records. Brunswick's method of electrical recording had been originally developed by the General Electric Company for use in recording motion picture soundtracks directly on film. This feature was stressed by Brunswick's Vice President, P. L. Deutsch, in advance publicity for the "Panatrope":

> The disc record will be used at present because we want to adapt the product to the use of the millions of phonographs now in existence, but the reproduction can be done by films, on which the sound waves are photographed. By this method the record can be made to play for any length of time.
>
> In order to reproduce the film records, the instrument must be equipped with the apparatus for sending a beam of light through the film to a photographic cell so as to turn the sound waves into electricity, after which the electrical waves are amplified by the vacuum tubes. This apparatus, however, is not costly or cumbersome, and there is no reason why the device using the film records may not become an ordinary household musical instrument. In all developments of this kind, however, it is necessary to protect the owners of existing apparatus as fully as possible.

As 1926 dawned, it seemed that the talking machine industry was shaking off its doldrums.

7-3
The Victrola "Credenza" (later known as the "8-30") was the flagship machine of the new "Orthophonic" line. For $275.00 the customer received an imposing mahogany or walnut cabinet with a six-foot long horn "folded" inside. *Courtesy of Norm and Janyne Smith.*

7-4
The "Viva-Tonal" was Columbia's answer to the "Orthophonic". This Model No. "601" was powered by a double-spring motor, used a "Viva-Tonal" No. 15 soundbox and sold for $90.00. *Courtesy of Lou Caruso.*

7-5
The playing compartment of the "Viva-Tonal"
Model No. "601". Most "Viva-Tonal" soundboxes
were made of brass, unlike the "Orthophonics",
which often used "pot-metal". *Courtesy of Lou
Caruso.*

Even in West Orange, things were happening. Although electrical recording was not to be offered commercially by Edison until September 1927, experimental 450 threads-per-inch long play discs were made in August 1925. The "Edison Long Playing Records" were offered to the public in November 1926. Theodore Edison, the inventor's youngest son, worked on the "LP" project throughout 1927, introducing such refinements as electrical recording. The "Edison Long Playing Records" were available in 10" and 12" sizes, the only 12" records commercially released by Edison. Console "Edison Disc Phonographs" with "LP" attachments were offered, as well as conversion attachments to allow existing Edison owners to play "LPs" on their machines. Unfortunately, it soon became apparent that performance of the "Long Playing Records" was a problem. The 2 1/2 ounce weight and stylus linkage used on the "LP" reproducer was too heavy for the fragile 450 tpi grooves. From the first, skipping and repeating were persistent problems. Sales were discouraging, and Edison's groundbreaking work on "Long Playing Discs" yielded little reward for the company.

By the twenties the entertainment cylinder was an anachronism. The Industructible Record Company of Albany, New York, lost its factory to fire in 1922. Edison alone carried on the cylinder format, although clearly as a poor relation to the "Diamond Discs". Still available from the Edison Company were the same rather tired Amberolas introduced in 1915: the "30", "50", and "75". In 1926, a table model Amberola "60" using surplus "Disc Phonograph" cabinets from the unpopular "London" series was briefly offered. An upright Amberola in the "Sheraton sans inlay" ("S-19") disc cabinet was offered in late 1928, designated the Amberola "80". Despite the overall quality of the Edison "Blue Amberol" record (dubbed from electrically-recorded "Diamond Discs" starting November 1927), the marketing of cylinders throughout the twenties represented a considerable financial drain on the company. In mid-1926, initial press runs for most "Blue Amberol" titles were eight hundred copies, miniscule even by the standards of the day. Demand fell off so drastically that by the end, in the summer of 1929, initial press runs were only one hundred copies of each title. It was obvious to everyone in the talking machine industry that the entertainment cylinder had come and gone. Obvious to everyone except perhaps the great inventor who stood at the helm of the Edison organization as it plowed relentlessly toward disaster.

7-6
The "Edison Long Playing Records" were conceptually ahead of their time, but fell short technically. The 12" record shown played for twenty minutes on each side. An "Edisonic" (with larger floating weight to increase volume) and conventional "Diamond Disc" reproducer are shown to the left. *Courtesy of George F. Paul.*

7-7
The Amberola "60" was the final
table model cylinder Phonograph
offered by Edison. It was released in
1926 at $60.00 and would be
followed by the floor model Amberola
"80" ($80.00) in 1928. Surplus
"Diamond Disc" cabinets were
pressed into service for both
instruments. The final Amberolas
used the Diamond "D" reproducer
which, like the "Edisonic", increased
volume with a heavier floating
weight. *Courtesy of Norm and Janyne
Smith.*

The advent of electrical recording had given new
life to the entire disc industry, including many independent labels which seemed to spring up almost daily.
As a result of Victor's new "Orthophonic" Victrolas and
electrically-recorded "Orthophonic" records, as well as
the RCA radios installed in many Victrolas, sales of Victor products jumped to $48,000,000 in 1926.

So sweeping were the new industry-wide innova-
tions that previous "old-fashioned" talking machines,

some less than a year old, lost their value virtually over-
night. The public clamored to trade in their current instruments for the new models which performed with
such unprecedented realism. Swamped with trade-in re-
quests, dealers struggled to standardize values for older
models. In December 1925, the Philadelphia Victor
Dealers' Association circulated a Victrola Exchange Price
Guide which attached values to nearly eighty different
Victor Victrola models in mahogany, oak or walnut cabinets. Just how popular the "Orthophonic" Victrolas had
become could be represented in the resultant devalua-
tion of the earlier Victrolas. The popular Victrola "IV"
which originally sold for $15.00-$25.00 was now ap-
praised for $4.25. The 1906 "VTLA" which had ushered
in the genre originally sold for $200.00, but was now
worth no more than $16.75. Although it is understand-
able that a nineteen-year-old Victrola would be worth
but a fraction of its original cost, even the Victrola "215"
manufactured in 1925 and having sold for $150.00 was
valued at only $25.40 by the end of the year. Such de-
valuation was testimony to the hegemony of the
"Orthophonic" Victrolas.

Once again offering a superb product line in the face
of a booming economy, Victor itself became an attractive investment possibility. The banking houses of J.&
W. Seligman and Company and Speyer and Company
offered to buy Victor outright. Eldridge Johnson, suffer-
ing from years of clinical depression and at least one
nervous breakdown, decided that the time was right to
let go. On December 7, 1926, the Victor Talking Machine Company was sold for a total of $40,000,000.
Johnson's share of the sale was $28,000,000. He spent
his nineteen remaining years in haphazard pursuit of one
interest after another, lamenting all along that he ever
sold Victor.

Victor as a separate entity had but two years to live.
On January 4, 1929, the Radio Corporation of America
bought the Victor Talking Machine Company from its
financier owners. Nipper and his Gramophone thus completed a journey from Berliner's June 1900 record catalogue to the world's largest manufacturer of radios. The
little fox terrier would continue to represent the RCA
Victor Division of the Radio Corporation of America.

AN IGNOMINIOUS END TO THE
EDISON PHONOGRAPH

On October 4, 1928, West Orange finally offered a
radio under the Edison name to the public. That the
company founded by America's pioneer electrician
should have delayed so long is one of the ironies of the
recording industry. Edison's first electrically-recorded
records had made their debut a year earlier, to the
public's general apathy. The company's record sales con-

tinued to suffer under Thomas Edison's stubborn allegiance to the vertically recorded format. Then, in August, 1929, Edison introduced a lateral electrically-recorded disc. These "needle type" discs were excellently recorded and featured up-to-date music, obviously not subject to Edison's personal approval. As crowed by Weekly List No. N-1 for August 16, 1929: "Edison invades the needle record field! Edison Recording quality is now available to the whole world! What a whale of an opportunity for every record dealer who thinks—and acts!"

7-8
The Edison electrically-recorded "Needle" type record. A superb product developed too late to save the world's oldest name in talking machines. *Courtesy of George F. Paul.*

Unfortunately, what had previously denied "Edison Recording quality" to the world was one man's ascetic refusal to subordinate his own feelings to the demands of business and public preference. Had Edison been defending real issues of morality or principle, his steadfastness would have been admirable. As it was, Edison's bull-headedness could not stop the evolution of the world around him. If the Edison "Needle Records" had been available four years earlier along with the rest of the industry, the company might have been saved. The "Needle Records" were on sale for only two months be-

fore the stock market crashed. On October 29, 1929, the Radio-Phonograph Division of Thomas A. Edison, Incorporated announced to the trade:

> After a careful weighing of the record business and its prospects, we have decided to discontinue the production of records, except for special purposes, and to devote our great record plant to the production of radio, and kindred new developments in the radio and home entertainment field.
>
> This step is being taken regretfully because the phonograph for home entertainment was one of Mr. Edison's favorite inventions. But, this is a case where sound business judgment must prevail over sentiment.

Thus did the oldest name in talking machines pass into oblivion through the belated application of "sound business judgment." Nevertheless, as written by Roland Gelatt in the 1965 edition of his book, *The Fabulous Phonograph*:

> "It is the young inventor of Menlo Park hurrying into New York to demonstrate his new tin-foil phonograph whom we should remember, not the octogenarian businessman of West Orange puttering in his outmoded laboratory and deserting his invention after years of bumbling mismanagement."

Regardless of Edison's disappointing lack of business acumen in his later years, it had been a thirty-year-old Edison who introduced the world to the reality of a machine that talks. Through his invention, a whole parade of performers and producers in what would become the talking machine industry found their bearings and made their mark. Edison's activities throughout his first sixty years of life were the catalyst by which a mighty industry was born, with artists, publishers, and songwriters living under its umbrella.

Indeed, the earlier years, when the talking machine was in its youth, hold the greater charm for many of us. It was a time when a machine exhibiting one peculiar human trait, that of speech, could evoke disbelief among spectators; when the workshop labors of a determined few resulted in new, revolutionary products. It was a time when brave men risked everything to own a piece of the dream; when pioneers themselves became captains of industry, besieged by plucky new entrepreneurs. It was an era of crude machinery evolving into brilliant efficiency; of vibrant colors and florid decals; of polished wood and gleaming brass; of distant voices and breathtaking realism. It was a brief period of innocence and avarice, wealth and poverty, oak and mahogany, wax and shellac, steel, sapphire, and diamonds.

7-9
The "Orthophonic" Victrola "4-7". At
$125.00 it was near the bottom of an
expensive line which the public
nevertheless embraced wholeheart-
edly. *Courtesy of Dan and Sandy Krygier.*

7-10
The Victrola "50", introduced in
1921, was the company's first
portable or "suitcase" Victrola. Just
the thing for Sunday picnics in the
Ford. Offered in mahogany or oak for
$50.00, it was emphatically a Victor
product: solidly built and reliable.
Courtesy of Lou Caruso.

7-11
At $50.00 in 1926 the Victrola "1-70"
featured a double-spring motor and a
Victrola No. 4 soundbox in a rectan-
gular mahogany cabinet with
Moorish-looking grille. *Courtesy of Lou
Caruso.*

7-12
The Victrola "1-1" was the least-expensive Victrola available in 1925. At $17.50, it was an obvious successor to the venerable "VV-IV", with a single-spring motor, a 10" turntable and mahogany cabinet. *Courtesy of Lou Caruso.*

7-13
The "Orthophonic" Victrola "8-4" (introduced 1926) was powered by a four-spring motor and featured gold-plated hardware. Priced at $235.00, the machine was available in a mahogany or walnut cabinet enclosing a "folded" horn nearly the size of the "Credenza". *Courtesy of Lou Caruso.*

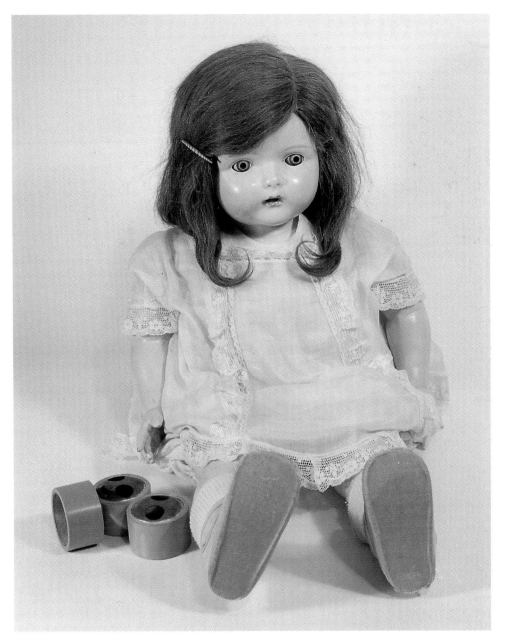

7-14
This "Madame Hendron" composition doll of 1922 featured a spring-driven mechanism concealed in its body which played removable celluloid cylinders. Six nursery rhymes were available. The mechanism was produced by the Averill Manufacturing Company of New York, and was also found in the similar (if slightly cheaper) Mae Starr doll. *Courtesy of Dan and Sandy Krygier.*

7-15
Toy talking machines became quite popular during the 1920s. On the left, a German "Gamaphola"; center, a decorated wood-cased machine with an Orthophonic-inspired arm; right, a colorful German Bing "Kiddyphone". *Courtesy of Dan and Sandy Krygier.*

7-16
From left to right: "Dixyphone"; "Nirona"; Bing "Pigmyphone".
Courtesy of Norm and Janyne Smith.

7-17
"Nirona" was a German-manufactured line of inexpensive disc machines. The graphics of this original box suggest they were intended as much for adults as for children. *Courtesy of Dan and Sandy Krygier.*

7-18
From left to right: "Genola",
"Bingophone", and an unmarked
machine with cardboard horn.
Courtesy of Norm and Janyne Smith.

7-19
The "Schubert" Edisonic was
introduced in 1927 for $135.00. This
model and its slightly larger sibling,
the "Beethoven", were the first
Edison Phonographs to use doors to
conceal the horn opening. They were
also the last acoustic "Diamond Disc"
Phonographs offered by the company.
Courtesy of Dan and Sandy Krygier.

241

7-20
The Sonora "Symphony" featured cabinetry of the "Orthophonic" style which became *de rigeur* in the late twenties. The Sonora Company had up until then taken a highly singular approach to cabinet design, most notably in its bombé models. *Courtesy of Dan and Sandy Krygier.*

7-21
In the capacious playing compartment of the Sonora "Symphony", the turntable and tone-arm are nearly lost. The Art Deco soundbox is typical of the die-cast models of the period. *Courtesy of Dan and Sandy Krygier.*

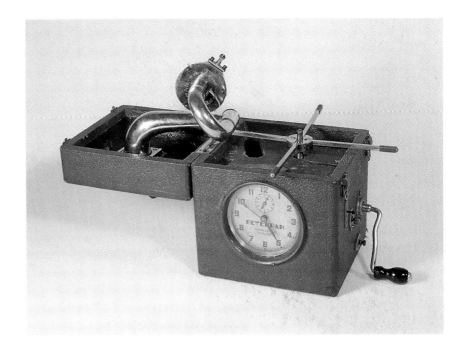

7-22
"Peter Pan" was a line of portable talking machines of European manufacture. This one, circa 1929, included an alarm clock which triggered the record rather than a bell. The most common "Peter Pan Gramophones" were the "cameraphones": that is, miniature talking machines designed to resemble box cameras when closed. *Courtesy of Allen Koenigsberg.*

7-23
The Brunswick "105" was a good example of a talking machine from the early 1920s, with a Victrola-like lid and cabinet. Classic Brunswick features included the white-painted wooden internal horn, and the sophisticated "Ultona" soundbox which was capable of playing any type of disc record manufactured; even the "Diamond Disc". Brunswick was a major producer and innovator during the 1920s. *Courtesy of Lou Caruso.*

243

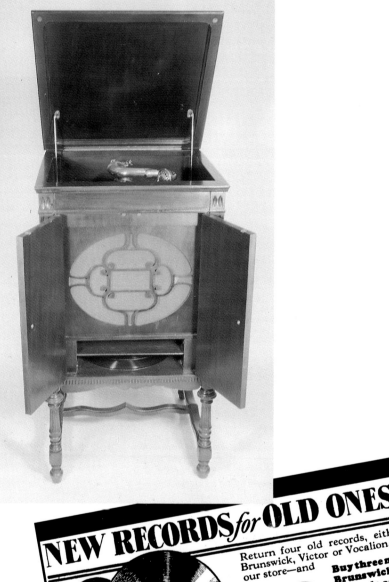

7-24
By the mid-twenties, Brunswick had
succumbed to the "Orthophonic" look.
Like the two Edisonic models, this
Brunswick "Seville" utilized doors to
conceal the horn. Expiration of the
Victor patent controlling this feature
allowed other companies to incorporate
such doors into their designs. *Courtesy
of Dan and Sandy Krygier.*

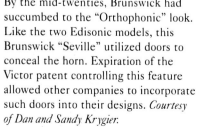

7-25 (Right)
The Pathé "Actuelle" ("up-to-date")
was one of the cleverest talking
machine designs of this period. The
machine projected sound via a large
paper cone diaphragm rather than a
horn. The exposed diaphragm was
fragile, but gave remarkably loud and
clear results. *Courtesy of Lou Caruso.*

All that the Victrola gives to others it will give to *you*

HIS MASTER'S VOICE
REG. U.S. PAT. OFF.

246

7-26
An artist's depiction of the many rewards of owning the Victrola. Let us rephrase the sentiments of this Victor jigsaw puzzle from the twenties: "May the talking machine give to you all that it has given us." *Courtesy of the William Kocher Collection.*

GLOSSARY

Amberol: The first four-minute cylinder developed by Edison, 1908-1912. These cylinders are black in color, made of especially hard metallic soap, and were usually sold in green and white containers.

Amberola: The name denoting Edison's line of internal-horn cylinder Phonographs, 1909-1929.

Back Mount: A term used to describe a talking machine which uses a back bracket which supports the horn and thus removes its inertia from the soundbox.

Bedplate: The plate (usually metal) to which the upper mechanism of a cylinder talking machine is mounted.

Blank: A smooth, grooveless unrecorded cylinder.

Blue Amberol: The blue celluloid four-minute cylinder sold by Edison, 1912-1929. The containers for these cylinders were blue until 1917, orange and blue thereafter.

Carriage: The assembly which "carries" the reproducer of a cylinder talking machine across the recording.

Carrier Arm: Edison nomenclature for the carriage. The half-nut and spring are attached directly to the carrier arm on nearly all Edison machines.

Combination Attachment: Devices offered by Edison to convert pre-1908 Phonographs to play four-minute cylinders in addition to the two-minute variety.

Concert: Edison's trade name for the five-inch diameter cylinder and the Edison Phonograph designed to play it.

Crane: The support used to mount horns of 15-inch length or greater to cylinder talking machines.

Cylinder: A geometric form on which entertainment recordings were made, 1877-1929. The earliest sheets of tinfoil were followed by self-supporting cylinders of ozocerite-covered cardboard, stearic acid/paraffin, hard metallic soap, and celluloid. Advantages of the cylinder format included a constant surface speed and the ability to make home recordings.

Diamond Disc: Edison's line of disc records and machines, 1912-1929. The Diamond Discs were vertically recorded, and the Diamond Disc Phonographs were one of the very few disc talking machines to use a feedscrew.

Diaphragm: The flexible, circular vibrating membrane of a soundbox or reproducer which converts mechanical energy to acoustic energy or sound waves. Mica, glass, compressed paper, copper, and aluminum were commonly used as diaphragms in early talking machines.

Elbow: The connection between the horn and the soundbox or tone arm of a disc talking machine. Earliest elbows are made of leather, gradually giving way to metal elbows after 1900.

Endgate: A swinging arm which supports one end of the mandrel on some cylinder talking machines. To mount or remove a cylinder it is therefore necessary to open and close the endgate.

Feedscrew: A threaded rod which usually drives a half-nut fixed to the carriage of a cylinder talking machine, thus guiding the reproducer across the record grooves. Certain disc machines used feedscrews to drive the soundbox across the record or to move the turntable beneath a fixed soundbox. Similarly, some cylinder machines used feedscrews to drive a mandrel longitudinally beneath a fixed reproducer.

Front Mount: A term used to describe a disc machine where the horn attaches directly to the soundbox, and the support arm (or mount) runs directly below and parallel to the horn. In such an arrangement the support arm points in the same general direction as the bell of the horn.

Gramophone: Originally the name by which Emile Berliner's disc talking machine was known, it became a generic term to denote any disc playing talking machine, but fell out of use in the United States.

Grand: Columbia's trade name for the five-inch diameter cylinder and the various Columbia machines designed to play it.

Governor: The mechanical assembly in a talking machine motor which regulates the speed, usually by limiting the outward movement of spinning weights.

Gutta-Percha: A substance made from the juice of certain Malaysian trees, which can be colored and moulded into rigid objects such as the reproducers of early Graphophones.

Half-Nut: An internally threaded metal piece usually in the form of a nut which has been cut in half. The threads of the half-nut correspond to the threads of the feedscrew. As the feedscrew revolves, the half-nut will be propelled along it, thus driving the carriage of a talking machine.

Mandrel: The tapered drum upon which the cylinder record is placed for playing.

Needle: The point (usually steel) of the soundbox which rides the grooves of the recording and transmits vibrations to the diaphragm.

Reproducer: The component comprising stylus, linkage, and diaphragm, which reproduces the sound from the record grooves. This term is most frequently applied to cylinder machines. (See *soundbox*)

Stylus: The point (usually sapphire or diamond) of the reproducer which rides the grooves of the recording and transmits vibrations to the diaphragm.

Tone Arm: A movable hollow tube which conducts sound to the horn from the soundbox.

Trunnion: Rightly, the sleeve visible on either side of the carriage which slides over the feedscrew shaft on a Graphophone, but commonly used to denote the entire carriage.

BIBLIOGRAPHY

Barnum, Frederick O. III. *His Master's Voice in America*. Camden, General Electric Company, 1991.

Barr, Steven C. *The Almost Complete 78 RPM Record Dating Guide (II)*. Huntington Beach, Yesterday Once Again, 1992.

Baumbach, Robert W. *Columbia Phonograph Companion, Vol. II (Disc Graphophones and the Grafonola)*. Woodland Hills, Stationery X-Press, 1996.

Baumbach, Robert W. *Look for the Dog*. Woodland Hills, Stationery X-Press, 1996.

Bayly, E., ed. *The EMI Collection*. Bournemouth (GB), Talking Machine Review, 1977.

_____. *The Talking Machine Review International*. Bournemouth (GB), various issues beginning 1970.

Bryan, Martin, ed. *The New Amberola Graphic*. St. Johnsbury (VT), various issues 1973-1997.

Chew, V.K. *Talking Machines*. London, Her Majesty's Stationery Office, 1967 (and subsequent editions).

City of London Phonograph and Gramophone Society, various eds. *The Hillandale News*. Various issues 1960s to present.

Conot, Robert. *A Streak of Luck*. New York, Seaview Books, 1979.

Dethlefson, Ronald, ed. *Edison Blue Amberol Recordings, 1912-1914*. Brooklyn, APM Press, 1980.

Dethlefson, Ronald, ed. *Edison Blue Amberol Recordings, 1915-1929*, Brooklyn, APM Press, 1981.

Fagan, Ted, compiled by. *The Encyclopedic Discography of Victor Recordings, Pre-Matrix Series*. Westport, Greenwood Press, 1983.

Fagan, Ted, compiled by. *The Encyclopedic Discography of Victor Recordings*. Westport, Greenwood Press, 1986.

Frow, George L. *Edison Cylinder Phonograph Companion*. Woodland Hills, Stationery X-Press, 1994.

_____. *The Edison Disc Phonographs and the Diamond Discs*, Sevenoaks, Kent (GB), George L. Frow, 1982.

Gaisberg, Frederick W. *The Music Goes Round*. North Stratford (NH), Ayer Company Publishers, Inc., 1977 (1942 reprint).

Gelatt, Roland. *The Fabulous Phonograph, revised*. New York, Appleton-Century, 1965 (three eds. 1955-1977).

Gracyk, Tim, ed. *Victrola and 78 Journal*. Roseville (CA), various issues 1994-1997.

Hatcher, Danny, ed. *Proceedings of the 1890 Convention of Local Phonograph Companies*. Nashville, Country Music Foundation Press, reprint, 1974.

Hazelcorn, Howard. *A Collector's Guide to the Columbia Spring-Wound Cylinder Graphophone, 1894-1910*. Brooklyn, APM Press, 1976.

Hunting, Russell, ed. *The Phonoscope*. New York, Phonoscope Publishing Company, various issues 1896-1900.

Johnson, E. R. Fenimore. *His Master's Voice Was Eldridge R. Johnson*. Milford (DE), State Media, Inc., 1975.

Koenigsberg, Allen, ed. *The Antique Phonograph Monthly*. Brooklyn, APM Press, various issues 1972-1993.

_____. *Edison Cylinder Records, 1889-1912, 2nd ed.* Brooklyn, APM Press, 1988.

_____. *The Patent History of the Phonograph, 1877-1912*. Brooklyn, APM Press, 1991.

Maken, Neil. *Hand-Cranked Phonographs*. Huntington Beach, Promar Publishing, 1995.

Marco, Guy A. and Andrews, Frank, eds. *Encyclopedia of Recorded Sound in the United States*. New York, Garland Publishing, Inc., 1993.

Marty, Daniel. *Histoire Illustrée du Phonographe (Illustrated History of the Phonograph)*. Lausanne/Paris, Edita/Lazarus, 1979 (reprinted in various English language editions with slight modifications of the title).

Moore, Jerrold Northrop. *A Matter of Records*. New York, Taplinger Publishing Company, 1977.

Moore, Wendell, ed. *The Edison Phonograph Monthly*. Various anthologies 1903-1916, New Albany (IN), Wendell Moore Publications.

Proudfoot, Christopher. *Collecting Phonographs and Gramophones.* New York, Mayflower Books, 1980.

Read, Oliver and Welch, Walter L. *From Tinfoil to Stereo.* Indianapolis, Howard W. Sams and Company, Inc., 1959.

Reiss, Eric L. *The Compleat Talking Machine.* Chandler (AZ), Sonoran Publishing, 1996.

Rust, Brian, compiled by. *Discography of Historical Records on Cylinders and 78s.* Westport, Greenwood Press, 1979.

Sherman, Michael W. (with Moran, William R. and Nauck, Kurt R. III). *Collector's Guide to Victor Records.* Dallas, Monarch Record Enterprises, 1992.

Sutton, Allan. *Directory of American Disc Record Brands and Manufacturers, 1891-1943.* Westport, Greenwood Press, 1994.

Welch, Walter L. and Burt, Leah Brodbeck Stenzel. *From Tinfoil to Stereo, 1877-1929.* Gainesville, University Press of Florida, 1994.

Wile, Raymond R. and Dethlefson, Ronald. *Edison Diamond Disc Recreations, Records and Artists 1910-1929.* Brooklyn, APM Press, 1985.

Selected Primary References

The American Graphophone Company, *Annual Report. 1888, 1889, 1890, 1899, 1900, 1901, 1902, 1903, 1904, 1905, 1906, 1907, 1908, 1909, 1910, 1911, 1912, 1913, 1914, 1915.*

Wm. J. Rahley vs. The Columbia Phonograph Company, in equity No. 457.

The United States Phonograph Company vs. The Chicago Talking Machine Company, in equity No. 24,293.

The American Graphophone Company vs. Edward H. Amet, in equity No. 23,986.

The Volta Graphophone Company and The American Graphophone Company vs. The Columbia Phonograph Company, in equity No. 14,533.

The American Graphophone Company vs. Cleveland Walcutt et al, affidavit of Cleveland Walcutt, December 10, 1894.

The Columbia Phonograph Company vs. The North American Phonograph Company and George E. Tewksbury and Leonard Garfield Spencer, in equity No. 14580.

The American Graphophone Company, *Minutes*, various extracts 1887-1891, taken from *The American Graphophone Company vs. The Edison Phonograph Works*, 1895.

Contract between The Victor Talking Machine Company of Camden, N.J. and The Burt Conpany of Milburn, N.J., January 18, 1902.

Suit on Jones Patent No. 688,739. *The American Graphophone Company vs. The Universal Talking Machine Manufacturing Company*, 1909.

Suit on Berliner Gramophone Patent No. 534,543. *The Victor Talking Machine Company and The United States Gramophone Company vs. The American Graphophone Company*, in equity No. 8627.

Suit on Berliner Gramophone Patent No. 534,543. *The Victor Talking Machine Company et. al. and The United States Gramophone Company vs. The Talkophone Company*, 1906.

Suit on Berliner Gramophone Patent No. 534,543. *The Victor Talking Machine Company et. al. vs. The Leeds and Catlin Company*, in equity No. 8797, 1906.

The Victor Talking Machine Company et. al. vs. William H. Hoschke, Individually &c., December 27, 1907.

The Victor Talking Machine Company and The United States Gramophone Company vs. The Duplex Phonograph Company, March 27, 1909.

Suit on Berliner Gramophone Patent No. 534,543. *The Victor Talking Machine Company and The United States Gramophone Company vs. The Duplex Phonograph Company*, in equity No. 1611, March 11, 1907.

Suit on Berliner Gramophone Patent No. 534,543. *The Victor Talking Machine Company and the United States Gramophone Company vs. The Aretino Company*, June 11, 1909.

U.S. Supreme Court, *The Leeds and Catlin Company vs The Victor Talking Machine Company and The United States Gramophone Company*, 1909.

VALUE GUIDE

ABOUT PRICES

Value Guides are like politicians: quote one and you'll start an argument. Why are guides to prices so controversial? Because prices vary and fluctuate from machine to machine, and from situation to situation. As well, an old real estate axiom can be adapted as an admonition to either buyers or sellers: "Condition. Condition. Condition."

Yet, there are many factors which affect a sale. Man "A" sells his talking machine for $300; man "B" gets $450 for the same model in the same general shape. The second man got more money, but the first has probably not been cheated. It is impossible to recreate the specific circumstances of any particular sale. You might say man "B" was a little more fortunate, and luck is a big part of the antique business.

WHAT NOT TO DO

It's tempting to flip through this book to a photo that seems familiar, turn to the Value Guide and declare, "That's it! That's the one up in Uncle Charlie's attic. Wow, $3,500!" We hope you will adopt a more cautious approach. Many similar-looking machines are actually very different. Proceed carefully when using this Guide and in a choice between two models which look similar, never assume the higher price.

BUYING

When buying a talking machine ask questions, shop around. However, don't make it an endless quest. If you find a reputable dealer or auction service act with confidence. Talking machine specialists usually sell instruments with reconditioned reproducers and motors, two "invisible" factors which can drastically affect performance. Remember, a "bargain" may just mean making someone else's problem your own.

SELLING

The prices shown are for spotless or restored talking machines. When selling be realistic. Unless you pay the rent on a fancy shop in an expensive part of town you might not get absolute top dollar. If a collector or dealer makes a sincere offer, consider it seriously. And do remember condition and completeness are the essence of any transaction.

WHAT IF I FIND A MACHINE PRICED HIGHER (OR LOWER) THAN LISTED HERE?

This is going to happen. Prices fluctuate. It doesn't automatically mean the price is wrong. Nothing "books" for a set price. We discourage the use of this expression.

IN CLOSING

This Guide is intended as a basic aid to buyers and sellers. It is not, nor could it be, gospel. The antique business is "alive"; what is written here reflects the relationship between values as much as the specific dollar amounts. Many machines which uncommonly change hands or likely do so only between knowledgeable collectors will be listed as "very rare" (VR). Some very expensive items, however, will be priced for purposes of comparison within the hobby. It would be inaccurate to suggest that the rarer machines are not available at any price. Consistent with the theme of this book, only talking machines will be priced.

FIG. #	PRICE IN $
1-1	-
1-2	VR
1-3	VR
1-4	VR
1-5	8,000.
1-6	-
1-7	VR
1-8	VR
1-9	12,000.
1-10	VR
1-11	10,000.
1-12	VR
1-13	10,000.
1-14	VR
1-15	7,500.
1-16	VR
1-17	-
1-18	VR
1-19	-
1-20	-
1-21	VR
1-22	-
1-23	-
1-24	VR
1-25	-
1-26	10,000.
1-27	VR
1-28	VR
1-29	-
1-30	VR
1-31	VR
1-32	-
1-33	VR
1-34	VR
1-35	-
1-36	VR
1-37	VR
1-38	-
1-39	15,000.
1-40	-
1-41	-
1-42	11,000.
1-43	VR
2-1	-
2-2	-
2-3	VR
2-4	6,500.
2-5	-
2-6	VR
2-7	12,000.
2-8	1000.
2-9	3000.
2-10	VR
2-11	VR
2-12	-
2-13	-
2-14	4,500.
2-15	-
2-16	750.
2-17	850.
2-18	450.
2-19	6000.
2-20	14,000.
2-21	VR
2-22	12,000.
2-23	VR
2-24	12,000.
2-25	12,000.
2-26	-
2-27	10,000.
2-28	10,000.
2-29	10,000.
2-30	VR
2-31	6,500.
2-32	8,000.
2-33	7,500.
2-34	-
2-35	-
2-36	7,500.
2-37	VR
2-38	-
2-39	VR
2-40	VR
2-41	6,000.
2-42	VR
2-43	VR
2-44	4,500.
2-45	4,000.
2-46	-
2-47	1,500.
2-48.	-
2-49	650.
2-50	5000.
2-51	-
2-52	8,500.
2-53	-
2-54	-
2-55	-
2-56	10,000.
2-57	10,000.
2-58	VR
2-59	-
2-60	3,500.
2-61	-
2-62	VR
2-63	VR
2-64	VR
2-65	6,500.
2-66	VR
2-67	VR
2-68	3,000.
2-69	1,200.
2-70	650.
2-71	-
2-72	1,500.
2-73	600.
2-74	VR
2-75	-
2-76	-
2-77	1,200. w/o horn
2-78	6,500.
2-79	-
2-80	VR
2-81	-
2-82	VR
2-83	-
2-84	4,500.
2-85	550.
2-86	6,500.
2-87	-
2-88	-
2-89	750.
2-90	VR
2-91	VR
2-92	VR
2-93	4,000.
2-94	7,000.
2-95	-
2-96	7,500.
2-97	1,000.
2-98	-
2-99	VR
2-100	-
2-101	-
2-102	-
3-1	VR
3-2	-
3-3	-
3-4	-
3-5	-
3-6	-
3-7	-
3-8	-
3-9	-
3-10	-
3-11	-
3-12	-
3-13	-
3-14	3,500.
3-15	VR
3-16	10,000.
3-17	VR
3-18	VR
3-19	-
3-20	VR
3-21	-
3-22	2,500.
3-23	3,500.
3-24	12,000.
3-25	-
3-26	2,500.
3-27	5,500.
3-28	VR
3-29	-
3-30	8,500.
3-31	10,000.
3-32	1,000.
3-33	5,000.
3-34	VR
3-35	VR
3-36	-
3-37	2,200.
3-38	4,500.
3-39	-
3-40	VR
3-41	-
3-42	7,500.
3-43	-
3-44	-
3-45	4,500.
3-46	-
3-47	6,000.
3-48	2,500.
3-49	1,600.
3-50	2,200.
3-51	3,000.
3-52	-
3-53	5,500.
3-54	-
3-55	VR
3-56	7,500.
3-57	5,500.
3-58	5,500.
3-59	3,500.
3-60	1,800.
3-61	VR
3-62	-
3-63	-
3-64	-
3-65	-
3-66	7,500.
3-67	1,000.
3-68	1,600.
3-69	800.
3-70	2,500.
3-71	VR
3-72	-
3-73	2,500.
3-74	600.
3-75	550.
3-76	550.
3-77	-
3-78	VR
3-79	750.
3-80	1,250.
3-81	VR
3-82	2,800.
3-83	2,500.
3-84	10,000.
3-85	8,500.
3-86	3,500.
3-87	2,200.
3-88	1,000.
3-89	1,800.
3-90	6,500.
3-91	VR
3-92	-
3-93	1,400.
3-94	1,600.
3-95	VR
3-96	1,200.
3-97	1,500.
3-98	1,400.
3-99	3,800.
3-100	2,000.
3-101	1,500.
3-102	-
3-103	-
3-104	1,400.
3-105	1,600.
3-106	1,800.
3-107	2,200.
3-108	3,200.
3-109	2,200.
3-110	2,500.
3-111	-
3-112	1,800.
3-113	1,250.
3-114	1,500.
3-115	1,250.
3-116	550.
3-117	-
3-118	650.
3-119	700.
3-120	450. excl. aluminum horn
3-121	1,200.
3-122	400. machine only
3-123	650.
3-124	700.
3-125	1,400.
3-126	550.
3-127	550.
3-128	2,500.
3-129	VR
3-130	VR
3-131	-
3-132	2,500.
3-133	2,500.
3-134	-
3-135	-
3-136	-

Item	Price		Item	Price		Item	Price		Item	Price		Item	Price
3-137	-		4-56	-		4-109	-		5-42	275.		6-24	500.
4-1	3,200.		4-57	-		1-110	1,400.		5-43	275.		6-25	425. w/o special cab
4-2	1,400.		4-58	-		4-111	1,500.		5-44	275.		6-26	-
4-3	1,600.		4-59	-		4-112	3,800.		5-45	-		6-27	600.
4-4	1,500.		4-60	600.		4-113	-		5-46	450.		6-28	800.
4-5	1,400 excl. carrying case		4-61	-		4-114	650.		5-47	-		6-29	400.
4-6	1,100.		4-62	VR		4-115	-		5-48	2,000.		6-30	-
4-7	2,500.		4-63	-		4-116	12,000.		5-49	3,500.		6-31	-
4-8	2,200.		4-64	-		4-117	12,000.		5-50	800.		6-32	450.
4-9	1,500.		4-65	3,000.		4-118	-		5-51	2,000.		6-33	2,800.
4-10	1,200.		4-66	VR		4-119	-		5-52	650.		6-34	1,500.
4-11	1,500.		4-67	7,500.		4-120	-		5-53	9000.		6-35	-
4-12	1,000.		4-68	300.		4-121	-		5-54	VR		6-36	3,800.
4-13	1,300.		4-69	$750. with horn		5-1	-		5-55	-		6-37	3,000.
4-14	2,000.		4-70	-		5-2	800.		5-56	1,500.		6-38	-
4-15	650.		4-71	1,500.		5-3	1,500.		5-57	1,800.		6-39	VR
4-16	650.		4-72	VR		5-4	1,700. with correct horn		5-58	1,400.		6-40	-
4-17	1,000.		4-73	1,300.		5-5	1,200.		5-59	-		6-41	-
4-18	900.		4-74	1,400.		5-6	2,800.		5-60	-		6-42	-
4-19	-		4-75	1,200.		5-7	1,200.		5-61	-		6-43	-
4-20	800.		4-76	2,700.		5-8	3,200.		5-62	-		6-44	-
4-21	-		4-77	1,800.		5-9	-		5-63	-		7-1	350.
4-22	-		4-78	1,600. machine only		5-10	1,800.		5-64	1,600.		7-2	-
4-23	850.		4-79	2,900.		5-11	2,200.		5-65	650.		7-3	1,000.
4-24	-		4-80	2,200. machine only		5-12	-		5-66	150. for common vers.		7-4	500.
4-25	-		4-81	2,000.		5-13	9,000.		5-67	250. oak		7-5	-
4-26	1,500.		4-82	4,500.		5-14	5,000.		5-68	-		7-6	-
4-27	-		4-83	VR		5-15	6,000.		5-69	700.		7-7	900.
4-28	2,500.		4-84	VR		5-16	2,800.		5-70	1,600.		7-8	-
4-29	750.		4-85	VR		5-17	-		5-71	3,000.		7-9	300.
4-30	-		4-86	VR		5-18	2,500.		5-72	1,600.		7-10	250.
4-31	-		4-87	-		5-19	VR		5-73	-		7-11	250.
4-32	900.		4-88	-		5-20	-		5-74	VR		7-12	150.
4-33	1,800.		4-89	1,000. if marked VTLA		5-21	650.		6-1	900.		7-13	700.
4-34	900.		4-90	-		5-22	550.		6-2	175.		7-14	850.
4-35	3,500.		4-91	-		5-23	450.		6-3	VR		7-15	L to R: 250. 250. 300.
4-36	1000.		4-92	1,600.		5-24	700.		6-4	-		7-16	L to R: 250. 350. 300. green version
4-37	650.		4-93	2,200.		5-25	-		6-5	900.		7-17	-
4-38	1,500.		4-94	VR		5-26	1,800.		6-6	VR		7-18	L to R: 350. 450. 150.
4-39	VR		4-95	-		5-27	1,800.		6-7	-		7-19	650.
4-40	2,500.		4-96	1,500.		5-28	600.		6-8	1,800.		7-20	800.
4-41	-		4-97	800.		5-29	700.		6-9	650.		7-21	-
4-42	1,000.		4-98	VR		5-30	-		6-10	650.		7-22	Clock VR, ordinary PP 300.
4-43	750.		4-99	900.		5-31	-		6-11	250.		7-23	350.
4-44	650.		4-100	900.		5-32	-		6-12	450.		7-24	300.
4-45	VR		4-101	1,000.		5-33	1,400.		6-13	450.		7-25	900.
4-46	2,500.		4-102	900.		5-34	2,800.		6-14	400.		7-26	-
4-47	1,500.		4-103	1,200.		5-35	10,000.		6-15	850.			
4-48	1,200.		4-104	1,200.		5-36	250.		6-16	750.			
4-49	3,500.		4-105	3,000.		5-37	150.		6-17	-			
4-50	2,500.		4-106	-		5-38	-		6-18	-			
4-51	1,800.		4-107	-		5-39	900. "L", 1,200. "H"		6-19	-			
4-52	-		4-108	2,200.		5-40	750.		6-20	650.			
4-53	3,500.					5-41	1,000.		6-21	350.			
4-54	750.								6-22	-			
4-55	1,000.								6-23	800.			

INDEX

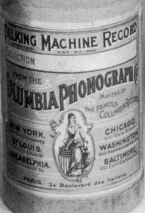